LYONS PRESS

GREAT
AMERICAN
SHIPWRECK
STORIES

EDITED BY

TOM McCARTHY

GUILFORD
CONNECTICUT

An imprint of Globe Pequot

Distributed by NATIONAL BOOK NETWORK

British Library Cataloguing in Publication Information available

Library of Congress Cataloging-in-Publication Data available

ISBN 978-1-4930-3371-3 (paperback)
ISBN 978-1-4930-3372-0 (e-book)

The paper used in this publication meets the minimum requirements
of American National Standard for Information Sciences—Permanence of
Paper for Printed Library Materials, ANSI/NISO Z39.48-1992.

Printed in the United States of America

CONTENTS

INTRODUCTION

Being aboard a ship that has crashed into a reef in the middle of nowhere is not an ideal ending for any cruise. One moment you're aboard and alert and feeling safe; the next you're engulfed in sheer panic. Throw in some hostile weather, say freezing temperatures and unrelenting winds, and the sudden change of plans a shipwreck brings can be nothing short of hell.

As you'll see in the stories in this collection, the wrecking and sinking and the terror they bring are only just the start of things. If you survive the crash, you will have much worse things to look forward to.

But that is the amazing thing about the sailors you'll read about here. They took the worst things that fate could throw at them and they persevered. Many survived the worst thing the sea can do to a sailor, then they went on to perform some incredible feats—amid daily threats of death and starvation and a slow, suffocating fear that they would never again be home and safe—and they thrived.

Other tales in this collection—fires aboard the *Morro Castle* and the *General Slocum*, the angry whale that crushed the *Essex*—are heart-wrenching accounts of unspeakable tragedy, silent deaths, and amazing heroism.

Going to sea requires a leap of faith, a wink and a nod at the odds that all will be well and a safe passage home is all but assured. More than anything, these stories show vulnerability, the fragile and fickle nature of fate. If bad luck intervened, and it often did, sailors had to be resilient and innovative and strong—mentally as well as physically. Surviving a shipwreck was only the start.

These tales show the indomitable spirit of the American sailor, often far from home and thrown into the worst of conditions. These survivors shrug their shoulders as if the wreck and the sinking are but minor irritations. They build sextants from old clocks, construct new boats from thick trees, they survive with rigid discipline. They move on.

They were tough enough to being with. Going to sea called for that. Then they become tougher.

The accounts of the sailors in these tales are of men who lived with little ego, who were confident and competent and did not need to pat themselves on the back. Their stories are studies in modesty and told with little flair or fanfare. That in fact might have been a common hallmark in the survivors. They put their sense of self aside and worked with others toward a common goal. They often did so with wry sense of observation.

Take this account of the chaos on the deck of the stern-wheeler *Equator* as it was going down on the upper Mississippi:

In the meantime the deck hands, or many of them, were in a panic, some of them on their knees on the forecastle, making strong vows of religious reformation should they come safe to land. This was a commendable attitude, both of body and spirit, had there been nothing else to do. In this particular province it would seem that much might have been expected from a captain who was also a preacher. On the contrary his manner of meeting the exigency was decidedly and profoundly out of drawing with preconceived notions of what might be expected from such a combination. An old man from Prescott, the richest man in town, and also one of the meanest, nearly seventy years old, crept up the companion way to the upper deck, and clasping Captain Green about the legs cried: "Save me! for God's sake save me! and I will give you a thousand dollars!"

"Get away you d—d cowardly old cur. Let go of me and get down below or I will throw you overboard," was Captain Green's exhortation as he yanked him to his feet by his collar and kicked him to the stairway.

Or how about this introductory remark from the New Bedford captain whose ship was rammed and sunk by a whale?

"Having been requested to give an account of the sinking of the Bark *Kathleen* by a whale I will do the best I can, though I think that those who have read the papers know as much or more about it than I do."

There is much in the collection to give readers pause, to make them sit back and try to imagine what it was like for Owen Chase, staring dumbfounded as a whale turned and prepared to stove in the hull of the *Essex*. He was 1,000 miles from the closest land and knew immediately that his next days would be the most trying of his life. Or to struggle with Daniel Collins of Wiscassett, Maine, who watched as his shipwrecked crewmates were massacred by pirates off Cuba. Or to try to imagine what it was like to spend nine months in the frigid Arctic with the surviving crew of the *Citizen*.

Some accounts are poignant, wrenching. You'll read of the *General Slocum*, a drifting inferno as mothers screamed and threw children from the decks. Or the doomed *Morro Castle*, so achingly close to its final destination of New York City.

Great American Shipwreck Tales is a testament to quiet heroism and remarkable human beings. Enjoy and admire these heroic, unsung figures and the adventures that made them so.

1

THE WRECK OF
THE *EQUATOR*

GEORGE BYRON MERRICK

A cruise down the Mississippi for a ship captain who was also a preacher presents an interesting challenge to his faith.

While some men were to be found on the Mississippi in the sixties who did not hesitate to avow themselves religious, and whose lives bore witness that they were indeed Christians, the combination of a Methodist preacher and a steamboat captain was one so incongruous that it was unique, and so far as I know, without a parallel on the river. There appeared to be no great incompatibility between the two callings, however, as they were represented in the person of Captain Asa B. Green. He was a good commander, as I had personal opportunity of observing at the time of the incident described in this chapter; and a few years later, when the great drama of the Civil War was on,

I again had an opportunity to observe Captain Green in his alternate rôle of minister of the gospel, he having been appointed chaplain of the Thirtieth Wisconsin Infantry in which I served as a private soldier. In this capacity he showed rare good sense and practical wisdom. He preached to the boys when a favorable opportunity offered on a Sunday, when there was not too much else going on; but his sermons were short, and as practical as was the man himself.

Of his conversion, or early life, on the river as a missionary, little seemed to be known by any one whom I ever met. He ran the Chippewa in the early days, during the summer months, and in the winter did missionary work among the lumbermen, following them to their camps in the woods, preaching and ministering to them; not as an alien, and in an academic fashion, but as one "to the manner born." It is likely that his young manhood was passed on the river and in the lumber camps, and when he was converted his thoughts turned naturally to the needs of these particular classes, for none knew better than he just how great their needs were. Of how or where he was ordained to preach I know nothing; but as he was in good standing with the Methodist conference there is no question as to the regularity of his commission. His master's certificate authorizing him to command a steamboat certified to his standing as a river man.

Probably he divided his time between commanding a steamboat and preaching the gospel, two callings so dissimilar, because the river work was quite remunerative, financially, while the other was quite the reverse. It probably took all the money he earned during the summer to support himself and his philanthropies during the winter. If his expenditures among the boys in the lumber camps were as free-handed as were his gifts to poor, sick, wounded, and homesick soldiers during his service with the Thirtieth Wisconsin during the war, it would easily require the seven months' pay of a river captain to sustain the other five months' liberality of the quondam preacher. Certain it is, that after three years' service as chaplain he came out as poor as he went in—in money. If the respect and high regard of his brother officers were worth anything; or better yet, if the love and gratitude of hundreds of plain boys in blue, privates in the ranks, might be counted as wealth, then Captain Green was rich indeed. And that was what he did count as real wealth. To be hugged by one of his "boys" at a Grand Army reunion, one whom he had nursed back to life in an army hospital by his optimistic cheerfulness and Christian hope and comfort—was to him better than gold or silver. He has gone to his reward; and whether he now is telling the "old, old story" to other men in other spheres, or pacing the deck of a spectre steamboat on the River of Life—whichever may be his work—beyond a peradventure he is doing that work well.

In the spring of 1858, in April, in his capacity as captain, Asa B. Green was commanding the steamer "Equator." She was a stern-wheel boat of about a hundred and twenty tons, plying on the St. Croix between Prescott and St. Croix Falls. The lake opened early that season, but the opening was followed by cold and stormy weather, with high winds. There was some sort of celebration at Stillwater, and as was customary in those days an excursion was organized at Hastings and Prescott to attend the "blow-out." About three hundred people crowded the little steamer, men, women, and children. She started off up the lake in the morning, fighting her way against a high wind right out of the north. Charley Jewell was pilot, the writer was "cub," John Lay was chief engineer. I have forgotten the name of the mate, but whatever may have been his name or nationality, he was the man for the place. He was every inch a man, as was the captain on the roof, and so in fact was every officer on the boat.

Everything went well until we had cleared Catfish bar, at Afton. From there to Stillwater is about twelve miles, due north. The wind had full sweep the whole length of this reach. The lake is two and a half miles wide just above Catfish bar. The sweep of the wind had raised a great sea, and the heavily-laden boat crawled ahead into the teeth of the blizzard—for it began to snow as well as blow. We had progressed very slowly, under an extra head of steam, for about three miles above the bar, when the port "rock-shaft," or eccentric rod, broke with a snap, and the wheel stopped instantly; in fact, John Lay had his hand on the throttle wheel when the rod broke, and in an instant had shut off steam to save his cylinders.

As soon as the wheel stopped the boat fell off into the trough of the sea. The first surge caught her on the quarter, before she had fully exposed her broadside, but it rolled her lee guards under water, and made every joint in her upper works creak and groan. The second wave struck her full broadside on. The tables had just been set for dinner. As the boat rolled down, under stress of wind and wave, the tables were thrown to leeward with a crash of broken glass and china that seemed to be the end of all things with the "Equator." Women and children screamed, and many women fainted. Men turned white, and some went wild, scrambling and fighting for life preservers. Several persons—they could hardly be called men—had two, and even three, strapped about their bodies, utterly ignoring the women and children in their abjectly selfish panic. The occasion brought out all the human nature there was in the crowd, and some that was somewhat baser than human.

As a whole, however, the men behaved well, and set about doing what they could to insure the safety of the helpless ones before providing for their own safety. It has always been a satisfaction to me that I had this opportunity, while a boy, to witness and take part in an accident which, while it did not result in the loss of a single life, had every element of great danger, and the imminent probability of the loss of hundreds of lives. It was an object lesson in what constituted manhood, self-reliant courage, official faithfulness, and the prompt application of ready expedients for the salvation of the boat.

When the crash came, Mr. Lay called up through the speaking-tube, stating the nature and extent of the accident. Mr. Jewell reported it to Captain Green, who ordered him to go to the cabin and attempt to allay the fright of the passengers, and to prevent a panic. As he started, Jewell ordered me to remain in the pilot house and listen for calls from the engine-room.

In the meantime the deck hands, or many of them, were in a panic, some of them on their knees on the forecastle, making strong vows of religious reformation should they come safe to land. This was a commendable attitude, both of body and spirit, had there been nothing else to do. In this particular province it would seem that much might have been expected from a captain who was also a preacher. On the contrary his manner of meeting the exigency was decidedly and profoundly out of drawing with preconceived notions of what might be expected from such a combination. An old man from Prescott, the richest man in town, and also one of the meanest, nearly seventy years old, crept up the companion way to the upper deck, and clasping Captain Green about the legs cried: "Save me! for God's sake save me! and I will give you a thousand dollars!"

"Get away you d——d cowardly old cur. Let go of me and get down below or I will throw you overboard," was Captain Green's exhortation as he yanked him to his feet by his collar and kicked him to the stairway. Both the language and the action were uncanonical in the extreme; but then, he was acting for the time in his capacity as captain, and not as preacher. I didn't laugh at the time, for I was doing some thinking on my own hook about the salvation business; and my estimate of the chances for getting to the shore, two miles away, in that wind and sea, was not flattering. I have laughed many times since, however, and wondered what the old miser thought of the orthodoxy of Chaplain Green when he answered his prayer.

The deck hands also met with a surprise from the mate, and that in less than a minute. Men think fast in such an emergency, especially those schooled amid dangers and quickened in mind and body by recurring calls for prompt action. A dozen seas had not struck the "Equator" before the mate was on the forecastle, driving the panic-stricken deck hands to work. Dropping the two long spars to the deck, with the assistance of the carpenter and such men as had gathered their wits together, he lashed them firmly together at each end. Then bending on a strong piece of line extending from end to end, and doubled, he made fast the main hawser, or snubbing line, to the middle, or bight of the rope attached to the spars, and then launched the whole overboard, making a "sea-anchor" that soon brought the bow of the vessel head to sea, and eased the racking roll of the hull, steadying the craft so that there was little further danger of her sinking. In the ten or fifteen minutes that it had taken to get the drag built and overboard, the waves had swept over the lower deck and into the hold, until there was a foot of water weighing her down, which the bilge pumps operated by the "doctor" were unable to throw out as fast as it came in. Had it continued to gain for fifteen minutes longer, the boat would have gone to the bottom with all on board. The drag saved the vessel; the coolness and quickness of the mate and carpenter were the salvation of the steamer and its great load of people.

In the meantime other incidents were occurring, that made a lasting impression upon my mind. I did not witness them myself, but I learned of them afterwards. All this time I stood at the side of the useless wheel in the pilot house, listening for sounds from the engine-room. Mr. Lay was doing all that was possible to remedy the break. He cut off the steam from the useless cylinder, and with his assistant and the firemen, was at work disconnecting the pitman, with the intent to try to work the wheel with one cylinder, which would have been an impossibility in that sea. In fact it would have been impossible under any circumstances, for the large wheel of a stern-wheel boat is built to be operated by two engines; there is not power enough in either one alone to more than turn it over, let alone driving the steamboat. When the crash came, Engineer Lay's wife, who was on board as a passenger, ran immediately to the engine-room to be with her husband when the worst should come. He kissed her as she came, and said: "There's a dear, brave, little woman. Run back to the cabin and encourage the other women. I must work. Good-bye." And the "little woman"—for she was a little woman, and a brave little woman, also—without another word gave her husband a good-bye kiss, and wiping away the tears, went back to the cabin and did more than all the others to reassure the frightened, fainting women and little children—the very antithesis of the craven old usurer who had crept on his knees begging for a little longer lease of a worthless life.

It took an hour or more to drift slowly, stern first, diagonally across and down the lake to the shore above Glenmont, on the Wisconsin side, where she struck and swung broadside onto the beach. The men carried the women ashore through four feet of water, and in another hour the cabin was blown entirely off the sunken hull, and the boat was a total wreck. Her bones are there to-day, a striking attestation of the power of wind and wave, even upon so small a body of water as Lake St. Croix.

Big fires were built from the wreckage to warm the wet and benumbed people. Runners were sent to nearby farm houses for teams, as well as to Hudson, seven or eight miles way. Many of the men walked home to Prescott and Hastings. Captain Green, who owned the boat, stayed with his crew to save what he could from the wreck, in which he lost his all; but he had only words of thanksgiving that not a life had been lost while under his charge. Through it he was cool and cheerful, devoting himself to reassuring his passengers, as soon as the drag was in place, and giving orders for getting the women and children ashore as soon as the boat should strike. His only deviation from perfect equipoise was exhibited in his treatment of the old man, a notoriously mean, and exacting money-lender, with whom he had no sympathy at any time, and no patience at a time like this.

2

THE *ESSEX* AND THE WHALE

OWEN CHASE

A Nantucket ship far from home and 1,000 miles from land is rammed and sunk by an angry whale. The true story of what later happened to the crew was long in coming, but the incident did catch the attention of a writer named Herman Melville.

The town of Nantucket, in the State of Massachusetts, contains about eight thousand inhabitants; nearly a third part of the population are Quakers, and they are, taken together, a very industrious and enterprising people. On this island are owned about one hundred vessels, of all descriptions, engaged in the whale trade, giving constant employment and support to upwards of sixteen hundred hardy seamen, a class of people proverbial for their intrepidity.

This fishery is not carried on to any extent from any other part of the United States, except from the town of New Bedford, directly opposite to Nantucket, where are owned probably twenty sail. A voyage generally lasts about two years and a half, and with an entire uncertainty of success. Sometimes they are repaid with speedy voyages and profitable cargoes, and at others they drag out a listless and disheartening cruise without scarcely making the expenses of an outfit.

The business is considered a very hazardous one, arising from unavoidable accidents, in carrying on an exterminating warfare against those great leviathans of the deep; and indeed a Nantucket man is on all occasions fully sensible of the honor and merit of his profession; no doubt because he knows that his laurels, like the soldier's, are plucked from the brink of danger. Numerous anecdotes are related of the whalemen of Nantucket; and stories of hair-breadth escapes, and sudden and wonderful preservation are handed down amongst them, with the fidelity, and no doubt many of them with the characteristic fictions of the ancient legendary tales.

A spirit of adventure amongst the sons of other relatives of those immediately concerned in it takes possession of their minds at a very early age; captivated with the tough stories of the elder seamen, and seduced as well by the natural desire of seeing foreign countries, as by the hopes of gain, they launch forth six or eight thousand miles from home, into an almost untraversed ocean, and spend from two to three years of their lives in scenes of constant peril, labour, and watchfulness.

The profession is one of great ambition, and full of honorable excitement: a tame man is never known amongst them; and the coward is marked with that peculiar aversion that distinguishes our public naval service. There are perhaps no people of superior corporeal powers; and it has been truly said of them that they possess a natural aptitude, which seems rather the lineal spirit of their fathers than the effects of any experience.

The town itself, during the war, was (naturally to have been expected) on the decline; but with the return of peace it took a fresh start, and a spirit for carrying on the fishery received a renewed and very considerable excitement. Large capitals are now embarked; and some of the finest ships that our country can boast of are employed in it. The increased demand, within a few years past, from the spermaceti manufactories, has induced companies and individuals in different parts of the Union to become engaged in the business; and if the future consumption of the manufactured article bear any proportion to that of the few past years, this species of commerce will bid fair to become the most profitable and extensive that our country possesses.

From the accounts of those who were in the early stages of the fishery concerned in it, it would appear that the whales have been driven, like the beasts of the forest, before the march of civilization into remote and more unfrequented seas, until, now they are followed by the enterprise and perseverance of our seamen even to the distant coasts of Japan.

The ship *Essex*, commanded by Captain George Pollard, junior, was fitted out at Nantucket, and sailed on the 12th day of August, 1819, for the Pacific Ocean, on a whaling voyage. Of this ship I was first mate. She had lately undergone a thorough repair in her upper works, and was at that time, in all respects, a sound, substantial vessel: she had a crew of twenty-one men, and was victualled and provided for two years and a half.

We left the coast of America with a fine breeze, and steered for the Western Islands. On the second day out, while sailing moderately on our course in the Gulf Stream, a sudden squall of wind struck the ship from the SW and knocked her completely on her beam-ends, stove one of our boats, entirely destroyed two others, and threw down the cambouse. We distinctly saw the approach of this gust, but miscalculated altogether as to the strength and violence of it.

It struck the ship about three points off the weather quarter, at the moment that the man at the helm was in the act of putting her away to run before it. In an instant she was knocked down with her yards in the water; and before hardly a moment of time was allowed for reflection, she gradually came to the wind, and righted. The squall was accompanied with vivid flashes of lightning and heavy and repeated claps of thunder. The whole ship's crew were, for a short time, thrown into the utmost consternation and confusion; but fortunately the violence of the squall was all contained in the first gust of the wind, and it soon gradually abated, and became fine weather again.

We repaired our damage with little difficulty, and continued on our course, with the loss of the two boats. On the 30th of August we made the island of Flores, one of the western group called the Azores. We lay off and on the island for two days, during which time our boats landed and obtained a supply of vegetables and a few hogs: from this place we took the NE trade-wind, and in sixteen days made the Isle of May, one of the Cape de Verds. As we were sailing along the shore of this island, we discovered a ship stranded on the beach, and from her appearance took her to be a whaler.

Having lost two of our boats, and presuming that this vessel had probably some belonging to her that might have been saved, we determined to ascertain the name of the ship, and endeavour to supply if possible the loss of our boats from her. We accordingly stood in towards the port, or landing place. After a short time three men were discovered coming out to us in a whale boat. In a few moments they were alongside, and informed us that the wreck was the *Archimedes* of New York, Captain George B. Coffin, which vessel had struck on a rock near the island about a fortnight previously; that all hands were saved by running the ship on shore, and that the captain and crew had gone home. We purchased the whale boat of these people, obtained some more pigs, and again set sail.

Our passage thence to Cape Horn was not distinguished for any incident worthy of note. We made the longitude of the Cape about the 18th of December, having experienced head winds for nearly the whole distance. We anticipated a moderate time in passing this noted land, from the season of the year at which we were there, being considered the most favourable; but instead of this, we experienced heavy westerly gales, and a most tremendous sea, that detained us off the Cape five weeks, before we had got sufficiently to the westward to enable us to put away.

Of the passage of this famous Cape it may be observed that strong westerly gales and a heavy sea are its almost universal attendants: the prevalence and constancy of this wind and sea necessarily produce a rapid current, by which vessels are set to leeward; and it is not without some favourable slant of wind that they can in many cases get round at all. The difficulties and dangers of the passage are proverbial; but as far as my own observation extends (and which the numerous reports of the whalemen corroborate), you can always rely upon a long and regular sea; and although the gales may be very strong and stubborn, as they undoubtedly are, they are not known to blow with the destructive violence that characterizes some of the tornadoes of the western Atlantic Ocean.

On the 17th of January, 1820, we arrived at the island of St. Mary's, lying on the coast of Chili, in latitude 36° 59' S., longitude 73° 41' W. This island is a sort of rendezvous for whalers, from which they obtain their wood and water, and between which and the main land (a distance of about ten miles) they frequently cruise for a species of whale called the right whale.

Our object in going in there was merely to get the news. We sailed thence to the island of Massafuera, where we got some wood and fish, and thence for the cruising ground along the coast of Chili, in search of the spermaceti whale. We took there eight, which yielded us two hundred and fifty barrels of oil; and the season having by this time expired, we changed our cruising ground to the coast of Peru.

We obtained there five hundred and fifty barrels. After going into the small port of Decamas, and replenishing our wood and water, on the 2d October we set sail for the Gallipagos Islands. We came to anchor, and laid seven days off Hood Island, one of the group; during which time we stopped a leak which we had discovered, and obtained three hundred turtle. We then visited Charles Island, where we procured sixty more. These turtle are a most delicious food, and average in weight generally about one hundred pounds, but many of them weigh upwards of eight hundred.

With these, ships usually supply themselves for a great length of time, and make a great saving of other provisions. They neither eat nor drink, nor are the least pains taken with them; they are strewed over the deck, thrown under foot, or packed away in the hold, as it suits convenience. They will live upwards of a year without food or water, but soon die in a cold climate.

We left Charles Island on the 23d of October, and steered off to the westward, in search of whales. In latitude 1° 0' S., longitude 118° W. on the 16th of November, in the afternoon, we lost a boat during our work in a shoal of whales. I was in the boat myself, with five others, and was standing in the fore part, with the harpoon in my hand, well braced, expecting every instant to catch sight of one of the shoal which we were in, that I might strike; but judge of my astonishment and dismay, at finding myself suddenly thrown up in the air, my companions scattered about me, and the boat fast filling with water. A whale had come up directly under her, and with one dash of his tail had stove her bottom in, and strewed us in every direction around her.

We, however, with little difficulty, got safely on the wreck, and clung there until one of the other boats which had been engaged in the shoal came to our assistance, and took us off. Strange to tell, not a man was injured by this accident. Thus it happens very frequently in the whaling business, that boats are stove; oars, harpoons, and lines broken; ankles and wrists sprained; boats upset, and whole crews left for hours in the water, without any of these accidents extending to the loss of life.

We are so much accustomed to the continual recurrence of such scenes as these, that we become familiarized to them, and consequently always feel that confidence and self-possession, which teaches us every expedient in danger, and inures the body, as well as the mind, to fatigue, privation, and peril, in frequent cases exceeding belief. It is this danger and hardship that makes the sailor; indeed it is the distinguishing qualification amongst us; and it is a common boast of the whaleman that he has escaped from sudden and apparently inevitable destruction oftener than his fellow. He is accordingly valued on this account, without much reference to other qualities.

I have not been able to recur to the scenes which are now to become the subject of description, although a considerable time has elapsed, without feeling a mingled emotion of horror and astonishment at the almost incredible destiny that has preserved me and my surviving companions from a terrible death.

Frequently, in my reflections on the subject, even after this lapse of time, I find myself shedding tears of gratitude for our deliverance, and blessing God, by whose divine aid and protection we were conducted through a series of unparalleled suffering and distress, and restored to the bosoms of our families and friends. There is no knowing what a stretch of pain and misery the human mind is capable of contemplating, when it is wrought upon by the anxieties of preservation; nor what pangs and weaknesses the body is able to endure, until they are visited upon it; and when at last deliverance comes, when the dream of hope is realized, unspeakable gratitude takes possession of the soul, and tears of joy choke the utterance.

We require to be taught in the school of some signal suffering, privation, and despair, the great lessons of constant dependence upon an almighty forbearance and mercy. In the midst of the wide ocean, at night, when the sight of the heavens was shut out, and the dark tempest came upon us, then it was that we felt ourselves ready to exclaim, "Heaven have mercy upon us, for nought but that can save us now."

But I proceed to the recital.—On the 20th of November (cruising in latitude 0° 40' S., longitude 119° 0' W.) a shoal of whales was discovered off the lee-bow. The weather at this time was extremely fine and clear, and it was about 8 o'clock in the morning that the man at the mast-head gave the usual cry of, "there she blows." The ship was immediately put away, and we ran down in the direction for them. When we had got within half a mile of the place where they were observed, all our boats were lowered down, manned, and we started in pursuit of them.

The ship, in the meantime, was brought to the wind, and the main-top-sail hove aback, to wait for us. I had the harpoon in the second boat; the captain preceded me in the first. When I arrived at the spot where we calculated they were, nothing was at first to be seen. We lay on our oars in anxious expectation of discovering them come up somewhere near us. Presently one rose, and spouted a short distance ahead of my boat; I made all speed towards it, came up with, and struck it; feeling the harpoon in him, he threw himself, in an agony, over towards the boat (which at that time was up alongside of him), and, giving a severe blow with his tail, struck the boat near the edge of the water, amidships, and stove a hole in her.

I immediately took up the boat hatchet, and cut the line, to disengage the boat from the whale, which by this time was running off with great velocity. I succeeded in getting clear of him, with the loss of the harpoon and line; and finding the water to pour fast in the boat, I hastily stuffed three or four of our jackets in the hole, ordered one man to keep constantly bailing, and the rest to pull immediately for the ship; we succeeded in keeping the boat free, and shortly gained the ship.

The captain and the second mate, in the other two boats, kept up the pursuit, and soon struck another whale. They being at this time a considerable distance to leeward, I went forward, braced around the mainyard, and put the ship off in a direction for them; the boat which had been stove was immediately hoisted in, and after examining the hole, I found that I could, by nailing a piece of canvas over it, get her ready to join in a fresh pursuit, sooner than by lowering down the other remaining boat which belonged to the ship.

I accordingly turned her over upon the quarter, and was in the act of nailing on the canvas, when I observed a very large spermaceti whale, as well as I could judge about eighty-five feet in length; he broke water about twenty rods off our weather-bow, and was lying quietly, with his head in a direction for the ship. He spouted two or three times, and then disappeared.

In less than two or three seconds he came up again, about the length of the ship off, and made directly for us, at the rate of about three knots. The ship was then going with about the same velocity. His appearance and attitude gave us at first no alarm; but while I stood watching his movements, and observing him but a ship's length off, coming down for us with great celerity, I involuntarily ordered the boy at the helm to put it hard up; intending to sheer off and avoid him.

The words were scarcely out of my mouth, before he came down upon us with full speed, and struck the ship with his head, just forward of the fore-chains; he gave us such an appalling and tremendous jar, as nearly threw us all on our faces. The ship brought up as suddenly and violently as if she had struck a rock, and trembled for a few seconds like a leaf.

We looked at each other with perfect amazement, deprived almost of the power of speech. Many minutes elapsed before we were able to realize the dreadful accident; during which time he passed under the ship, grazing her keel as he went along, came up alongside of her to leeward, and lay on the top of the water (apparently stunned with the violence of the blow) for the space of a minute; he then suddenly started off, in a direction to leeward. After a few moments reflection, and recovering, in some measure, from the sudden consternation that had seized us, I of course concluded that he had stove a hole in the ship, and that it would be necessary to set the pumps going.

Accordingly they were rigged, but had not been in operation more than one minute before I perceived the head of the ship to be gradually settling down in the water; I then ordered the signal to be set for the other boats, which, scarcely had I despatched, before I again discovered the whale, apparently in convulsions, on the top of the water, about one hundred rods to leeward. He was enveloped in the foam of the sea, that his continual and violent thrashing about in the water had created around him, and I could distinctly see him smite his jaws together, as if distracted with rage and fury.

He remained a short time in this situation, and then started off with great velocity, across the bows of the ship, to windward. By this time the ship had settled down a considerable distance in the water, and I gave her up for lost. I, however, ordered the pumps to be kept constantly going, and endeavoured to collect my thoughts for the occasion.

I turned to the boats, two of which we then had with the ship, with an intention of clearing them away, and getting all things ready to embark in them, if there should be no other resource left; and while my attention was thus engaged for a moment, I was aroused with the cry of a man at the hatchway, "here he is—he is making for us again."

I turned around, and saw him about one hundred rods directly ahead of us, coming down apparently with twice his ordinary speed, and to me at that moment, it appeared with tenfold fury and vengeance in his aspect. The surf flew in all directions about him, and his course towards us was marked by a white foam of a rod in width, which he made with the continual violent thrashing of his tail; his head was about half out of water, and in that way he came upon, and again struck the ship.

I was in hopes when I descried him making for us, that by a dexterous movement of putting the ship away immediately, I should be able to cross the line of his approach, before he could get up to us, and thus avoid what I knew, if he should strike us again, would prove our inevitable destruction. I bawled out to the helmsman, "hard up!" but she had not fallen off more than a point, before we took the second shock. I should judge the speed of the ship to have been at this time about three knots, and that of the whale about six. He struck her to windward, directly under the cathead, and completely stove in her bows. He passed under the ship again, went off to leeward, and we saw no more of him.

Our situation at this juncture can be more readily imagined than described. The shock to our feelings was such, as I am sure none can have an adequate conception of, that were not there: the misfortune befell us at a moment when we least dreamt of any accident; and from the pleasing anticipations we had formed, of realizing the certain profits of our labour, we were dejected by a sudden, most mysterious, and overwhelming calamity.

Not a moment, however, was to be lost in endeavouring to provide for the extremity to which it was now certain we were reduced. We were more than a thousand miles from the nearest land, and with nothing but a light open boat, as the resource of safety for myself and companions. I ordered the men to cease pumping, and every one to provide for himself; seizing a hatchet at the same time, I cut away the lashings of the spare boat, which lay bottom up across two spars directly over the quarter deck, and cried out to those near me to take her as she came down.

They did so accordingly, and bore her on their shoulders as far as the waist of the ship. The steward had in the meantime gone down into the cabin twice, and saved two quadrants, two practical navigators, and the captain's trunk and mine; all which were hastily thrown into the boat, as she lay on the deck, with the two compasses which I snatched from the binnacle. He attempted to descend again; but the water by this time had rushed in, and he returned without being able to effect his purpose. By the time we had got the boat to the waist, the ship had filled with water, and was going down on her beam-ends: we shoved our boat as quickly as possible from the plank-shear into the water, all hands jumping in her at the same time, and launched off clear of the ship. We were scarcely two boat lengths distant from her, when she fell over to windward, and settled down in the water.

Amazement and despair now wholly took possession of us. We contemplated the frightful situation the ship lay in, and thought with horror upon the sudden and dreadful calamity that had overtaken us. We looked upon each other, as if to gather some consolatory sensation from an interchange of sentiments, but every countenance was marked with the paleness of despair. Not a word was spoken for several minutes by any of us; all appeared to be bound in a spell of stupid consternation; and from the time we were first attacked by the whale, to the period of the fall of the ship, and of our leaving her in the boat, more than ten minutes could not certainly have elapsed!

God only knows in what way, or by what means, we were enabled to accomplish in that short time what we did; the cutting away and transporting the boat from where she was deposited would of itself, in ordinary circumstances, have consumed as much time as that, if the whole ship's crew had been employed in it. My companions had not saved a single article but what they had on their backs; but to me it was a source of infinite satisfaction, if any such could be gathered from the horrors of our gloomy situation, that we had been fortunate enough to have preserved our compasses, navigators, and quadrants.

After the first shock of my feelings was over, I enthusiastically contemplated them as the probable instruments of our salvation; without them all would have been dark and hopeless. Gracious God! what a picture of distress and suffering now presented itself to my imagination. The crew of the ship were saved, consisting of twenty human souls. All that remained to conduct these twenty beings through the stormy terrors of the ocean, perhaps many thousand miles, were three open light boats.

The prospect of obtaining any provisions or water from the ship, to subsist upon during the time, was at least now doubtful. How many long and watchful nights, thought I, are to be passed? How many tedious days of partial starvation are to be endured, before the least relief or mitigation of our sufferings can be reasonably anticipated? We lay at this time in our boat, about two ship lengths off from the wreck, in perfect silence, calmly contemplating her situation, and absorbed in our own melancholy reflections, when the other boats were discovered rowing up to us.

They had but shortly before discovered that some accident had befallen us, but of the nature of which they were entirely ignorant. The sudden and mysterious disappearance of the ship was first discovered by the boat-steerer in the captain's boat, and with a horror-struck countenance and voice, he suddenly exclaimed, "Oh, my God! where is the ship?"

Their operations upon this were instantly suspended, and a general cry of horror and despair burst from the lips of every man, as their looks were directed for her, in vain, over every part of the ocean. They immediately made all haste towards us. The captain's boat was the first that reached us. He stopped about a boat's length off, but had no power to utter a single syllable: he was so completely overpowered with the spectacle before him that he sat down in his boat, pale and speechless.

I could scarcely recognise his countenance, he appeared to be so much altered, awed, and overcome with the oppression of his feelings, and the dreadful reality that lay before him. He was in a short time however enabled to address the inquiry to me, "My God, Mr. Chase, what is the matter?" I answered, "We have been stove by a whale." I then briefly told him the story. After a few moment's reflection he observed that we must cut away her masts, and endeavour to get something out of her to eat. Our thoughts were now all accordingly bent on endeavours to save from the wreck whatever we might possibly want, and for this purpose we rowed up and got on to her. Search was made for every means of gaining access to her hold; and for this purpose the lanyards were cut loose, and with our hatchets we commenced to cut away the masts, that she might right up again, and enable us to scuttle her decks.

In doing which we were occupied about three quarters of an hour, owing to our having no axes, nor indeed any other instruments, but the small hatchets belonging to the boats. After her masts were gone she came up about two-thirds of the way upon an even keel. While we were employed about the masts the captain took his quadrant, shoved off from the ship, and got an observation. We found ourselves in latitude 0° 40' S., longitude 119° W. We now commenced to cut a hole through the planks, directly above two large casks of bread, which most fortunately were between decks, in the waist of the ship, and which being in the upper side, when she upset, we had strong hopes was not wet.

It turned out according to our wishes, and from these casks we obtained six hundred pounds of hard bread. Other parts of the deck were then scuttled, and we got without difficulty as much fresh water as we dared to take in the boats, so that each was supplied with about sixty-five gallons; we got also from one of the lockers a musket, a small canister of powder, a couple of files, two rasps, about two pounds of boat nails, and a few turtle. In the afternoon the wind came on to blow a strong breeze; and having obtained everything that occurred to us could then be got out, we began to make arrangements for our safety during the night.

A boat's line was made fast to the ship, and to the other end of it one of the boats was moored, at about fifty fathoms to leeward; another boat was then attached to the first one, about eight fathoms astern; and the third boat, the like distance astern of her. Night came on just as we had finished our operations; and such a night as it was to us! so full of feverish and distracting inquietude, that we were deprived entirely of rest.

The wreck was constantly before my eyes. I could not, by any effort, chase away the horrors of the preceding day from my mind: they haunted me the live-long night. My companions—some of them were like sick women; they had no idea of the extent of their deplorable situation. One or two slept unconcernedly, while others wasted the night in unavailing murmurs. I now had full leisure to examine, with some degree of coolness, the dreadful circumstances of our disaster. The scenes of yesterday passed in such quick succession in my mind that it was not until after many hours of severe reflection that I was able to discard the idea of the catastrophe as a dream.

Alas! it was one from which there was no awaking; it was too certainly true, that but yesterday we had existed as it were, and in one short moment had been cut off from all the hopes and prospects of the living! I have no language to paint out the horrors of our situation. To shed tears was indeed altogether unavailing, and withal unmanly; yet I was not able to deny myself the relief they served to afford me.

After several hours of idle sorrow and repining I began to reflect upon the accident, and endeavoured to realize by what unaccountable destiny or design (which I could not at first determine) this sudden and most deadly attack had been made upon us: by an animal, too, never before suspected of premeditated violence, and proverbial for its insensibility and inoffensiveness. Every fact seemed to warrant me in concluding that it was anything but chance which directed his operations; he made two several attacks upon the ship, at a short interval between them, both of which, according to their direction, were calculated to do us the most injury, by being made ahead, and thereby combining the speed of the two objects for the shock; to effect which, the exact manoeuvres which he made were necessary. His aspect was most horrible, and such as indicated resentment and fury.

He came directly from the shoal which we had just before entered, and in which we had struck three of his companions, as if fired with revenge for their sufferings. But to this it may be observed, that the mode of fighting which they always adopt is either with repeated strokes of their tails, or snapping of their jaws together; and that a case, precisely similar to this one, has never been heard of amongst the oldest and most experienced whalers.

To this I would answer, that the structure and strength of the whale's head is admirably designed for this mode of attack; the most prominent part of which is almost as hard and as tough as iron; indeed, I can compare it to nothing else but the inside of a horse's hoof, upon which a lance or harpoon would not make the slightest impression. The eyes and ears are removed nearly one-third the length of the whole fish, from the front part of the head, and are not in the least degree endangered in this mode of attack.

At all events, the whole circumstances taken together, all happening before my own eyes, and producing, at the time, impressions in my mind of decided, calculating mischief on the part of the whale (many of which impressions I cannot now recall) induce me to be satisfied that I am correct in my opinion. It is certainly, in all its bearings, a hitherto unheard of circumstance, and constitutes, perhaps, the most extraordinary one in the annals of the fishery.

3

MAINERS MAROONED AND MURDERED

DANIEL COLLINS

~~~~~~

A winter cruise to Cuba for some resolute Mainers from Wiscasset turns out very badly for all but one amazing man.

~~~~~~

On the 28th of November, 1824, I sailed from Wiscasset, (Me.) for Matanzas, in the Island of Cuba, on board the brig *Betsey*, laden with lumber; our officers and crew consisting of seven, viz. ELLIS HILTON, of Wiscasset, master; JOSHUA MERRY, of Edgecomb, 1st mate; DANIEL COLLINS, of Wiscasset, 2d mate; CHARLES MANUEL, (a Portuguese), SETH RUSSELL, and BENJ. BRIDGE, seamen; and DETREY JEOME, cook.

On the 18th of December we passed the Berry Islands, and early next morning came to anchor within a league of Orange Key, on the Bahama Banks. It was the morning of the Sabbath, so calm and clear that even the lengthened billows of the Gulf Stream seemed sleeping around us, and the most untutored son of Neptune could not but remember that it was a holy day, consecrated to devotion and rest. Here we continued until noon, when a fresh breeze from the North invited us to weigh anchor and unfurl our sails, which, swelling with a fair wind, were as buoyant as our own spirits, at the increasing prospect of reaching our port of destination.

Our course was W. S. W. that afternoon and night. At 4 o'clock next morning, by order of Capt. Hilton, who had been sick most of the passage out, and was now unable to appear on deck during the night, we kept her away one point, steering S. W. by W. calculating the current easterly at three knots, which he supposed would clear us of the Double Headed Shot Keys.

About sunset, a dark and stormy night approaching, I suggested to our Captain the propriety of shortening sail, to which he would not assent, presuming we might get into Matanzas the next day. The night was so dark that we could not discover objects distinctly beyond the length of the vessel, and the wind blew more than an usual wholesale breeze, which drove her, heavy-laden as she was, at the rate of 9 knots, calculating ourselves more than 6 leagues to the windward of the Double Headed Shot Keys. At half past 2 o'clock I was relieved at the helm, and after casting a glance over the lee side and discovering no alteration in the appearance of the water, I observed to my shipmate at the helm, "there is no fear of you"—went below and turned in with my clothes on. No one was below at this time except the Captain, who stood at the foot of the companion way viewing the appearance of the weather.

I had been in my birth about half an hour when I felt a tremendous shock, which covered me with the muskets that were over head, boxes, barrels and other cabin articles; the water pouring into my birth through the quarter. I cleared myself by a violent effort, ran for the companion way—it was gone—turned—leaped through the sky light, and was on deck in an instant. We were in the hollow of a sea, and I could just discern over our main peak the dark top of the rock, which we had struck, stem on, then going at the rate of nine knots. This rock, which some of our crew supposed to be a wreck, was concealed from the helmsman by the mainsail. Two of the crew were at the pumps—the deck load, which consisted of boards, scantlings and oars, piled on each side as high as their heads—the other two people were probably on the quarter deck. It was a careless watch for a dark night, even at our supposed distance from the Keys; but we were now in no situation to complain. A part of our stern and the yawl at the davits, had gone together. I ran forward to clear the anchors in order to prevent her from ranging ahead on another rock which I could perceive among the surf; but a greater part of the bows were gone, and with them the anchors.—The water was already groaning under the deck—she arose for the last time on the crest of another sea nearly to the top of the rock, quivering like a bird under its death-wound. Our Captain and crew were around the long-boat endeavoring to cut the leashings and right her, while I secured a compass, an axe, a bucket and several oars. The next sea we descended she struck; opened fore and aft, the masts and spars, with all sails standing, thundering against the rock, and the lumber from below deck cracking and crashing in every direction. We were all launched overboard on the lumber that adhered together, clinging hold of the long-boat as the seaman's last ark of refuge, and endeavoring to right her, which we did in a few moments; but not without the misfortune of splitting a plank in her bottom. We all sprang in, bearing with us nothing but the sea clothes we had on, the few articles before named, and some fragments of the boat's leashings. The Captain's dog, which a few moments before had been leaping from plank to plank after the cat, with as determined an enmity as though the pursuit had been through a farmyard, followed us; a companion by no means unwelcome to those, who, without provision or water, might have been compelled to depend on this faithful animal for the preservation of their lives.

A new difficulty now presented itself: Our boat leaked so fast that three hands, two with hats and one with the bucket, were unable to free her; but with the aid of the only knife we had saved, and the fragments of the leashings, I filled some of the seams, which helped to free her; but not so effectually as to relieve a single hand from bailing.

About a league from the rock we hung on our oars, watching the sea that ran mountains high, until day-light, when we pulled up under its lee, but could discover neither fresh water nor a particle of provisions, except a few pieces of floating bread that we dared not eat. Fragments of boards and spars were floating here and there, but the only article either of convenience or comfort we could preserve was a large blanket, which was converted into a sail and set; and being compelled by the violence of the sea, we put her away before the wind, steering S. half E.—a course that must have carried us far East of our intended track, had it not been for the strong Westerly current in St. Nicholas' Channel.

The rock on which we were wrecked, and from which we took our departure in the boat, proved to be one of the N. E. range of the Double Headed Shot Keys.

We steered the above course all that day, bailing and rowing without a moment's cessation, and approaching, as was then supposed, the Island of Cuba, the coast of which, except the entrance of Matanzas and Havana, was unknown to us. We knew, however, that the whole coast was lined with dangerous shoals and keys, though totally ignorant of the situation of those East of Point Yeacos. An hundred times during the day, were our eyes directed to every point of the compass, in search of a sail, but in vain—we were too far to the eastward of the usual track to Matanzas.

As night approached the danger of our situation increased. We had all been fatigued—some of us much bruised, by the disasters of the preceding night; and our toils during the day, as may well be conceived, were not much relieved by an incessant rowing and bailing, without a particle of food to assuage our hunger or one drop of fresh water to cool our parched tongues. Anxiety was depicted in every visage, and our spirits were clouding like the heavens over them. Capt. Hilton, whose sickness and debility had been increased by fatigue and hunger, could no longer smother the feelings that were struggling within.—The quivering lip, the dim eye, the pallid cheek, all told us, as plainly as human expression could tell, that the last ray of that hope which had supported him during the day, was now fading away before the coming night. I had seen much more of rough service and weather than any one on board, and having been blessed with an excellent constitution, made it my duty to encourage the rest, by representing our approach to the Island as certain and safe; this seemed to stimulate increased exertion at the oars, and the breeze continuing fair, we made good head-way. About midnight, Capt. Hilton's oar touched something which he supposed bottom, but which the blade of the oar discovered to be a shark that followed us next morning. Deeming us, therefore, over some dangerous shoal, he gave full vent to his feelings, by observing, that if even we were to escape these dangerous shoals, our distance from the Island was so great, that we could never endure hunger, thirst and the fatigue of bailing long enough to reach it. I endeavored to convince him that we must reach the land by another night, in the direction we were steering. The disheartened crew soon caught the contagious and fatal despair which the Captain had incautiously diffused among them. In vain did I expostulate with him on the necessity of continuing our exertions at the oars—he burst into tears, kneeled down in the bottom of the boat and implored Divine protection. It is true our hold on life was a frail one. In an open boat, that from leaking and the violence of the sea we could scarcely keep above water—without food, drink, or clothing sufficient to defend us from the cold and rain of a December *Norther*—in an irregular and rapid current that prevented any correct calculation of our course—on an unknown and dangerous coast, without a chart to guide us.

In a state of mind bordering on that insanity which is sometimes caused by hunger, thirst and despair united, we passed a most perilous night. At the very first dawn of light every eye was again in search of a sail. A small dark speck on the ocean was descried ahead, about 5 leagues distant! The joyful sound of land ran through our nerves like an electric shock, and gave new life to the oars. The wind being fair, the aid of our sail, which was equal to two additional oars, gave us such head way, that as the rays of the rising sun sported over the tops of the waves and fell on the small spot of land ahead, we found ourselves nearing one of the Cuba Keys.

The land we first discovered was a little Island of about three acres, that arose above the surrounding key, as high as the tops of the mangroves. The name of this key—the largest of its group—was of so sacred an import, that one would have supposed it had been a refuge no less from the storms of persecution, than those of the element around it.

Cruz del Padre, or *Cross of our Father*, situated in W. long. 80° 5′ and N. lat. 23° 11′—is about 27 leagues E. by N. from Matanzas. It is a long, narrow key, of whose size we could not accurately judge.— Around its North side about a league distant from the shore, was a semi-circular reef, over which the sea broke as far as the eye extended. It was a tremendous battery in a storm, and were I approaching it in an American squadron, I should fear its ground tier more than all the cabanas of the Morro. But hunger and thirst are powerful antidotes to fear. We therefore boldly approached it with confidence in that divine interposition which had been recently so signally displayed towards us. Availing ourselves of the deepest water and the swell of a sea, we were hurried on the top of a breaker, that shook our long-boat like an aspin leaf and nearly filled her with water; but in a moment she was floating on a beautiful bay that presented to the eye "the smooth surface of a summer's sea."

The Northern boundary of this bay was formed by the reef, making the inner part of a crescent—the Southern, by two long lines of mangroves on each side, and a small beach of beautiful white pipe clay, that formed the front of the little Island in the centre. The distance across was about three miles, two of which we had already passed, directly for the beach, a few rods from which as we had previously discovered, were two huts, inhabited by fishermen, whom we could now see passing in and out. When at the above distance from the reef, our attention was suddenly arrested by the appearance of two wrecks of vessels, of too large a size, one would have supposed, to have beaten over the reef. As the water grew shoaler I could see an even pipe clay bottom, on which our boat grounded an hundred yards from the shore. One of the inhabitants came off in a flat bottom'd log canoe about 25 feet long and 2-½ wide, hailed us in Spanish, demanding who we were, and was answered by Manuel our Portuguese.

As this Spaniard, who was the head fisherman, came along side, he was recognized by Capt. Hilton as the same of whom he had purchased some sugars the voyage before at Matanzas.

The two huts we have named were formed of the planks and cabin boards of wrecks, about 7 feet high, and 10 by 15 on the ground, with thatched roofs. At the N. E. corner was a group of old weather-beaten trees, the only ones above the height of a mangrove on the Island, on which the fishermen hung their nets. In front of the beach was a *turtle troll* about 15 feet square, surrounded by a frame, from which were suspended a great number of wooden hooks, on which their fish were hung, and partially preserved, by drying in the sea breeze. It was about 8 o'clock in the morning when we were conducted into one of the huts, and as we had had neither food nor drink for nearly two days and nights, some refreshment, consisting of turtle and other fish, hot coffee, &c. was immediately provided.

After our refreshment, some sails were spread on the ground, on which we were invited to repose. My shipmates readily accepted the invitation; but I had seen too much of Spanish infidelity, under the cloak of hospitality, to omit an anchor watch, even in our present snug harbour.

There were five fishermen, all stout, well built Spaniards, the master of whom was over six feet, and had much the appearance of an American Indian.—My companions were soon in a "dead sleep," and when the fishermen had left the hut, I walked out to explore our new habitation. The two huts were so near that a gutter only separated them, which caught the water from the roofs of each and conducted it into a hogshead bedded in the sand, from which other casks were filled against a drought; the fresh water thus obtained being all the Island furnished. West of the beach was a small bay, in the centre of which was an Island about a mile in circumference. At the head of this bay a creek made up several rods into the mangroves, which served as a harbour for a small fishing vessel of about twelve tons, decked over, in which they carried their fish to Matanzas and elsewhere about the Island of Cuba.

East of the beach was a cove that extended about a quarter of a mile into the bushes, forming a kind of basin at its head, which was as still as a millpond. This basin was surrounded by thick mangroves, and completely concealed from every thing without by the jutting out of a point at its entrance. A more lonely place I never saw. Around its borders a "solitary guest," you might see the *Flamingo* strutting in all the pride of its crimson plumage, as erect and nearly as high as a British soldier. The bottom of this Cove was like that of the bay.

The mangroves are very thick,—their trunks covered with oystershells that adhere to them like barnacles to a vessel's bottom, which annoy those who attempt to pass among them, by tearing their clothes and wounding the flesh as high up as the hips.

Among the bushes were concealed two clinker-built boats, remarkably well constructed for rowing, with their bottoms greased or soaped; in one of which I found a handkerchief filled with limes: I took one and brought it into the house;—this displeased the fishermen, who afterwards told Manuel that the boats and limes belonged to some people at a small distance, who would return in a few days. There were also two yawls moored in front of the huts, that appeared to have belonged to American vessels.

When I returned to the hut, my shipmates were yet asleep, and we did not awake them until supper was prepared, which was much the same with our breakfast, except the addition of plantain. After supper we all set around the table devising means to get to Matanzas. Through Manuel, Capt. Hilton offered the master fisherman our long-boat and forty dollars in cash, on our arrival at Matanzas, which was accepted, and we were to sail in their small schooner as soon as the weather would permit. About 8 or 9 o'clock, we all turned in, but my suspicions would not allow me to sleep; for when all was silent, I could hear the Spaniards conversing with each other in a low tone, on which I spake to Manuel with the hope that he might understand the subject of their consultation; but he, like his companions, was too sound asleep to be easily awakened. A lamp of fish oil had been dimly burning for two or three hours, when the master fisherman arose and extinguished it. About this time an old dog belonging to the fishermen, commenced a most hideous howling without, that was occasionally answered by our dog within. Supposing some boat might be approaching, I went out, but could discover no living being in motion. It was a star light-night, the wind blowing fresh with a few flying scuds. When I returned into the hut, I set down between two barrels of bread, against one of which I leaned my head, prepared to give an early warning of any foul play that might befal us; but the night passed without any incident to interrupt the slumbers of my weary messmates.

Early in the morning they turned out and we went down to the Cove before described, in order to bathe. While we were clothing ourselves on the shore at the head of the Cove, we discovered, at high-water mark, a number of human skeletons—(except the skulls)—bleached and partly decayed. The bones of the fingers, hands and ribs were entire. To me this was no very pleasant discovery, and I observed to Mr. Merry that "we might all be murdered in such a place without the possibility of its being known"; but the bones were, at the time, supposed to have belonged to seamen that might have been shipwrecked on the reef near this part of the key.

On our return to the hut we found breakfast awaiting us. This day we spent in rambling about the Island, and were generally followed by two of the fishermen, who manifested more than usual vigilance. During this as well as the preceding day they suspended their usual occupation, and passed their time in loitering about. My suspicions were increased by a number of circumstances to such a degree, that I urged Capt. Hilton to depart in our own boat bad as she was; but he expressed great confidence in the head fisherman, from his previous acquaintance with him at Matanzas.

As we had made arrangements to depart the next morning, all hands were preparing to turn in at an early hour when the master fisherman observed, it was too *hot* to sleep in the house, drew his blanket over his shoulders and went out.

It is a little singular that such a circumstance should not have produced on the minds of my shipmates the same effect it did on mine, as the weather was then uncomfortably cool to me within the hut. But in justice to them I ought to add, that a singular dream the night before our shipwreck, had produced on my mind a kind of sailor's superstition, which banished sleep from my eyes, even now while they were enjoying its refreshing influence.

After I had paced the room several times, one of the fishermen arose and extinguished the light, and when all was still, I went to the door that had been fastened after the master fisherman, drew the bolt without disturbing any one, and went out. At the threshold of the door I found an axe which I took in my hand, walked around the hut several times, but could not discover the object of my search. I at length found his blanket tucked up among the thatch under the eaves of the hut, and immediately re-entered the room to tell my companions I was apprehensive that this strange departure of the Spaniard was influenced by another motive than that expressed.

He could not go far without wading in the water, which was two or three feet deep all over this extensive key, except the spot around the huts, on which he was not to be found; and it is well known to mariners, that these keys are dissected by numerous creeks like the one already described, which in some instances extend miles among the mangrove bushes, where a sea robber might conceal himself for months without the fear of detection.

Without disturbing the Spaniards, I shook Mr. Merry and whispered to him my suspicions, on which we both went to the door and sat down to await the fisherman's return. When I first awaked him he trembled with fear that some unnatural fate awaited us. But the night passed without any further disturbance, and at day-light we all, by previous arrangement, commenced loading the two canoes, (which were of the same dimensions of that already described) by wading off to them with the fish in our arms. It was about sunrise when we had completed loading, and while we were all in the huts, the master fisherman suddenly entered—saluted Capt. Hilton in Spanish, and requested all our people and three of his own to accompany him to the schooner before named, in order to haul her out of the creek and moor her off, preparatory to our departure: this we did with no little labor, wading into the mud and water breast high. After we had anchored her about half a mile abreast of the huts, and discharged the fish from the canoes into her, we returned to the huts to breakfast.

When the master fisherman returned in the morning, I observed that his trowsers were wet up to his hips, and he appeared as though he had been wading several miles.

After breakfast we finished loading the little schooner, and returned to the huts to bring down some small stores. As we were all standing before the huts, the master fisherman was seen pointing to the Eastward and laughing with his companions. On looking in the direction he was pointing, I discovered the object of his amusement to be a small vessel just doubling an Easterly point of the key, about seven miles distant *within the Reef,* and bearing away for us. I had too often seen the grin of a Spaniard accompanied with the stab of his stiletto, to pass the circumstance unnoticed. By my request Manuel inquired of the Spaniards what vessel it was, and received for answer, that "it was the King's Cutter in search of Pirates." This answer satisfied us, and in a short time we were all hands, the master fisherman and three of his crew, on board our vessel. As soon as we were ready to weigh anchor, observing the Spaniard intent on watching the "Cutter," and delaying unnecessarily to get under way, I began to hoist the foresail, on which, he, for the first time, sang out to me in broken English, "no foresail, no foresail." By this time the sail was within three quarters of a mile of us. As I stood on the forecastle watching her, I saw one of her people forward, pointing at us what I supposed a spy glass; but in an instant the report of a musket and whistle of a bullet by my ears, convinced me of my mistake. This was followed by the discharge of, at least, twenty blunderbusses and muskets, from which the balls flew like hail-stones, lodging in various parts of our schooner; one of which pierced my trowsers and another Mr. Merry's jacket, without any essential injury.

At the commencement of the firing the four fishermen concealed themselves below deck, out of danger, and our Portuguese attempting to follow their example was forced back. I remained on the forecastle watching the vessel until the whistleing of six or seven bullets by my ears, warned me of my danger. At first I settled down on my knees, still anxious to ascertain the cause of this unprovoked outrage, until they approached within two or three hundred feet of us, when I prostrated myself on the deck, soon after which, the master fisherman arose, waved his hat at them, and the firing ceased. About forty or fifty feet abreast of us, she dropped anchor and gave orders for the canoe at our stern to come along side, which one of our fishermen obeyed, and brought on board of us their Captain and three men. The supposed Cutter was an open boat of about thirty-five feet keel, painted red inside and black without, except a streak of white about two inches wide; calculated for rowing or sailing—prepared with long sweeps, and carrying a jib, foresail, mainsail, and squaresail. She was manned by ten Spaniards, each armed with a blunderbuss, or musket, a *machete*, long knife, and pair of pistols. They were all dressed with neat jackets and trowsers, and wore palm-leaf hats. Their beards were very long, and appeared as though they had not been shaved for eight or nine months.

One of them had an extremely savage appearance, having received a blow, probably from a cutlass, across his face, that had knocked in all his front teeth and cut off a part of his upper lip, the scar extending some distance beyond the angles of the mouth—three of the fingers of his left hand, with a part of the little finger, were cut off, and the thumb was badly scarred. He was tall, well proportioned, and appeared to have some authority over the others. The Captain was stout, and so corpulent that I should not underrate his weight at 260 pounds. He reminded me strongly of a Guinea Captain I had formerly seen. He was shaved after the manner of the Turks; the beard of his upper lip being very long—was richly dressed—armed with a machete and knife on one side, and a pair of pistols on the other; besides which, he wore a dirk within his vest. After examining our papers, which had been accidentally saved by Capt. Hilton, he took out of a net purse, two doubloons, and presented them to the master fisherman in presence of all hands. This, we at first supposed to be intended as some compensation for the injury done, by firing at us. The account of our shipwreck, sufferings, and providential escape to the Island, was now related to him, by Manuel, which he noticed, by a slight shrug of the shoulders, without changing a single muscle of his face. He had a savage jeer in his look during the recital of our misfortunes, that would have robbed misery of her ordinary claims to compassion, and denied the unhappy sufferer even a solitary expression of sympathy.

After he had ascertained who we were, he returned to his own boat with three of his men, leaving one on board of us as a kind of prize master. Our master fisherman, who also accompanied him, was greeted by all on board the armed vessel in a manner that denoted him to have been an old acquaintance. We could see them passing to each other a long white jug, which, after they had all drank, they shook at us, saying in broken English, "Anglois, vill you have some *Aquedente?*" to which we made no reply. When they had apparently consulted among themselves about half an hour, they sent two men, with the jug, on board of us, from which we all drank sparingly, in order to avoid offence, and they returned to their own vessel, took in two more men and proceeded to the huts, which they entered and went around several times, then came down to our long boat and examined her carefully. After this they came off to our vessel with the *two canoes*, one of which, went to the armed boat and brought on board of us, all but the Captain and two of his men. Our little crew had thus far been the anxious spectators of these mysterious manœuvres.

There were circumstances which at one time encouraged the belief that we were in the hands of friends, and at another, that these pretended friends were calmly preparing for a "foul and most unnatural murder." Capt. Hilton was unwilling yet to yield his confidence in the treacherous Spaniard, who, I did not doubt, had already received the price of our blood. In this state of painful suspense, vibrating between hope and fear, we remained, until the master fisherman threw on the deck a ball of cord, made of tough, strong bark, about the size of a man's thumb, from which they cut *seven* pieces of about nine feet each—went to Capt. Hilton and attempted to take off his over-coat, but were prevented by a signal from their Captain. They now commenced binding his arms behind him just above the elbows with one of the pieces of cord, which they passed several times round, and drew so tight, that he groaned out in all the bitterness of his anguish.

My fears that they were pirates were now confirmed; and when I saw them, without temptation or provocation, cruelly torturing one whom shipwreck had thrown among them, a penniless sailor, reduced by sickness to an almost helpless condition, and entreating with all the tenderness of a penitent that they would not cut him off in the blossom of his sins, and before he had reached the meridian of life—reminding them of the wife and parents he left behind, I burst into tears and arose involuntarily as if to sell my life at the dearest rate, but was shoved back by one of the Pirates who gave me a severe blow on the breast with the muzzle of his cocked blunderbuss. A scene of woe ensued which would have tried the stoutest heart, and it appeared to me that even they endeavored to divert their minds from it, by a constant singing and laughing, so loud as to drown the sound of our lamentations—After they had told Manuel they should carry us to Matanzas as prisoners of war, they proceeded to pinion our arms as they had Capt. Hilton's, so tight as to produce excruciating pain.

We were now completely in their power, and they rolled us about with as much indifference as though we had been incapable of feeling, tumbling us into the canoes without mercy. They threw me with such force that I struck the back of my neck against the seat of the canoe and broke it. Capt. Hilton, Mr. Merry, Bridge, and the Cook were in one canoe; Russell, Manuel, and myself in the other. For the first time they now informed us that they were about to cut our throats, which information they accompanied with the most appaling signs, by drawing their knives across their throats, imitating stabbing and various other tortures. Four Pirates accompanied the other canoe and three ours, besides the four fishermen, two to manage each canoe. We were thus carried along side the piratical schooner, when all their fire arms were passed on board of her; the arm chest, which was in the stern sheets and covered with a tarpaulin, opened, several long knives and machetes taken out, their keen edges examined with the greatest scrutiny and passed on board the canoes for the expressed purpose of murdering us all.

The seven Pirates and four fishermen, as before, now proceeded with us toward the beach until the water was about three feet deep, when they all got out; the two fishermen to each canoe, hauling us along, and the Pirates walking by the side of us, one to each of our crew, torturing us all the way by drawing their knives across our throats, grasping the same, and pushing us back under the water which had been taken in by rocking the canoes. While some of us were in the most humiliating manner beseeching of them to spare our lives, and others with uplifted eyes were again supplicating that Divine mercy which had preserved them from the fury of the elements, *they* were singing and laughing, and occasionally telling us in broken English, that "Americans were very good beef for their knives." Thus they proceeded with us nearly a mile from the vessel, which we were now losing sight of by doubling a point at the entrance of the cove before described; and when within a few rods of its head, *where we had before seen the human bones*, the canoes were hauled abreast of each other, from twelve to twenty feet apart, preparatory to our execution.

The stillness of death was now around us—for the very flood-gates of feeling had been burst asunder and exhausted grief at its fountain. It was a beautiful morning—not a cloud to obscure the rays of the sun—and the clear blue sky presented a scene too pure for deeds of darkness. But the lonely sheet of water, on which, side by side, we lay, presented that hopeless prospect which is more ably described by another.

We had scarcely passed the last parting look at each other, when the work of death commenced.

They seized Captain Hilton by the hair—bent his head and shoulders over the gun-wale, and I could distinctly hear them chopping the bone of the neck. They then wrung his neck, separated the head from the body by a slight draw of the sword, and let it drop into the water;—there was a dying shriek—a convulsive struggle—and all I could discern was the arms dangling over the side of the canoe, and the ragged stump pouring out the blood like a torrent.

There was an imploring look in the innocent and youthful face of Mr. Merry that would have appealed to the heart of any one but a Pirate. As he arose on his knees, in the posture of a penitent, supplicating for mercy even on the verge of eternity, he was prostrated with a blow of the cutlass, his bowels gushing out of the wound. They then pierced him through the breast in several places with a long pointed knife, and cut his throat from ear to ear.

The Captain's dog, repulsed in his repeated attempts to rescue his master, sat whining beside his lifeless body, looking up to these blood hounds in human shape, as if to tell them, that even brutal cruelty would be glutted with the blood of two innocent, unoffending victims.

Bridge and the Cook, they pierced through the breast, as they had Merry, in several places with their knives, and then split their heads open with their cutlasses.—Their dying groans had scarcely ceased, and I was improving the moment of life that yet remained, when I heard the blow behind me—the blood and brains that flew all over my head and shoulders, warned me that poor old Russel had shared the fate of the others; and as I turned my head to catch the eye of my executioner, I saw the head of Russel severed in two nearly its whole length, with a single blow of the cutlass, and even without the decency of removing his cap. At the sound of the blow, Manuel, who sat before me, leaped over board, and four of the Pirates were in full chase after him. In what manner he loosed his hands, I am unable to say—his escape, I shall hereafter explain. My eyes were fixed on my supposed executioner, watching the signal of my death—he was on my right and partly behind me—my head, which was covered with a firm tarpaulin hat, was turned in a direction that brought my shoulders fore and aft the canoe—the blow came—it divided the top of my hat, struck my head so severely as to stun me, and glanced off my left shoulder, taking the skin and some flesh in its way, and divided my pinion cord on the arm. I was so severely stunned that I did not leap from the canoe, but pitched over the left side, and was just arising from the water, not yet my length from her, as a Pirate threw his knife which struck me, but did not retard my flight an instant; and I leaped forward through the water, expecting a blow from behind at every step.

The shrieks of the dying had ceased—the scene of horrid butchery in the canoes was now over—Manuel and I were in the water about knee deep—two of the Pirates after me, and all the rest, with the fishermen, except one Pirate, after Manuel. We ran in different directions; I, towards the mouth of the Cove, making nearly a semicircle in my track, to keep them over my shoulder, which brought me back again towards the canoes; and as the remaining Pirate came out in order to cut me off, I was obliged to run between the canoes, so near the last Pirate, that he made a pass at me and fell, which gave me the start. At the first of our race, I was after Manuel, with Pirates before and behind. My object was to gain the bushes as soon as possible, supposing their cutlasses would be an obstacle, which I had the good fortune to prove.

I lost sight of Manuel just as I entered the bushes; he was up to his breast in water, and the Pirates near him. When I entered the bushes one of the Pirates was within ten feet of me, and continued striking, hoping to reach me; and all of them yelling in the most savage manner, during the whole distance. The most of the way, the water and mud was nearly up to my hips—the mangroves were very thick, covered, as I before observed, with oyster shells up to high-water mark. It was about noon when I entered these bushes, my course Westerly, the Pirates after me, repeatedly in view, one of them frequently within three rods of me. Had it been on cleared land, I should soon have been overtaken by them; but the bushes were so large and thick as frequently to entangle their swords. I was barefoot; and had I worn shoes, they would soon have been lost in the mud.

My feet and legs were so badly cut with the oyster shells, that the blood flowed freely; add to this, my head was very painful and swollen, and my shoulder smarted severely. In this manner and direction I ran till the sun about an hour high, when I lost sight of the Pirates and paused for a moment, pulled off my jacket (the cord being yet on my right arm, which I slipped off) in which I rolled my hat, and taking it under my arm, I settled down on my knees, which brought the water up to my chin, in order to secrete myself. In this way I crept till nearly sunset, when, to my astonishment, I discovered the ocean, and just as the sun was setting, I crawled out to the border of the Island. I looked round and saw a very large bush of mangroves, the highest near, among the roots of which, I concealed myself. When the sun was setting, I could distinctly hear the splashing of water and cracking of bushes, and the Pirates hallooing to each other, which increased my apprehensions, supposing they might discover my track through the muddy water. I was almost exhausted from a severe pain in my side, caused by running so long, though I had determined not to yield to them until I fell under the blow of their cutlass. Soon after the sun was down their noise ceased, and I crept up to the top of the tall mangrove, put on my hat and jacket, where I set all night, until the sun rose the next morning, that I might discover if they had come round the Island to intercept my passage.

As I ran through the bushes, I disturbed numberless birds, among which was the Flamingo, who was extremely bold, flying around me with such a noise, that I feared it would betray me, by serving as a guide to my pursuers.

When the sun had arisen, without a cloud, I could discover nothing to increase my apprehension. I descended the mangrove and proceeded to the border of the Key—looked across the water before me, where lay another Key, which I judged 2½ or 3 miles distant. Here I stripped myself to my shirt, the sleeves of which I tore off, and with my trowsers, threw them into the sea. I then tied my jacket, which was of broad cloth, by means of the cord that was on my arm, slung it over my neck, and put my hat on, to protect my wounded head from the sun. In this plight I committed myself to the sea, first supplicating, on my knees, a Divine blessing on my undertaking; but doubting whether I should ever reach the opposite Key. Being, however, an excellent swimmer, having before swum nearly 2 miles on a wager, I reached the opposite Key without any other injury than the galling my neck with the cord; and with much less fatigue than I could have supposed. This Key was much of the description of the last, but smaller. I made but little pause, continuing my course South Westerly across it, which was, I should suppose, about three miles; and as I had not hurried, owing to my fatigue, when I arrived at its border, it was about the middle of the afternoon.

At about 2 miles distance, I descried another Key, to which I swam, slinging my jacket as before. When I arrived at this, which was the third Key, it was a little before sunset. I proceeded into the bushes about three-fourths of a mile, it being a small Key, and came out nearly to its margin, where I passed the night, leaning against a bunch of mangroves, with the water up to my hips. Such had been my fatigue and mental excitement, that even in this unpleasant situation, I slept soundly, until I was disturbed by a vision of the horrible scene in the canoes—the images of Capt. Hilton and Mr. Merry, mangled as when I last saw them, came before my eyes; and in my fancied attempt to rescue them, I awoke, but could not convince myself it was a dream, until I grasped my own flesh. Again I slept interruptedly until day-light. Being excessively hungry, for this was the third day since I had taken a single particle of food or drink, I plucked some of the greenest of the leaves; this relieved my hunger but increased my thirst. About sun-rise I departed from this Key, wading with the water, at times, up to my neck, for nearly a mile, when it grew deeper.

The next and fourth Key, being about another mile distant, I swam to. This day I kept on about the same course, South Westerly, and crossed three more small Keys, about a mile distant from each other. I had now arrived at the seventh and last Key; on this I passed the night, having prepared a kind of flake of old roots, on which I slept soundly, for the first time out of water, since I left Cruz del Padre. Between day-light and sun-rise, having eaten of the green leaves as before, and having been refreshed by sleep, I departed from the last Key; by this time so weak that I could scarcely walk. The water was not so deep but I could wade until within half a mile of what afterward proved to be Cuba; but of which I was ignorant at the time.

While I was crossing this last passage, I had to contend with a strong current probably from the mouth of the very river I afterward forded; and when but a few rods from the shore a shark approached within a rod; but to my great joy, he turned and left me.

I had now swam about nine miles beside the distance I had trav-elled through mud and water, and the hunger and thirst I had endured, having tasted neither food nor drink, except a few salt leaves of man-groves, during my flight. And to add to my sufferings, my almost naked body was covered with moschetoes, attracted by the blood and sores produced by my escape from Cruz del Padre.

Observing that this shore varied a little from those I had passed, I followed it in an Easterly direction, which was reversing my former course, for nearly two miles, when I came to a large yawl, with her foremast standing. As I set me down on her gun-wale, the thought struck my mind that this boat, like our own, might have preserved some unfortunate crew from the fury of the storm, in order to offer them up to the pitiless Pirate, who, perhaps, had not suffered a solitary individual to escape and say, that the vengeance of man, on these encrimsoned shores, had sacrificed those whom the mercy of God had spared amid the dangers of his "mighty deep." While I was employed by these reflections, the gnawings of hunger were suddenly aroused by the appearance of two Craw-fish under the stern sheets; one of which, I caught and devoured with such greediness, that it was very soon rejected; and although I at first thought I could have eaten a dozen of them, the exhaustion, produced by my efforts to vomit, destroyed all relish for the other.

I again proceeded on my old course, South Westerly, until about the middle of the afternoon, when I approached dry land, and set me down on a wind-fall to contemplate my situation; to a description of which, I might well have adapted the language of JOB: "My flesh is clothed with worms and clods of dust; my skin is broken and become loathsome." Near the roots of this tree, as I sat viewing some holes formed by land crabs, I observed water issuing from one of them. A more grateful and unexpected sight the Israelites could not have witnessed at the smitten rock; for I soon found the water proceeded from a boiling spring: and without it, I am sure I could not have survived another day; for it will be recollected that this was the first fresh water I had tasted since the morning my shipmates were murdered. But pure as it was, my parched stomach would not retain it, until after repeated trials, I succeeded in quenching my thirst. I again proceeded South Westerly, the land gradually elevating, until there suddenly opened upon me an immense plain, where the eye could reach over thousands of acres without the obstruction of a tree, covered with cattle of every age and description; some of which came snuffing around, so near, that in my crippled condition, I feared they might *board me.* But a swing of my hat set them capering and snorting in every direction. The number and variety of wild cattle collected on these plains is immense. I should think I saw more than five hundred hogs, chiefly of a dark colour, and more than half that number of horses, principally white; bulls, and cows with calves by their sides, goats, mules, &c.

I travelled on my course with as much rapidity as my feeble and exhausted condition would allow, until dusk, when I arrived at the bank of a small River; here I reposed uninterruptedly until day-light next morning. When I first attempted to arise, my limbs refused their duty; and I was compelled to seize hold of a bush that was near, in order to raise myself upon my feet. This is not strange, when we consider the fatigue and hunger I had endured, the wounds all over my limbs, and the numbness produced by sleeping without a covering, exposed to the dampness that arises from a fresh water river, in a climate like that of Cuba.

I paused on the bank a few moments observing the current, in order to ascertain the direction of its source, towards which, I proceeded, travelling on the bank until noon, when I entered a beautiful lime grove, the fruit of which, completely strewed the ground. After I had devoured as many of these, rind and all, as satisfied the cravings of hunger, I filled my jacket pockets, fearing I might not again meet with such a timely supply.

By this time I had discovered a winding foot path, formed by droves of wild cattle; but in vain did I search for the impression of a human foot step. This path I followed until it lead to a fording place in the river, where I paused, dreading the effect of fresh water on my sores, some of which had begun to scab over. But my situation would not admit delay; I therefore forded the river, which had been so swollen by

recent rains, that I was compelled to wade up to my arm-pits. This produced the apprehended effect; for I had no sooner reached the opposite shore, than my sores began to bleed afresh, and smart severely. My
supply of limes recruited my strength sufficiently to pursue my path
until sunset, when I again halted and set me down on a log.

The only article of clothing I had to cover my nakedness, was my
jacket; for the body of my shirt, I had left on one of the Keys, fearing
that the blood stains upon it, might bring on me some unjust suspicion. My numerous sores, owing to the alternate influence of heat
and fresh water, had now become so offensive as to occasion a violent
retching, that nearly overcame the feeble powers of my stomach; and
had it not been for my providential supply of limes, that afterward, in
some degree corrected their fœtor, I must have laid me down by this
log, a mass of corruption, and given my body up a prey to the birds
and wild beasts of the forest. The reader will not think this an exag-
geration; for while I was sitting here, the numerous Turkey-buzzards
that were roosting over my head, attracted by my offensive smell,
alighted within a few feet of me, and began to attack each other
with as much ferocity as if they were already contending for their
prey. I arose, as if to convince them that I yet possessed the power
of motion; though I doubted within myself whether they would not
have possession of me before the setting of another sun. But onward
I travelled as far and as fast as my feeble condition would permit, until
it was too dark to follow the path, when I laid down and passed a restless night, annoyed, as usual, with moschetoes. In the morning I arose
feeble and dejected; and in my prayers, which I had daily addressed to
HIM whose mercy-seat had so often covered me from the tempest,
and whose "pillar of cloud by day and pillar of fire by night" had not
yet forsaken me in the wilderness, I desired that I might meet this day,
(the sixth of my miraculous escape,) some being to whom I could

relate my sufferings, and the murder of my companions, as an appeal to my country, (bound as she is, to protect the humblest of her citizens,) to arise in the majesty of her naval power, and stay the hands of those who are colouring these barbarous shores with the blood of her enterprising seamen.

My life glass appeared to be nearly up, and I now began to yield all hopes of being relieved. My feet and limbs began to swell, from the inflammation of the sores, and my limes, the only sustenance I had, although they preserved life, began to create gnawing pains in my stomach and bowels. I however wandered on, following the intricate windings of the path, until the middle of the forenoon, when I discovered, directly in the way, several husks of corn, and soon after, some small sticks like bean poles, that had evidently been sharpened at one end by some human hand. This discovery, trifling as it may appear, renewed my spirits and strength to such a degree, that I made very little pause until about sun-set, when I espied in the path, not a great distance ahead, a man on horse back, surrounded by nearly twenty dogs! Fearing he might not observe me, I raised my hat upon my walking stick, as a signal for him to approach. The quick-scented dogs were soon on the start, and when I saw that they resembled blood hounds, I had serious apprehensions for my safety; but a call from their master, which they obeyed with prompt discipline, put my fears to rest. The man was a negro, mounted on a kind of mat, made of the palm leaf, and generally used for saddles by the plantation slaves on this Island.— When within a few rods of me he dismounted, approached with his drawn sword (machete) and paused in apparent astonishment; I pointing to the sores on me, fearing from his attitude he might mistake me for some highway robber. He now began to address me in Spanish, of which I knew only enough to make him understand I had been shipwrecked; on which he made signs for me to mount the horse. This I attempted, but was unable to do, until he assisted me. He then pointed in the direction of the path for me to go on, he following the horse, with his sword in his hand.

After travelling nearly three miles, I discovered a number of lights, about half a mile distant; and when we came up with them we halted near a large bamboo grove, where, with his aid, I dismounted, and by a signal from him, set down until he went to a hut and returned with a shirt and pair of trowsers, with which he covered my nakedness. He now took me by the hand and led me into a large house, occupied by his master, the owner of the plantation. A bench was brought me, on which I seated myself, and the master of the house, a grey headed Spaniard, probably turned of seventy, came toward me with an air of kindness, understanding that I had been shipwrecked.

As the old man was examining my sores, he discovered on my arm a handsome impression of the *Crucifix* that had been pricked in with indelible ink, in the East Indies some years before, which he kissed with apparent rapture, saying to me, "Anglois very much of the Christian," supposing me to be a Roman Catholic.—This drew around me all the members of the family, who kneeled in succession, kissing the image and manifesting their sensibility by tears, at the sufferings which they perceived by my sores and emaciated appearance, I must have endured. I was then conducted by an old lady, whom I took to be his wife, into another apartment, in the corner of which, was a kind of grate where a fire was kindled on the ground. Here a table was spread that groaned under all the luxuries which abound on the plantations of this Island; but it was perhaps fortunate for me, that my throat was so raw and inflamed I could swallow nothing but some soft-boiled rice and coffee.

After this refreshment, the kind old Spaniard stripped me, dipped a clean linen cloth into pure virgin honey and rubbed it over my sores.

He then pointed to the bed, which had been prepared for me in the same room. I gave him to understand, by signs, that I should besmear his clean sheets; but this was negatived by a shake of the head; so without further ceremony I turned in—it was the softest pillow I ever did, or expect to, lay my head on;—yet it was rest, not sleep.

The old man had ordered a servant to attend me during the night, fearing the little food I had taken, after so long an abstinence, might produce some serious illness. Every time I groaned or turned, this servant would run to me with a bowl of strong hot coffee, which I could not refuse without disobeying his master's orders. Early in the morning, before I arose, the old planter came to my bed side, examined my pulse and tongue, and brought me a quart bowl of fresh tamarinds, more than half of which, he compelled me to eat, in order to prepare my stomach for the after reception of food, and prevent those symptoms of inflammation, which his intimate knowledge of the healing art had enabled him to discover.

I arose, put on my clothes and walked out to survey the possessions of this wealthy old planter, to whose hospitality I had been indebted for my life.

4

DEATH ON THE COLUMBIA BAR

GABRIEL FRANCHÈRE

They thought they had completed a dangerous sea passage and were safe. But they were wrong.

Having taken on board a hundred head of live hogs, some goats, two sheep, a quantity of poultry, two boat-loads of sugar-cane, to feed the hogs, as many more of yams, taro, and other vegetables, and all our water-casks being snugly stowed, we weighed anchor on the 28th of February, sixteen days after our arrival at Karaka-koua.

We left another man (Edward Aymes) at Wahoo. He belonged to a boat's crew which was sent ashore for a load of sugar canes. By the time the boat was loaded by the natives the ebb of the tide had left her aground, and Aymes asked leave of the coxswain to take a stroll, engaging to be back for the flood. Leave was granted him, but during his absence, the tide having come in sufficiently to float the boat, James Thorn, the coxswain, did not wait for the young sailor, who was thus left behind. The captain immediately missed the man, and, on being informed that he had strolled away from the boat on leave, flew into a violent passion. Aymes soon made his appearance alongside, having hired some natives to take him on board; on perceiving him, the captain ordered him to stay in the long-boat, then lashed to the side with its load of sugar-cane.

The captain then himself got into the boat, and, taking one of the canes, beat the poor fellow most unmercifully with it; after which, not satisfied with this act of brutality, he seized his victim and threw him overboard! Aymes, however, being an excellent swimmer, made for the nearest native canoe, of which there were, as usual, a great number around the ship. The islanders, more humane than our captain, took in the poor fellow, who, in spite of his entreaties to be received on board, could only succeed in getting his clothes, which were thrown into the canoe. At parting, he told Captain Thorn that he knew enough of the laws of his country, to obtain redress, should they ever meet in the territory of the American Union.

While we were getting under sail, Mr. M'Kay pointed out to the captain that there was one water-cask empty, and proposed sending it ashore to be filled, as the great number of live animals we had on board required a large quantity of fresh water. The captain, who feared that some of the men would desert if he sent them ashore, made an observation to that effect in answer to Mr. M'Kay, who then proposed sending me on a canoe which lay alongside, to fill the cask in question: this was agreed to by the captain, and I took the cask accordingly to the nearest spring.

Having filled it, not without some difficulty, the islanders seeking to detain me, and I perceiving that they had given me some gourds full of salt water, I was forced also to demand a double pirogue (for the canoe which had brought the empty cask, was found inadequate to carry a full one), the ship being already under full sail and gaining an offing. As the natives would not lend a hand to procure what I wanted, I thought it necessary to have recourse to the king, and in fact did so. For seeing the vessel so far at sea, with what I knew of the captain's disposition, I began to fear that he had formed the plan of leaving me on the island. My fears, nevertheless were ill-founded; the vessel made a tack toward the shore, to my great joy; and a double pirogue was furnished me, through the good offices of our young friend the French schoolmaster, to return on board with my cask.

Our deck was now as much encumbered as when we left New York; for we had been obliged to place our live animals at the gangways, and to board over their pens, on which it was necessary to pass, to work ship. Our own numbers were also augmented; for we had taken a dozen islanders for the service of our intended commercial establishment. Their term of engagement was three years, during which we were to feed and clothe them, and at its expiration they were to receive a hundred dollars in merchandise. The captain had shipped another dozen as hands on the coasting voyage. These people, who make very good sailors, were eager to be taken into employment, and we might easily have carried off a much greater number.

We had contrary winds till the 2d of March, when, having doubled the western extremity of the island, we made northing, and lost sight of these smiling and temperate countries, to enter very soon a colder region and less worthy of being inhabited. The winds were variable, and nothing extraordinary happened to us till the 16th, when, being arrived at the latitude of 35° 11' north, and in 138° 16' of west longitude, the wind shifted all of a sudden to the S.S.W., and blew with such violence, that we were forced to strike top-gallant masts and top-sails, and run before the gale with a double reef in our foresail. The rolling of the vessel was greater than in all the gales we had experienced previously.

Nevertheless, as we made great headway, and were approaching the continent, the captain by way of precaution, lay to for two nights successively. At last, on the 22d, in the morning, we saw the land. Although we had not been able to take any observations for several days, nevertheless, by the appearance of the coast, we perceived that we were near the mouth of the river Columbia, and were not more than three miles from land. The breakers formed by the bar at the entrance of that river, and which we could distinguish from the ship, left us no room to doubt that we had arrived at last at the end of our voyage.

The wind was blowing in heavy squalls, and the sea ran very high; in spite of that, the captain caused a boat to be lowered, and Mr. Fox (first mate), Basile Lapensee, Ignace Lapensee, Jos. Nadeau, and John Martin, got into her, taking some provisions and firearms, with orders to sound the channel and report themselves on board as soon as possible. The boat was not even supplied with a good sail, or a mast, but one of the partners gave Mr. Fox a pair of bed sheets to serve for the former. Messrs. M'Kay and M'Dougal could not help remonstrating with the captain on the imprudence of sending the boat ashore in such weather; but they could not move his obstinacy.

The boat's crew pulled away from the ship; alas! we were never to see her again; and we already had a foreboding of her fate. The next day the wind seemed to moderate, and we approached very near the coast. The entrance of the river, which we plainly distinguished with the naked eye, appeared but a confused and agitated sea: the waves, impelled by a wind from the offing, broke upon the bar, and left no perceptible passage. We got no sign of the boat; and toward evening, for our own safety, we hauled off to sea, with all countenances extremely sad, not excepting the captain's, who appeared to me as much afflicted as the rest, and who had reason to be so. During the night, the wind fell, the clouds dispersed, and the sky became serene. On the morning of the 24th, we found that the current had carried us near the coast again, and we dropped anchor in fourteen fathoms water, north of Cape Disappointment. The *coup d'oeil* is not so smiling by a great deal at this anchorage, as at the Sandwich islands, the coast offering little to the eye but a continuous range of high mountains covered with snow.

Although it was calm, the sea continued to break over the reef with violence, between Cape Disappointment and Point Adams. We sent Mr. Mumford (the second mate) to sound a passage; but having found the breakers too heavy, he returned on board about mid-day. Messrs. M'Kay and D. Stuart offered their services to go ashore, to search for the boat's crew who left on the 22d; but they could not find a place to land. They saw Indians, who made signs to them to pull round the cape, but they deemed it more prudent to return to the vessel. Soon after their return, a gentle breeze sprang up from the westward, we raised anchor, and approached the entrance of the river. Mr. Aikin was then despatched in the pinnace, accompanied by John Coles (sailmaker), Stephen Weeks (armorer), and two Sandwich-islanders; and we followed under easy sail.

Another boat had been sent out before this one, but the captain judging that she bore too far south, made her a signal to return. Mr. Aikin not finding less than four fathoms, we followed him and advanced between the breakers, with a favorable wind, so that we passed the boat on our starboard, within pistol-shot. We made signs to her to return on board, but she could not accomplish it; the ebb tide carried her with such rapidity that in a few minutes we had lost sight of her amidst the tremendous breakers that surrounded us. It was near nightfall, the wind began to give way, and the water was so low with the ebb, that we struck six or seven times with violence: the breakers broke over the ship and threatened to submerge her. At last we passed from two and three quarters fathoms of water to seven, where we were obliged to drop anchor, the wind having entirely failed us. We were far, however, from being out of danger, and the darkness came to add to the horror of our situation: our vessel, though at anchor, threatened to be carried away every moment by the tide; the best bower was let go, and it kept two men at the wheel to hold her head in the right direction. However, Providence came to our succor: the flood succeeded to the ebb, and the wind rising out of the offing, we weighed both anchors, in spite of the obscurity of the night, and succeeded in gaining a little bay or cove, formed at the entrance of the river by Cape Disappointment, and called *Baker's Bay*, where we found a good anchorage.

It was about midnight, and all retired to take a little rest: the crew, above all, had great need of it. We were fortunate to be in a place of safety, for the wind rose higher and higher during the rest of the night, and on the morning of the 25th allowed us to see that this ocean is not always pacific.

Some natives visited us this day, bringing with them beaver-skins; but the inquietude caused in our minds by the loss of two boats' crews, for whom we wished to make search, did not permit us to think of traffic. We tried to make the savages comprehend, by signs, that we had sent a boat ashore three days previous, and that we had no news of her; but they seemed not to understand us. The captain, accompanied by some of our gentlemen, landed, and they set themselves to search for our missing people, in the woods, and along the shore N.W. of the cape. After a few hours we saw the captain return with Weeks, one of the crew of the last boat sent out. He was stark naked, and after being clothed, and receiving some nourishment, gave us an account of his almost miraculous escape from the waves on the preceding night, in nearly the following terms:—

"After you had passed our boat;" said he, "the breakers caused by the meeting of the wind roll and ebb-tide, became a great deal heavier than when we entered the river with the flood. The boat, for want of a rudder, became very hard to manage, and we let her drift at the mercy of the tide, till, after having escaped several surges, one struck us midship and capsized us. I lost sight of Mr. Aiken and John Coles: but the two islanders were close by me; I saw them stripping off their clothes, and I followed their example; and seeing the pinnace within my reach, keel upward, I seized it; the two natives came to my assistance; we righted her, and by sudden jerks threw out so much of the water that she would hold a man: one of the natives jumped in, and, bailing with his two hands, succeeded in a short time in emptying her. The other native found the oars, and about dark we were all three embarked.

The tide having now carried us outside the breakers, I endeavored to persuade my companions in misfortune to row, but they were so benumbed with cold that they absolutely refused. I well knew that without clothing, and exposed to the rigor of the air, I must keep in constant exercise. Seeing besides that the night was advancing, and having no resource but the little strength left me, I set to work sculling, and pushed off the bar, but so as not to be carried out too far to sea. About midnight, one of my companions died: the other threw himself upon the body of his comrade, and I could not persuade him to abandon it. Daylight appeared at last; and, being near the shore, I headed in for it, and arrived, thank God, safe and sound, through the breakers, on a sandy beach.

I helped the islander, who yet gave some signs of life, to get out of the boat, and we both took to the woods; but, seeing that he was not able to follow me, I left him to his bad fortune, and, pursuing a beaten path that I perceived, I found myself, to my great astonishment, in the course of a few hours, near the vessel."

The gentlemen who went ashore with the captain divided themselves into three parties, to search for the native whom Weeks had left at the entrance of the forest; but, after scouring the woods and the point of the cape all day, they came on board in the evening without having found him.

The narrative of Weeks informed us of the death of three of our companions, and we could not doubt that the five others had met a similar fate. This loss of eight of our number, in two days, before we had set foot on shore, was a bad augury, and was sensibly felt by all of us. In the course of so long a passage, the habit of seeing each other every day, the participation of the same cares and dangers, and confinement to the same narrow limits, had formed between all the passengers a connection that could not be broken, above all in a manner so sad and so unlooked for, without making us feel a void like that which is experienced in a well-regulated and loving family, when it is suddenly deprived by death, of the presence of one of its cherished members. We had left New York, for the most part strangers to one another; but arrived at the river Columbia we were all friends, and regarded each other almost as brothers.

We regretted especially the two brothers Lapensée and Joseph Nadeau: these young men had been in an especial manner recommended by their respectable parents in Canada to the care of Mr. M'Kay; and had acquired by their good conduct the esteem of the captain, of the crew, and of all the passengers. The brothers Lapensée were courageous and willing, never flinching in the hour of danger, and had become as good seamen as any on board. Messrs Fox and Aikin were both highly regarded by all; the loss of Mr. Fox, above all, who was endeared to every one by his gentlemanly behavior and affability, would have been severely regretted at any time, but it was doubly so in the present conjuncture: this gentleman, who had already made a voyage to the Northwest, could have rendered important services to the captain and to the company. The preceding days had been days of apprehension and of uneasiness; this was one of sorrow and mourning.

The following day, the same gentlemen who had volunteered their services to seek for the missing islander, resumed their labors, and very soon after they left us, we perceived a great fire kindled at the verge of the woods, over against the ship. I was sent in a boat and arrived at the fire. It was our gentlemen who had kindled it, to restore animation to the poor islander, whom they had at last found under the rocks, half dead with cold and fatigue, his legs swollen and his feet bleeding. We clothed him, and brought him on board, where, by our care, we succeeded in restoring him to life.

Toward evening, a number of the Sandwich-islanders, provided with the necessary utensils, and offerings consisting of biscuit, lard, and tobacco, went ashore, to pay the last duties to their compatriot, who died in Mr. Aikin's boat, on the night of the 24th. Mr. Pillet and I went with them, and witnessed the obsequies, which took place in the manner following. Arrived at the spot where the body had been hung upon a tree to preserve it from the wolves, the natives dug a grave in the sand; then taking down the body, and stretching it alongside the pit, they placed the biscuit under one of the arms, a piece of pork beneath the other, and the tobacco beneath the chin and the genital parts. Thus provided for the journey to the other world, the body was deposited in the grave and covered with sand and stones.

All the countrymen of the dead man then knelt on either side of the grave, in a double row, with their faces to the east, except one of them who officiated as priest; the latter went to the margin of the sea, and having filled his hat with water, sprinkled the two rows of islanders, and recited a sort of prayer, to which the others responded, nearly as we do in the litanies.

That prayer ended, they rose and returned to the vessel, looking neither to the right hand nor to the left. As every one of them appeared to me familiar with the part he performed, it is more than probable that they observed, as far as circumstances permitted, the ceremonies practised in their country on like occasions. We all returned on board about sundown.

The next day, the 27th, desirous of clearing the gangways of the live stock; we sent some men on shore to construct a pen, and soon after landed about fifty hogs, committing them to the care of one of the hands. On the 30th, the long boat was manned, armed and provisioned, and the captain, with Messrs. M'Kay and D. Stuart, and some of the clerks, embarked on it, to ascend the river and choose an eligible spot for our trading establishment. Messrs. Boss and Pillet left at the same time, to run down south, and try to obtain intelligence of Mr. Fox and his crew. In the meantime, having reached some of the goods most at hand, we commenced, with the natives who came every day to the vessel, a trade for beaver-skins, and sea-otter stones.

Messrs. Ross and Pillet returned on board on the 1st of April, without having learned anything respecting Mr. Fox and his party. They did not even perceive along the beach any vestiges of the boat. The natives who occupy Point Adams, and who are called *Clatsops*, received our young gentlemen very amicably and hospitably. The captain and his companions also returned on the 4th, without having decided on a position for the establishment, finding none which appeared to them eligible. It was consequently resolved to explore the south bank, and Messrs. M'Dougal and D. Stuart departed on that expedition the next day, promising to return by the 7th.

The 7th came, and these gentlemen did not return. It rained almost all day. The day after, some natives came on board, and reported that Messrs. M'Dougal and Stuart had capsized the evening before in crossing the bay. This news at first alarmed us; and, if it had been verified, would have given the finishing blow to our discouragement. Still, as the weather was excessively bad, and we did not repose entire faith in the story of the natives—whom, moreover, we might not have perfectly understood—we remained in suspense till the 10th.

On the morning of that day, we were preparing to send some of the people in search of our two gentlemen, when we perceived two large canoes, full of Indians, coming toward the vessel: they were of the *Chinook* village, which was situated at the foot of a bluff on the north side of the river, and were bringing back Messrs. M'Dougal and Stuart. We made known to these gentlemen the report we had heard on the 8th from the natives, and they informed us that it had been in fact well founded; that on the 7th, desirous of reaching the ship agreeably to their promise, they had quitted *Chinook* point, in spite of the remonstrances of the chief, *Comcomly*, who sought to detain them by pointing out the danger to which they would expose themselves in crossing the bay in such a heavy sea as it was; that they had scarcely made more than a mile and a half before a huge wave broke over their boat and capsized it; that the Indians, aware of the danger to which they were exposed, had followed them, and that, but for their assistance, Mr. M'Dougal, who could not swim, would inevitably have been drowned; that, after the Chinooks had kindled a large fire and dried their clothes, they had been conducted by them back to their village, where the principal chief had received them with all imaginable hospitality, regaling them with every delicacy his wigwam afforded; that, in fine, if they had got back safe and sound to the vessel, it was to the timely succor and humane cares of the Indians whom we saw before us that they owed it. We liberally rewarded these generous children of the forest, and they returned home well satisfied.

5

THE BURNING OF THE *MORRO CASTLE*

RILEY BROWN

~~~~~~

An idyllic transatlantic cruise and the approaching of New York Harbor do not necessarily mean the best is yet to come.

~~~~~~

Thoughts of war and disaster were far from the minds of the 549 passengers and crew of the Ward Liner *Morro Castle* on the morning of September 8, 1934, as she plowed her way toward New York. Most of the passengers were still asleep; others were up, making ready to disembark as soon as the ship docked. Storm warnings threatened bad weather up and down the coast and, around two-thirty in the morning, the sea was making up rapidly. The *Morro Castle*, however, hoped to beat the storm, as she was making twenty knots and was due in New York within two hours.

George W. Rogers, chief radio operator, was in his cabin preparing to go to bed, when someone knocked hurriedly on the door and entered before Rogers could reply.

It was the third assistant radioman; his face was white and drawn, and he had difficulty in speaking coherently.

"Chief! You'd better come up to the radioroom! The whole ship's afire!"

Leaping from his bunk, Rogers donned some clothes, and dashed for the passageway. The ship was in an uproar. Clad in nightclothes, a woman near the lounge door was screaming hysterically. Seeing Rogers, she lunged for him, clutching his arm desperately.

"It's not so, is it? Tell me, please? The ship's not on fire, is it?"

"Madam, I don't know. Perhaps, it's not as bad as it seems. You'd better go to your cabin and get your things. Try to be calm."

She glanced at him for a moment, seemed to gather courage from his face, then nodded and turned abruptly away.

Rogers shook his head and leaped for the stairs. On "B" deck, now, he ran into a wall of smoke, through which he could see the red flames licking and spitting. People bumped into him, screaming, pushing—praying. Men fought to keep their wives and children around them, strove to calm their loved ones with voices that shook and broke.

Suddenly, out of the smoke and flames, a boy and girl loomed, hands clasped. They were scarcely out of their teens, the boy dark and slender, the girl blonde and tiny. Each wore a life preserver.

The boy said calmly: "You're an officer, aren't you? We're going to jump. How far are we from the beach?"

"Five or six miles," Rogers said, "I don't know. Maybe eight. But you should wait for a boat."

"No," said the boy, "we're going together. In a boat we might become separated. We're not afraid, are we, Judith?"

The girl smiled. "No, we're not afraid—together."

They were gone in an instant.

Rogers made his way to the radioroom. The smoke was hanging in wreaths throughout the ship. Near the radioroom, in the lounge, the flames roared. The radioman knew that nothing could save the ship now; there remained but one thing to do—summon help without delay.

The radioroom was also on "B" deck, and Rogers knew that the fire would soon cut the cables that supplied the main transmitters with power. That would mean relying upon a small emergency transmitter for sending out a distress call.

The second assistant operator, Alagna, was on watch when Rogers came into the radioroom. Alagna said: "The nearest ship is the *Luckenbach*, chief. I heard him talking a few moments ago." He got up and handed the phones to Rogers.

Nodding tersely, Rogers put the phones over his ears. Smoke was piling into the radioroom, the steel beneath their feet growing hot. The chief operator glanced beyond the doorway, where flames were crackling.

"Get a release on an SOS from the captain," he said to Alagna. "No time to waste! I must contact some ship!"

When Alagna had gone, Rogers heard the *Luckenbach* asking WSC, the Tuckerton, N. J., radio station, if he had received a report that a ship was on fire at sea. Evidently, someone had sighted the flames from the *Morro Castle* and had put a report on the air. Having received no such report, WSC informed the *Luckenbach* to that effect.

Rogers decided to send out a standby signal so that all ships and stations within range would be waiting for the distress call once authority was received from the captain to send one. Accordingly, he switched on his transmitter and pounded out the following:

CQ CQ de KGOV QRX QRX.

Within a few seconds after this signal went out, the air became still; the operators were obeying Rogers' instructions to stop sending and stand by.

At three-twenty, Alagna returned from the bridge. Lips tight, he flashed a look at Rogers.

"Hell, chief! The captain refuses to send out a distress call at this time. Claims there's still time—"

As the second assistant spoke, the power went off, plunging the radioroom into darkness. The fire had reached the cables—all power was cut from the main transmitters!

Grabbing a flashlight Rogers whirled to the emergency transmitter. Installed for just such an emergency, this equipment was worked from a bank of batteries outside the radioroom. If the fire had not reached them, there might still be a chance—

"Here, Alagna!" Rogers snapped. "Hold this flashlight while I tune the transmitters!"

"Make it snappy, chief," Alagna whispered through tight lips. "We can't stay here long! Look at that paint on the bulkhead!"

Under the heat, the paint was peeling away from the steel; smoke and flames billowed through the door.

Feverishly, the radioman adjusted his transmitter, praying that the flames had not yet exploded the batteries. He pressed the key and was rewarded when he saw the antenna current meter flicker upward. He was on the air again.

Once more, he whipped out the standby signal. The heat was unbearable, the smoke stifling. He pushed Alagna to the door.

"Tell the captain I can't keep this equipment on the air very much longer. Tell him to release an SOS, or by God, I'll release it myself!"

Alagna made his way through the smoke and fire toward the bridge. The flames had gained such headway that he had considerable difficulty in finding his way. Finally, he located the captain on the bridge, and shouted in his ear that Rogers would be burned alive in the radioroom if the captain did not immediately release the distress call. His face white and drawn, the captain seemed to ponder; then suddenly he nodded.

"Release an SOS. Our position's twenty miles south of Scotland Lightvessel."

Fighting his way back to the radioroom, Alagna shouted over the roaring flames to Rogers: "All right, chief! Send the SOS! Position's twenty miles south of Scotland light!"

Rogers nodded grimly and turned to his key. He had wrapped a towel around his face so that he could breathe in the stifling smoke. He had propped his feet on the table, the steel deck being too hot to stand on. The curtains on the port side of the radioroom were now in flames, lending to the scene a ghastly red glow.

The distress message flicked out on the air: SOS SOS DE KGOV ON FIRE 20 MILES SOUTH OF SCOTLAND LIGHT NEED ASSISTANCE.

As Rogers finished this transmission, the small generator went out. Eyes blank and hopeless, the two radiomen stared at each other.

"The batteries—" whispered Alagna.

Rogers shook his head. "No. They'll make plenty noise when they go."

He groped his way over to the panel where the leads from batteries were fastened to the switch. While Alagna held the flashlight, Rogers explored the panel and found that the intense heat had melted the solder in the lugs, allowing the leads to slip out and break the connection. Having bent the lead around the lug to the best of his ability, he staggered back to the table.

Again the small generator hummed and Rogers flung out his frantic call for help for the second time. But no more. With a terrific sound, the batteries exploded. The last means of communication was out of commission!

"Come on, Rogers!" Alagna husked through parched lips. "You can't do any more! Let's scram!"

But Rogers did not hear. He was slumped in his chair, unconscious; fumes from the exploding batteries having overpowered him.

Picking him up, Alagna struggled to the door. The steel was blistering the assistant radioman's feet. The heat and fumes were almost overpowering. Somehow, he managed to get out in the passageway. Here, the air was a trifle better, and Rogers revived somewhat. With Alagna supporting his chief, the two radiomen made their way to the bridge. It was deserted. Their job finished, they went down from the bridge to the forecastle head, and were subsequently rescued by a Coast Guard surf boat. They had done the best they could for the hundreds of passengers aboard the *Morro Castle* and had upheld the finest traditions of the sea.

Apparently, the *Morro Castle* caught fire at about two thirty in the morning, the conflagration starting in the lounge room of "B" deck. It spread so rapidly that at four o'clock the entire ship from the bridge to the stern was a blazing inferno. Passengers had no choice but to throw themselves into the water and pray that rescue ships would arrive soon enough to save them.

On watch in the lookout tower of the Shark River Coast Guard Station at this time, Surfman Stephen M. Wilson sighted a red glow in the sky, and a few seconds later, made out the shape of a vessel in flames. He called the officer in charge of the station, Chief Boatswain's Mate M. M. Hymer, and reported the fire. Hymer immediately mustered his crew, and after reporting to the commander of the Fifth Coast Guard District, proceeded to sea in the station's motor surfboat. He had left orders for Surfman Leonard M. Eno to follow him at daylight in the picket boat CG 831.

Bringing his surfboat within a quarter of a mile of the burning vessel, Hymer and his crew could feel the heat from the flames. "Good Heavens, chief," a surfman said hoarsely, "she's a passenger liner!"

Even as he spoke, a cry sounded from a point off the bow. An object was seen bobbing on the water. Nearer the ship and clearly visible in the glow from the flames, other objects dotted the sea.

The Coast Guardsman headed his boat in closer and ran up alongside the man in the water. The man, past middle age, was clad only in nightclothes, with a preserver fastened about his waist. Looking at his rescuers through glazed eyes, he said, "Thank God! you came! Hundreds of people are dying, burning to death!"

The Coast Guardsmen counted nearly two hundred persons in the water, some with life preservers on, others swimming desperately. The surfboat moved in among them, picking them up singly and sometimes in groups. People could be seen leaping from the ship, which was covered by flames from bridge to stern. Hymer loaded the surfboat to the danger point. Seeing the lights of a steamer about a mile away, he turned and headed for her.

She proved to be the *Luckenbach* and was already preparing to lower her boats when the Coast Guard surfboat drew alongside. Hymer transferred the survivors, at the same time requesting *Luckenbach*'s captain to move in closer, so that no time might be lost in getting boats to the *Morro Castle*. Then wasting no time, the Coast Guardsman headed his craft back to the scene of horror.

At five o'clock the picket boat from Shark River station, Surfman Eno in charge, arrived and at once began to pick up survivors from the water. Handling his boat with superb skill in the rising seas the surfman rescued thirty people. Stephen M. Wilson, the surfman who had originally sighted the *Morro Castle*, dived time and time again from the picket boat. Swimming to survivors who were too weak to help themselves, he assisted many of them to the picket boat.

The last person saved by the picket boat was a young girl who had been supported in the water by a youth. As the craft was now dangerously overloaded, the Coast Guardsman was obliged to proceed, telling the youth that he would have to wait for the surfboat which was even then approaching from the direction of the *Luckenbach*. Having a life preserver on, the youth was in no immediate danger.

"Right," he said, smiling. "Just take care of my wife. She's fainted."

As the picket boat moved away toward the Steamer City of Savannah, which was standing by taking survivors aboard, one of the surfmen bent to examine the girl.

"She's dead," he said quietly.

The surfboat under the command of Boatswain Hymer continued to pick up the *Morro Castle*'s survivors, and in addition, towed the *Luckenbach*'s lifeboats back and forth from the *Morro Castle*. All in all, the Shark River boat rescued eighty people, besides picking up numerous bodies.

In most instances the survivors were too shocked and stunned to voice opinions of the disaster. A few told how the fire had suddenly broken out; how, in a few moments, the flames had seemed to cover the entire ship. Others related stories of horror aboard the *Morro Castle*, how parents screamed for their children, and how a woman had dived back into the flames for her dog. They spoke in jagged voices about the utter madness that had reigned on deck; how the flames had whipped about, driving people to the rails, and then into the water to escape the searing blasts.

The surfboats from the Sandy Hook station, together with the pilot boat from New York harbor, had arrived at the *Morro Castle* just after daybreak, by which time the Coast Guard boats had already rescued more than one hundred and twenty persons, and were searching in ever widening circles around the burning vessel for additional survivors.

On duty some thirty-five miles east of the *Morro Castle*'s position, the Coast Guard patrol boat *Cahoone* received the standby signal from the distressed vessel at three twenty-one that morning, but due to trouble being experienced with the intermediate frequency receiver, failed to get the distress call at three twenty-eight. The operators worked feverishly on the receiver, and at three fifty, the *Cahoone* was back on the air.

Cape May Coast Guard Radio station contacted the *Cahoone* at 4 A.M. and notified her that the *Morro Castle* was afire off Asbury Park, N. J. The *Cahoone* proceeded immediately, and arriving at seven fifty-five, joined in the rescue work.

The Coast Guard Cutter *Tampa*, at the dock in Staten Island, did not receive the distress message direct because of the low power transmitter being used aboard the *Morro Castle*. At four thirty-six, orders came for the *Tampa* to proceed, which she did, after having recalled the liberty crew, at five forty. Making about eighteen knots, she completed the run in a little over two hours, arriving at about seven fifty-seven, a few minutes after the *Cahoone*.

The *Tampa*, being the senior vessel present, took command and directed the *Cahoone* and all but one surfboat to work in toward shore, for it was hoped that survivors had themselves drifted or swum in that direction.

Meanwhile, the Coast Guard surf stations along the beach were kept busy. A crew from the Monmouth Beach rescued sixteen people from the surf, the surfmen forming a life chain out in the water in order to bring the survivors in. Surfmen of the Squan Beach Station rescued four persons and picked up six bodies; Bay Head Station saved five people, but only after Surfmen Grayson J. Mears and Robert A. Gent had fought through the rolling surf to bring them in. These two men nearly lost their lives in the effort and afterwards required medical treatment.

Nearly thirty Coast Guard surf stations assisted in the *Morro Castle* rescue work, together rescuing one hundred and seventy-three persons, and recovering thirty-eight bodies. The Service itself was credited with saving a total of two hundred and fifty-nine survivors and recovering fifty-six bodies.

Captain W. H. Shea, commanding the New York Division of the Coast Guard, stated in a letter to Headquarters:

"In the opinion of the division commander, Chief Boatswain's Mate (L) M. M. Hymer was the outstanding man in the Coast Guard in the performance of effective duty during the *Morro Castle* disaster. The fire was reported to him at 3:15 A.M., standard time, and he immediately started in action, as seen from his report. Going to sea in conditions that required and obtained great skill and seamanship in small boat handling, he and his crew in the motor surfboat should receive special commendation from Headquarters. Also, Surfman Leonard M. Eno and the crew of the CG 831 should be commended for their fine work. Special mention is made here of Surfman Stephen M. Wilson, who swam to various survivors and helped them into small boats. Signed, W. H. Shea, Commander, New York Division."

The forepart of the *Morro Castle* was comparatively untouched by the flames, the fire having confined itself to the middle and afterpart of the ship. Boatswain Morin, in charge of the Sandy Hook surfboat, informed the *Tampa's* commander that fourteen men were still aboard the burning liner, having taken refuge on the forecastle head. Boatswain Morin was directed to go as close as possible to the *Morro Castle* and take these men off.

After establishing communications with the liner's acting commander, Warms, Boatswain Morin reported to the *Tampa* that Warms had requested a line be put aboard the burning ship and a tow attempted to New York harbor, where fire boats could extinguish the conflagration.

The *Tampa*, with the aid of the New York pilot boat, finally managed to get a running line across to the *Morro Castle*, and now began a real struggle. As the latter's engine room had long since been abandoned and there was accordingly no steam on the winches, the men on the liner's forecastle head had to pull in the hawser by hand. After an hour of struggle with the wet and heavy line, they managed to get it through the anchor eye and make it fast. Next, the anchors were let go and the *Morro Castle* swung round in the sea, the wind coming across her stern, bringing the smoke and heat down on the fourteen men on the forecastle head. The *Tampa* immediately took up a strain on the hawser, and slowly, the *Morro Castle*'s nose came a round. The wind was directly off the bow now, and a heavy pall of smoke clouded the sky behind the burning vessel. For the men on the forecastle head, this was a welcome relief, the intense heat being thus alleviated.

There remained nothing more for these survivors to do. Realizing that the increasing gale might shift and drive the flames upon them, the *Tampa*'s commander ordered the Sandy Hook surfboat to go alongside the *Morro Castle* and effect the rescue.

In charge of the surfboat, Boatswain Morin knew that here was a task that would try his seamanship to the limit. The *Morro Castle*, free from the weight of her anchors, was pitching heavily, yawing widely behind the Coast Guard cutter. It was absolutely necessary that the

Coast Guardsman approach close enough to the burning ship's side to permit rescue of the survivors as they clambered down a Jacob's ladder.

Actually, there seemed very little chance of doing this without staving in the surfboat against the *Morro Castle* blistered side, and throwing the Coast Guard crew into the sea. Boatswain Morin was fully aware of these risks, but he had his orders. He maneuvered the surfboat closer and closer to the *Morro Castle*, while around him mingling smoke and spray dangerously limited visibility. The men on the forecastle watched breathlessly, for this might be their last chance of salvation.

The surfboat was close in now. But—suddenly—the *Morro Castle*, like a maddened sea monster, lunged directly at the surfboat. Desperately, Morin whipped his wheel over, his eyes pinned on the mass above him. The distance narrowed; collision seemed inevitable. Then, at the last moment, the *Morro Castle* listed suddenly away, and, as though disgruntled with its failure to crush the surfboat, rolled restlessly in the troughs.

Morin brought his craft around for a second attempt. This time, he was more successful, and in a few moments lay under the *Morro Castle*'s rail. He held the surfboat there, with only a yard or so separating him from disaster, until the last one of the fourteen survivors were safe on board. It was nine o'clock—a gray morning with fine rain drifting in sheets before the increasing wind—when Morin headed away from the burning liner.

A storm, previously forecast, was making up in earnest and the seas were tossing angrily, when soon after Morin had rescued the last survivors, the hitherto mentioned *Tampa* got under way and steered for New York with her tow. She made little headway. The *Morro Castle*, without a rudder or any other means of guidance, kept yawing broadside behind the *Tampa*, stretching the hawser so tight that it droned like a reed in the wind. Anxious eyes aboard the Coast Guard cutter watched that line, waiting for the loud "crack!" that would come when it parted. Once that happened, all hopes of saving what was left of the palatial ocean liner would be lost, for there would be no chance whatever of placing another hawser aboard her.

The *Tampa*'s commander requested the New York pilot boat to pick up a line which was dangling from the *Morro Castle*'s stern, and in this manner act as a rudder, so that the vessel might be held as well as possible on the course.

This was done, and for a time it seemed that Coast Guard ingenuity and perseverance would bring the *Morro Castle* into the harbor, where fire boats could extinguish the fire. Such good fortune was not to be, however. After a day's struggle with the burning hulk, the pilot boat was forced by the now raging gale to abandon its post. Aboard the Coast Guard cutter, it was feared that the hawser would part at any moment, and precautions were therefore taken to prevent injury to the men in the event that the broken line should come hurtling back upon the *Tampa*.

Hardly had this been done, when the hawser snapped with a report like that of a three-inch gun. The *Tampa* surged ahead, trembling throughout her frame. Destruction threatened her. Writhing through the air, the hawser struck her stern and fouled the churning screw. The cutter trembled. Bells jangled frantically in the engineroom, as the commander rang STOP on telegraph.

Her screw now hopelessly fouled, the cutter took the seas broadside and at once began to drive toward the beach, from which sounded the thunder of the surf. Furthermore, a sand bar was known to bear a cable's length ahead.

In response to orders from the bridge, both anchors were let go in an effort to check the *Tampa*'s headlong plunge to destruction. The men wondered: Will she hold?

Those were anxious moments. The anchors dragged. Then, suddenly, they bit, took solid hold, and the cutter lay within a few hundred feet of the beach.

The *Tampa* flashed a call to Divisional Headquarters in New York, and the cutter *Sebago*, which had been undergoing repairs, was ordered to assist her into port. The *Tampa*'s work was done. Along the beach, however, weary patrols from the Coast Guard surf stations continued to search for bodies. This work went on for days, until the surfmen were ready to drop from fatigue. Not until hope for the recovery of the rest of the bodies had been abandoned did these men get rest. Some of them had been on their feet for seventy-six hours. The concerted efforts of the Coast Guard units resulted in the saving of two hundred and fifty-nine lives and the recovery of fifty-six bodies.

Meanwhile, the *Morro Castle* had been driven ashore and had brought up near the pier at Asbury Park, N. J. The flames were dying now, but tremendous pillars of smoke still belched from the charred hull—a grim, blackened reminder of one of the worst tragedies in maritime history.

6

ON THE ROCKS
IN ALASKA, TWICE

ARCHIBALD CAMPBELL

A September gale off the coast of Alaska can be more ominous than even the most experienced sailor can imagine.

We left Kamschatka on the 8th of August, and proceeded on our voyage to the northwest coast of America. Nothing material occurred till the 10th of September. On the morning of that day it blew hard from the south, and the ship was reduced to close reefed topsails; about three in the afternoon, the gale increased to such a degree that it became necessary to take in the fore and mizen topsails.

Whilst the men were on the yards, they discovered land off the lee bow, distant about five or six leagues; we conjectured it to be that part of the continent called Aliaska; the ship's course was immediately altered from N. E. to E. and the weather proving more moderate in the evening, stood on, close hauled, but did not set more sail. About ten at night, the alarm was given that there were breakers ahead, and on the lee bow. Mr. Brinkman, the chief mate, who had the charge of the watch, immediately went to the mizen topmast head, and observing there was room to wear the ship, hastened below to report the circumstance to the captain.

When he returned upon deck, he instantly went to the wheel and ordered us to our stations, with the intention of wearing; but the captain, who followed him, was of a different opinion; he said what we saw was only white water, and not breakers; that there was no danger, and ordered us to stand on our course. He had scarcely given this order before the ship plunged, and struck with such violence as to knock away the fore-foot, and the watch below were driven from their hammocks against the deck. The sea running very high, she beat so hard that in a few minutes the rudder was unshipped, and the stern-post forced up through the poop; as she still had way upon her, she shot over the reef into deep water: upon sounding we found seventeen fathoms.

It was immediately determined to let go the anchor, and remain by the ship as long as she would swim. In case she went down, we hoped to save our lives by the long-boat, which was accordingly cleared and hoisted out, that she might be ready; seven of the guns were at the same time thrown overboard, in order to keep her above water until daylight. The carpenter attempted to sound the well, but owing to some obstacle, could not get down the sounding rod. I was sent below with him to bore a hole beside the pump thro' the lower deck; but on taking off the after hatch, we found the water as high as the shifting boards.

Early on the morning of the 11th, to our great joy, we saw land to the leeward of us, distant about three or four leagues. It was immediately determined to watch the lull, slip the cable, and cast the ship's head in shore, and steer her for it with the jib and fore-topsail.—After she was under way, the captain ordered that any of the crew that could not swim should go into the long-boat astern, and be ready as soon as she struck to come alongside for the rest, as he expected that she would then go to pieces. As soon as she struck, all hands came into the boat, and went for the shore, the captain taking his quadrant, until the tide should ebb, when he expected she would be nearly dry. We landed between eleven and twelve o'clock in the forenoon.

The land upon which we were thrown presented a most dreary appearance; it was an extensive plain, intersected by pools of fresh water, stretching about five miles from the sea, and terminated by two mountains. The ground was covered with heath and moss; not a tree nor a bush could be seen, neither did we observe the least trace of human habitations. As the land afforded us no sustenance, we turned our attention to the sea, and when the tide ebbed found some large muscles.

Having satisfied our hunger with some raw muscles, we prepared to go off to the ship; but on our way off we had the mortification to see her fall over on her beam ends. When we reached the ship we found that we could do nothing with her, and were preparing to leave her, when we discovered in the bottom of the long-boat the carpenter's axe; we then cut the parrel and gear of the main-topsail yard, and let it drive clear of the wreck, while we went to cut away the topmasts, and then left her for that day. On our way ashore we found the main-topsail yard, and took it in tow, and landed again about six o'clock in the evening. The approach of night rendering some shelter necessary, we made a sort of tent with a sail, and lay down on the moss, cold and wet, and spent a most uncomfortable night.

Next morning, the 12th, we set off along shore in search of any thing that might have driven from the ship, and found, in a bay at no great distance from our tent, a barrel of rosin, the arm chest, with one or two small carbines, some swan-shot, and, what was of greater consequence to us, several calking irons and mallets; on finding these we went to the ship, but the sea was so high we could not come near her, and we returned to our tent.

On the 13th, 14th, and 15th, we were employed in repairing the boat, which had begun to get very leaky; having picked some oakum, we calked the seams as well as we could. Over the places where this was insufficient, we nailed pieces of boards, and calked round the edges. Although we could not pay the seams, having nothing to melt our rosin in, we succeeded in making her tolerably tight.

On the 16th several pieces of wreck and some sails were secured; this day was chiefly employed in preparations for going off to the wreck. We formed a grappling iron by lashing four bolts together, and bending them, and made a line out of the rigging that came ashore with the spars; this proved of great service in fishing up articles from the wreck. Every thing being ready, and the 17th proving fine, we set off at day-break, and taking the carpenter's axe with us, we cut a large hole in her side, just before the main channels.—With the grappling irons we hooked several sails, and a number of other articles, such as boxes of silks and nankeens, and made three different trips to the wreck this day.

On the 18th we were busy in making a larger tent with the sails we had got. We set up two small spars at each end, and laid a studding sail boom across the tops of them; over this we spread a topsail, hung smaller sails at the ends, and placed planks round the bottom, to prevent them from being blown up by the wind. With the soft moss of the island for beds, and planks to sit upon, we now found ourselves pretty comfortable in every respect but one: All our attempts to kindle a fire proved unavailing, and we were obliged to eat our victuals raw.

Observing a flight of large birds, resembling ravens, carrying something in their talons, we watched where they alighted, and going to the spot, found several parcels of pork and beef which they had picked up, the barrels being staved by the rocks. In this manner we procured about a dozen of pieces. We again went off to the wreck in the afternoon, to see what we could get on shore, as it had every appearance of a gale of wind, and managed to get three of our chests out of the vessel before dark; and amongst them mine. It contained only one shirt and my bible, which I had put into one of those squares, common in sailor's chests, for holding case bottles, and in which it was firmly fixed, in consequence of having swelled with the water.

I was at great pains in drying it in the sun, and succeeded so well that I could read any part of it. It was afterwards saved from a second wreck; and in my future hardships and sufferings, the perusal of it formed my greatest consolation. It is still in my possession, being the only article I brought with me when I returned to my native country.

We also secured this day, a barrel of fine biscuit; it was soaked with salt water, but was, nevertheless, a most acceptable addition to our store. In the night, between the 18th and 19th, it blew so hard from the south, that the ship went to pieces before morning. At day-break, we discovered on a small isle, separated from the land by a channel which was dry at low water, the fore part of the ship, which had driven high up on the beach. Had we been able to have moved it to a better situation, it would have made an excellent hut; but this was beyond our strength. It was broken up and gradually removed when we could afford time. Some more fragments of the wreck, consisting of knees and planks, came on shore this day. We also recovered a few packages of nankeens and chests of tea, which we spread on the moss to dry.

Our horizon to the south being interrupted by the reef, the captain and mate went out in the long-boat to determine the latitude by a meridian altitude of the sun. The result of the observations gave 54 deg. 52 min. north, as the latitude of the south side of the island.

We made a number of trips to the wreck in the course of the ten following days, and saved a considerable part of the cargo, consisting of chests of tea, packages of nankeens, and bags of rice. The last time we went off to the wreck, before the arrival of the Indians, the wind was off shore, and began to blow so fresh that we were obliged to desist from our labours. After having secured a few more sails, some coils of cordage, and two bales of silks, having only two oars and a heavy boat to row, we reached the shore before dark, after a most fatiguing pull. By this time so much of the wreck was recovered that we determined to build a vessel large enough to carry us to the Sandwich Islands, where we were certain of meeting with an American ship. Our principal attention was now turned to that object, and we began our preparations by collecting into one place planks and other pieces of wood suitable for the purpose.

Our necessary occupations, and the unpromising appearance of the country, had hitherto prevented us from leaving the neighbourhood of our hut; but we had seen nothing that led us to imagine that the island was inhabited. We were, however, visited on the 28th, by a party of natives, who had traced the fragments of wreck along shore.

About mid-day we saw them approach in three small skin canoes, with one Indian in each. One of them, who had a gold medal about his neck, came forward, and addressed us in the Russian language. The captain, who had made a former voyage to these settlements, and understood a few words of the language, contrived to make our situation known to him. He immediately despatched one of his companions to a village on the northern part of the island for assistance, and the other to Oonalaska to give information to the commandant of the Russian settlements on that island.

The chief himself remained, and most willingly gave us a share of his provisions, which consisted of a bladder of train oil, and a basket of berries, about the size of bilberries, preserved in oil. These, to people in any other situation, would scarcely have been deemed an acquisition. Even we, who had lived so long on raw muscles, found some difficulty in reconciling ourselves to train oil; but we thought the berries, which had been cured with seal oil, no small luxury. This friendly Indian, who had hooks and lines, went out in his canoe, and in a short time returned with a few small fish. He then kindled a fire in the following manner: he laid a piece of soft wood upon the ground, and took another within his teeth; between these he put an upright piece of a harder quality, which he twirled rapidly around with a thong of hide, as we would a drill; the friction soon kindled the soft wood, and by placing it in dried grass, and blowing it, it burst into a flame.

We lost no time in broiling the fish, and enjoyed the first comfortable meal we had since the shipwreck.

Next day about forty Indians, men and women, came and encamped beside us; they made huts for themselves, by setting up planks, leaning against each other at the top, and throwing earth upon them, over which they put a covering of grass.

They brought a supply of provisions, consisting of berries, oil, blubber, and dried salmon, and gave us a share of all they had with the utmost liberality.

By the assistance of the Indians, who towed our boat with their canoes, we made two more trips to the wreck, and were successful in saving a considerable quantity of the cargo, as well as several articles of greater use to us for our intended vessel; such as bolts of canvass, cordage, and other naval stores, being part of the rigging of the ship that was stranded in the harbor of St. Peter and St. Paul. In saving these articles, the grappling-irons proved of the greatest service; for though the wreck lay in about three fathoms, the water was so clear, when the wind was southerly, that we could distinctly see what lay at the bottom. A considerable part of the ship still held together.

In about a week after this, Mr. Bander, the Russian commandant of Oonalaska, arrived in a large skin canoe or baidarka, with twenty or thirty Indians, who also hutted themselves beside us. The presence of so many visitors formed a singular contrast to the solitude in which we had hitherto lived. Our tent was now in the centre of a busy and populous village.

Some of our new visitors erected huts, whilst others contented themselves with sleeping under their baidarka, which they placed bottom up, and raised by supports from the ground on the lee side.

We were now in no want of provisions.—In addition to what the Indians brought with them, they procured us a plentiful supply of fish and fowl, particularly geese, in which the island abounded; these they shot with their rifles, in the use of which they are very expert.

These rifles are no wider in the bore than our own; but the metal is extremely thick, particularly at the muzzle. They load them almost full of powder, over which they force a piece of lead, three or four inches long, with a mallet; this comes out like an arrow. The piece is rested upon two supports, which fold out, and are stuck in the ground. I have seen them fire at the geese, which usually sat in rows, and kill several at one shot.

Mr. Bander took possession of the ship's cargo. Under his directions we went off to her several times, in company with the Indians, and brought away a considerable quantity of the nankeens and cloth; but were not successful in getting provisions, for we secured nothing except a few casks of damaged bread, and half a puncheon of rum.

Our chief attention was now turned towards our vessel, and we had a reasonable prospect of completing her by the aid of our visitors.

From Oonalaska we procured twelve Indians who could use the axe, and Mr. Bander promised us the assistance of Russian carpenters from Kodiak. To obtain which, as well as to report the loss of the ship to the governor of the Russian settlements, the long-boat was fitted out for a voyage to Kodiak.—About the 6th of November the necessary repairs were begun.

The seams were payed with a composition of the rosin that had been saved from the wreck, and train oil, boiled to a consistence in the kettles of the Indians. A kind of spar deck was formed, by laying the boards of the hat boxes over the thwarts; and upon these we nailed a tarpaulin: a hatch way was left at the stern, by which we got below, and in which the man at the helm could stand. We laid a small platform on the bottom, and covered it with skins; this formed a birth into which we could creep, but it was too low to allow us to sit upright. Out of the ship's spanker I made a suit of sails. She was rigged a sloop, and provided with a cable and grapnel. She was small enough for a voyage of 500 miles at such a season, being only twenty-two feet long, and measuring about six ton. She, however, proved an excellent sea-boat.

Every thing being completed by the 17th, we laid in our stores, consisting of dried salmon, berries, and oil, with a cask of water, and sailed on the following morning. The crew consisted of Mr. Bartram, second mate, myself, and seven more of the crew, one Indian, who acted as pilot.

The island on which we had now remained two months, is called by the natives Sannack; by Captain Cook it is named Halibut Island. It is situated in latitude 54. 27. north, longitude 197. east, and lies 10 or 12 leagues to the south of the promontory of Aliaski, and about 60 east of Oonalaska. It is quite flat, with the exception of two mountains, is eight or ten miles long, and about six broad. The main land could be distinctly seen; and the remarkable volcano mentioned by

Captain Cook, bore N. N. W. from our tent. It was constantly smoking during the day, and at night we could frequently see the flames.

The land produces nothing eatable but berries. To the south lies the dangerous reef upon which we were wrecked; it is of great extent, for when at the ship we observed breakers a considerable distance to the southward.

There is a village of 12 or 15 Indian families at the northern extremity of the island.—These people are under the government of the Russians, for whom they provide furs for the American company. They are a quite inoffensive race, converts to the Greek Church, and if not very devout, are at least extremely attentive to the ceremonial part of crossing themselves.

Their appearance and manners will be afterwards more particularly described. As the whole of their sustenance, clothing, and, indeed, every article they make use of, except a few berries, are the produce of the sea, they are extremely expert in managing their canoes, and most ingenious in their modes of catching fish and other sea animals. They are excellent marksmen with the rifle and spear; to the latter they fix a bladder, which prevents the wounded animal from taking it under water, and dart it with great force and certainty by means of a throwing stick.

Like all other savages I have seen, they are immoderately fond of spirits and tobacco.

We sailed from Sannack, in the long-boat, on the morning of the 18th of November; but had scarcely been an hour at sea, before we discovered a leak in the counter, which forced us to put back.

Having repaired the damage, we again set sail next morning, with a fair southerly wind. Our little vessel made better weather than could have been expected, and so long as it continued moderate, she scudded before the sea perfectly dry; we boomed out the foresail on the weather side, and the wind being fair, proceeded on our voyage at a great rate.—About noon it freshened into a smart gale, and the sea rose considerably, frequently curling over the stern in an alarming manner. Our open cock-pit rendered this extremely dangerous, till we adopted an expedient of which I fortunately recollected having read in the voyages of some Dutch navigators, who used oil to smooth the sea. Upon trying the experiment, it proved an effectual remedy. We lashed a keg of oil upon the taffrail, allowing a small stream to run from it, which spread a scum over the surface in our wake, and completely prevented the waves from topping.

The coast of Aliaski which we passed this day, is very mountainous, and deeply indented with arms of the sea. Many small islands lie near the shore, which are covered with brushwood. Sometimes a temporary hut erected by the hunters is to be seen, but there were no other symptoms of inhabitants. Extensive reefs of rocks lie a considerable distance off the land; our pilot, who was well acquainted with the navigation, took us within them; but strangers should be very cautious in approaching this part of the coast.

About ten at night we were close in with an island of considerable height, and attempted to pass to leeward, but were prevented by breakers, which obliged us to tack and pass on the outside. A round lofty rock lies a quarter of a mile to the southwest; the channel within seemed also full of rocks, and we were obliged to make another tack before we could weather it. Our situation for about two hours after this, was very alarming; we passed many sunk rocks, and were repeatedly obliged to tack in order to avoid them.

At day-break we found ourselves near a barren island, four or five miles in length, lying to the south of a larger one called Ungar. We passed through the sound between them, and, coasting along the southern shore of Ungar, arrived about ten A. M. at a village, situated on the eastern part of the island, after a run of 160 miles.

We found the settlement here in the most distressing situation. The whole of the male inhabitants, except the Russian overseer and his son, and the Indian interpreter, having gone out to catch seals, about three weeks before this time, a severe gale of wind came on, which their slight canoes were unable to resist, and every one of them perished. This dreadful calamity did not prevent the survivors from receiving us with the kindest hospitality. We were lodged in the hot bath, which was effectually warmed by the steam of water thrown upon red-hot stones.

Ungar is nearly twenty miles in length; in the interior the country rises into lofty mountains; near the sea it is more level, and is covered with brushwood, but produces no vegetable food, except berries, and a root from which the Russians make the liquor called quass. We remained eight days at this place, during which we went out several times to shoot deer, with which the island abounds, accompanied by the son of the overseer and the interpreter; we had tolerable sport, and the venison made a most acceptable addition to our store.

The natives seem, in all respects, the same as those at Sannack. The settlement consisted of one Russian and about thirty Indian families. The houses of the latter were built of mud, in the form of a bee-hive, with a hole at the top instead of a door; they had no fire-places, but warmed themselves by means of lamps made out of flat hollow stones, with rush wicks, which when cold, they placed under their frocks. One cooking place served for the whole village.

This island is separated from the main land, by a strait nearly ten miles wide at high water, but so extremely shallow that it is said to dry at low ebbs, when deer frequently pass over from the continent.

The village is situated on the north side of a small, well sheltered harbour, the entrance to which is between two rocky heads, not above a cable's length asunder. Within it is a quarter of a mile broad, and divides, a short way above the village, into two branches, one of which extends a considerable distance to the west. There are three or four high pointed rocks a little to the south of the entrance, but there is deep water all round.

We sailed on the morning of the 28th, with the wind at N. W. and steered between the main land and a small isle to the east of Ungar. Before we reached the open sea, the wind headed us, and blew with such violence as to force us back to the harbour we left in the morning. Gales from the N. E. with heavy falls of snow, prevented us from sailing for the eight following days. I employed myself in making a squaresail out of a bolt of canvass we had for the purpose.

Having laid in a store of deer's flesh, dried and boiled, the only provisions the place afforded, we again sailed on the morning of the 6th of December; the wind strong from the west, with squalls, accompanied with snow showers. The excessive cold made us feel severely the want of a camboose, or fireplace in the boat.

We continued to coast along the main land, within half a mile of the shore. Nothing could exceed the barren aspect of the country, which consisted of a range of steep and rugged hills, destitute of wood, or almost any appearance of vegetation. Many reefs lie a considerable way off the land.

On the 7th we passed an island called St. Ivan, the weather still very cold, with snow.

In the afternoon, the wind veered to the N. E. and blew with such violence that we were driven out to sea; had the gale continued, our situation would have been highly critical; for our water was nearly expended, and we were unprovided with a compass to direct our course; fortunately, however, it abated towards morning, when we tacked and stood to the shore. About noon we were close in with the land, and being anxious to kindle a fire, anchored in a bay, where the brushwood grew down to the water's edge. One of the Indians landed to cut firewood, but, he was scarcely upon shore when three bears made their appearance, and forced him to swim back to the boat. We were reluctantly obliged to desist; and having weighed anchor, we went ten miles further, to a village called Schutcum.

A number of sunk rocks lie about half a mile to the south of this place, with an intricate and narrow channel, through which we were piloted by the overseer, who came out to meet us in a bidarka.

After remaining here three days, we sailed again on the 13th, having met with the same hospitable treatment we had uniformly experienced from these islanders. They liberally supplied us with berries and oil, bear's flesh, and dried salmon. Soon after leaving Schutcum, we doubled a bluff head, and opened up a strait that separates Kodiak from the main land; a short way beyond it passed a narrow entrance leading into a spacious bay or inlet; the pilot told us that it stretched twenty or thirty versts into the country, and afforded an excellent shelter for ships.

We then stood over to Kodiak, which we reached in the evening; the wind W. S. W. with fine weather; we run along shore during the night. Next day, about two o'clock, we passed near a rock, on which several outches, or sea-lions, were sitting; some of them swam towards us, uttering loud yells; but as the boat was going at a great rate through the water, we soon lost sight of them.

Soon after, whilst crossing a deep bay, the wind checked round to the northwest, and blew so hard at times as to oblige us to take in all our sails. We endeavored to run under the west point of the bay, where there seemed to be good shelter; but we fell to leeward, and were under apprehensions that we should not be able to weather the point that formed its eastern extremity. Mr. Bertram proposed to run the boat ashore, but the surf was so heavy, that the attempt would have been extremely hazardous. I was of opinion that we might weather the point by carrying sail, and he allowed me to take the helm. Having set our close-reefed mainsail and storm-jib, the whole crew, except myself, went below, and lay as much as possible to the weather side, by which means the boat was enabled to carry sail till we cleared the head. After this we had the wind upon our quarter, and the evening proving fine, we made great progress.

The channel or strait, which separates Kodiak from the continent, is about fifteen leagues in breadth, and as far as I could judge, is free from danger, except close in shore.

We entered by moonlight the strait between Kodiak and several smaller islands to the east, with a strong tide in our favor, and were clear of it before daylight.

Being in want of water, we landed early in the morning, and having kindled a fire, had a warm breakfast before embarking. The country here was well wooded with pines, but we saw no inhabitants. We made sail about eleven, and entered the harbour of Alexandria before dark. We hoisted a Russian jack which we had on board, upon which a baidarka came off and towed us in. There were two ships and a brig at anchor in the bay.

Alexandria is the principal Russian settlement in the Fox islands, and the residence of the governor, upon whom we waited immediately upon our landing, with our letters from Mr. Bander.

He gave each of us a tumbler of brandy, and sent us to the cazerne, or barracks, where the Russian convicts lodged.

The brig which lay in the harbour was ordered to be fitted out for Sannack, for the purpose of taking in that part of the cargo of the *Eclipse* which had been saved from the wreck. As it would take a considerable time before she could be got ready, the governor ordered us to return in the boat with the carpenters and tools required for our vessel, that no time might be lost.

We remained here three weeks, and during that time we were employed in preparations for our return. The boards we had nailed on the boat's bottom were stripped off, and she was thoroughly repaired by the Russian carpenters. A camboose for our fire was made, by sawing a cask in two, and filling it with gravel, and secured by lashing it to the mast. We also provided ourselves with a compass, the want of which we had experienced in our voyage thither, our view of the land having been almost constantly intercepted by fogs and snow showers.

Mr. Baranoff, the governor, gave us a chart of the Fox islands and adjoining continent; and furnished us with letters, in case we should find it necessary to touch at any of the Russian settlements; he also sent three carpenters to assist in the construction of our vessel.

By the 8th of January 1808, every thing was completed, and we had laid in a good stock of provisions, consisting of salted pork and bear's flesh, two skin bags of rusk, two casks of water, and a keg of rum, with preserved berries, and blubber for the Indians.

We quitted the harbour of Alexandria on the morning of the 9th of January, on our voyage back to Halibut Island.

With a fine breeze of southerly wind we coasted along the northeast shore of Kodiak, leaving on our right a cluster of islands which lie to the eastward. Upon the largest, which is called Afognac, I was informed there are several Russian settlements.

This is the finest part of the island I have seen, the country being covered with wood, chiefly of the pine tribe, and many of the trees of great size. The other islands are also well wooded.

In the evening the wind died away, and the tide turned against us when nearly half way through the straits. We anchored for the night in a cove on the larboard side.

Next morning at daylight, we weighed, with a strong breeze from the east, which soon carried us clear of the strait. Upon reaching the open sea, we shaped our course to the northwest.

The headland or cape, which forms the extremity on the starboard hand, is perfectly level on the summit for nearly a mile, and terminates in a lofty perpendicular cliff.

On the following day the wind changed to the northwest, and blew hard, with a heavy sea; as it was directly against us, with every appearance of a gale coming on, we were obliged to bear away for a harbour. At noon, we reached a well sheltered bay, on the northern side of Kodiak. From the threatening appearance of the weather, it was judged prudent to haul the boat on shore; and there being no habitations within reach, we were under the necessity of living on board.

The bay was surrounded by high mountains, with a rocky shore, except at our landing place, where there was a small extent of sandy beach. The whole country was at this time, many feet deep with snow, which prevented us from making any distant excursions. At this place we were forced by the weather to remain ten days.

The dread of famine at last obliged us to put to sea, although the state of the weather was by no means favourable for the prosecution of our voyage. The surrounding country produced no food of any kind, and our stock of provisions was nearly expended. We left the bay, in hopes of reaching a settlement called Karlouski, which lay at no great distance to the west.

We launched the boat on the morning of the 21st, and stood over towards the main land. When about mid-channel, we discovered that the boat had sprung a leak; at the same time a heavy fall of snow came on, accompanied with violent squalls. The leak gained so much upon us, that it became absolutely necessary to run for the nearest shore.

Had the day been clear, we might have got back to the harbour we had quitted in the morning; but the snow rendered it so dark that we could scarcely see a boat's length ahead; we had therefore no resource but to put before the wind, and trust our lives to Providence.

The first view we had of the shore was most alarming; we were completely embayed, with a heavy surf breaking amongst the rocks, whilst, at the same time, the violence of the gale, and the state of the boat, were such as to preclude any hopes of working out of the bay. We therefore turned the bow to that part of the shore which seemed clearest of rocks, and a sea carried us so far up, that when it retired, we were left almost dry; the next wave carried us a little further, upon which the second mate imprudently let go the anchor; when it retired we all jumped out, and reached the shore in safety. Upon the return of the swell, the boat swung round, with her head to the sea, and being prevented by the anchor from driving farther up, she almost immediately went to pieces upon the rocks.

That part of the island on which we were cast was quite barren, and many miles distant from the nearest settlement, the path to which lay across mountains covered with snow.

After collecting what we could save of the wreck of the boat, we set out in search of some place to shelter us for the night, and fortunately discovered, at no great distance, one of those huts that are constructed for the use of the fox and bear hunters. It was too small to admit of a fire in the inside; but the number of people crowded into it rendered the cold less intense; and we lighted a fire in the open air, at which we made ready our provisions.

Upon examining our remaining stock, we found, that with the utmost economy, it would not last above three or four days; it became therefore necessary to form some plan to extricate ourselves from so deplorable a situation.

The bay in which we were wrecked was surrounded with high mountains, which ran down to the shore, terminating in a steep range of rocks, or what sailors call an iron bound coast. Karlouski, the nearest settlement, lay, as we were informed by our Russian companions, at a considerable distance to the west. We deliberated whether we should attempt to reach it by crossing the mountains, or by going along shore at low water. The danger and difficulty of making our journey over the snow deterred us from adopting the first plan: we therefore fixed on the latter, and determined to set out on our journey next morning.

On the morning of the 22d we quitted the hut, leaving one of the Russians and our Indian pilot to take charge of what we had saved from the boat.

Having proceeded some distance, we were interrupted by a reef of rocks, over which it was necessary to wade. I was provided with strong seal-skin boots, but unfortunately in crossing they were filled with water, which, the cold being so severe, the exercise of walking did not prevent from freezing. In a short time I lost all feeling in my feet, but was able to keep up with my companions, till our progress along shore was completely stopped by a mountain which projected into the sea.

Finding it impossible to get round the base, we attempted to climb over the summit. It was very steep, and in many places crusted with ice. I had by this time entirely lost the use of my feet, and with all my exertions, was unable to keep pace with my companions. In many places I was forced to dig steps in the ice and snow, with a pair of boots I had on my hands for that purpose. At length, after great labour and fatigue, I gained what I imagined to be the summit; it proved, however, to be little more than half way up, and the higher part of the mountain was quite inaccessible. I endeavoured to descend again; but in a short time found that the state of my feet rendered the attempt unavailing.

I had no alternative but to slide down; and, therefore, throwing away the boots, and placing my hands behind me, to direct my course, I came down with such velocity, that at the foot of the hill, I sunk at least ten feet into the frozen snow.

I was at first almost suffocated, till I made a little room by pressing the snow from me. I called as loud as I was able for assistance, but could not make my companions hear me, although I heard their voices perfectly well calling upon me. I at length relieved myself, by compressing the snow till it became sufficiently hard to bear my weight. I then planted my feet into it, and reached the surface.

We turned back, and endeavoured to proceed by a valley which lay behind the mountain. My feet by this time were frozen, never to recover; and I was so ill able to ascend, that I was frequently blown over by the wind, and sometimes driven a considerable way down the hill. Exhausted by these fruitless trials to keep up with the rest, I became totally unable to proceed, and was left to my fate. I laid myself down on the snow in a state of despair. Having recovered a little, I resolved to make another attempt to follow the track of my companions, but had not proceeded far when I met them coming down the hill, which had proved to be impassable.

We now set off on our return to the hut, but were soon interrupted by a steep rock, which the rising tide prevented us from passing. We had no resource, but to wait till low water next day, and to pass the night where we were. This was a most unfortunate circumstance for me, for had I reached the hut, and got my feet dried, they would in all likelihood have recovered. It blew hard, and the night was piercingly cold; we therefore returned to the valley, where there was at least some shelter from the wind.

The Russians, who knew the effects of cold, informed us that the consequences of lying down would be fatal. Although well aware of this, I was so much overcome by cold and fatigue, that I several times dropt asleep upon my feet; but my companions, who had not suffered so much, took care to arouse me.

Next morning we again set off for the hut, and met with no interruption till we came to the reef where I had got my feet wet. In consequence of the high wind, the swell was heavier than it had been the day before, and my feet were so powerless that a wave washed me completely off the reef into deep water. It was fortunately towards the shore, and on the returning wave I recovered my footing, and succeeded in getting over.

I followed my companions as well as my exhausted strength and the state of my feet would permit, but fell considerably behind, and had entirely lost sight of them, when my progress was impeded by a projecting crag, through which a natural perforation formed the only passage. The entrance was elevated a considerable way from the ground, and that part of the rock over which it was necessary to scramble, was nearly perpendicular, and almost covered with ice.

With a little assistance I could have easily got over; but situated as I was, my own exertions were of little avail. My feet were of no use in climbing, and I was obliged to drag myself up by my hands, in doing which they also were frozen. After many ineffectual attempts, I had, as I thought, gained the top; but when I had tried to lay hold of a projection in the rock, my fingers refused to perform their office, and I fell to the ground.

The tide was fast rising, and the surge already washed the spot where I stood; in a few minutes it would have been too late, and I must have perished had I been obliged to remain another tide, with my feet and hands frozen, and my whole body wet. As a last resource, I collected a few stones, which I had just strength to pile sufficiently high to enable me to get over.

This took place early in the day, and the hut was only a few miles farther on, but I was so much enfeebled that I did not reach it till dusk.

I never again walked on my feet; but, by the blessing of God, recovered the use of my hands, with the loss of only two fingers.

I was treated with great humanity upon my arrival, by the Russians, who had preserved their clothes dry in seal skin bags. They gave me a suit, and having cut off my boots, wrapped my feet and hands in flannel drawers. I was laid upon a bed of dried grass, after having satisfied my hunger with some rusk and blubber, which were the only provisions that remained.

As our stock was so low, no time was to be lost in procuring assistance; accordingly, the two who had remained set out next morning to endeavor to reach the settlement by the mountains.

On the third day after their departure our provisions were completely exhausted; but the weather had been tolerable, and we knew that if they succeeded, they would lose no time in sending us relief.

On the 27th, those who had been on the look out brought the joyful intelligence that five canoes were in sight, which proved to have been sent by our companions, who had reached the village in safety.

We quitted the hut on the 28th, in the canoes, which were baidarkas, with three seats in each. In crossing a bay we encountered a heavy sea; in order to keep me dry I was put below, and the hole in which I sat was stuffed up with the gut frock.

It was a great relief to me when we got into smoother water, for the space into which I was crammed was so small that I had nearly been suffocated. We arrived at Karlouski in the evening.

This settlement consisted of about thirty Indian families, and several Russians; the latter lived together in a cazerne, and the Indians in huts, which at this place were built of logs, wood being plenty. I was carried to the cazerne, where I was laid upon a bed of skins, and treated with the utmost attention; but as the place afforded no medical assistance, my feet and hands began to mortify, and my health was otherwise so much impaired, that I was frequently in a state of delirium.

We remained here till about the 25th of February, when we took our passage in a baidarka, or large skin-boat, bound to Alexandria, with a cargo of furs, berries, oil, and fish.—They had for provisions the salmon-roe, preserved in train oil, and kept in bladders. This is by them esteemed a delicacy, but it was too strong for my stomach.

The first night we landed at a village constructed differently from any I had hitherto seen; the whole of the houses, except the roofs, were under ground, and communicated with each other by a subterraneous passage. Bad weather, and contrary winds, detained us at this place eleven days.

We sailed again on the 7th of March. The wind being fair we hoisted a squaresail, and ran before it at a great rate. There is a group of small islands abreast of the south point of North-Island, at which place the tides meet, causing a heavy breaking sea; and as the baidarka was deeply loaded, it had a frightful appearance. The frame of the vessel was so extremely slight, that when between the waves, she was bent into a deep curve, and whilst on the top of the wave the two ends were as much depressed. I was in constant apprehension that the frame would give way. She however, went through the sea drier than a stiffer vessel would have done, and we reached the harbour of Alexandria on the 9th, without any accident.

7

THE LAST OF THE *MONITOR*

J. L. WORDEN,
LT. S. D. GREENE, AND
H. ASHTON RAMSAY

~~~~~~

The lights go out on a ship that once held much hope for the Confederacy.

~~~~~~

On the 29th of December, 1862, nine months after her memorable combat with the *Merrimac*, the *Monitor*, Commander John P. Bankhead, left Hampton Roads in tow of the *Rhode Island*, commanded by Captain Stephen Decatur Trenchard, for Beaufort, North Carolina. The weather at the time of starting looked favorable for the trip, but on the following day, when nearing Cape Hatteras, the wind came out from the southeast and gradually freshened until by evening it was blowing a moderate gale, with a tolerably heavy sea running. It was soon seen that the *Monitor* was making heavy weather of it, and the engines were slowed down, but the course was still kept head to the wind and sea.

This was a mistake, for experience later on in towing other vessels of her class proved that the safest way to handle them in heavy weather was to let them lie in the trough of the sea, when the waves would wash over their decks and the roll would not be excessive. The *Monitor* was closely watched, all on board the *Rhode Island* feeling anxious for her safety. Toward the end of the first watch—between 8 P.M. and midnight—the signal of distress, a red lantern, was hoisted on the *Monitor*, and, unknown to those on the *Rhode Island*, the hawser was cut and the anchor of the *Monitor* let go.

The *Rhode Island* immediately stopped her engine, and three boats were called away with an officer in charge of each, and were sent to take off the *Monitor's* people. With the heavy sea running it was a difficult matter to go alongside of her, and the first boat to reach her was thrown by a wave upon the deck and a hole stove in her. The next wave washed the boat off, and with considerable difficulty she took on board as many of the men as in her leaky condition could make the return trip safely.

When the boats came alongside of the *Monitor*, her captain and executive officer went upon the deck and, clinging to the life-lines with the waves washing over them, called to the crew to come down from the turret and get into the boats, which they were reluctant to do at first. Some were able to jump into the boats, and some landed in the water and were hauled in. Seeing an old quartermaster with a large bundle under his arm, the executive officer, thinking that it was his clothes-bag, told him that that was no time to be trying to save his effects. He said nothing, but threw it into the boat. When the bundle was passed up over the side of the *Rhode Island* it proved to be a little messenger-boy—probably the smallest and youngest one in the service. The three boats were finally loaded and made their way back to the ship.

In the meanwhile the *Rhode Island*, in backing her engines, had fouled the hawser with her port paddle-wheel, and being directly to windward of the *Monitor*, with her engines helpless, drifted down upon her. It looked at one time as if she would strike the bow of the *Monitor*, but, fortunately, she just missed it, and, scraping along her side, drifted off to leeward.

Another boat was sent to bring off the remainder of the *Monitor's* crew, but, being to leeward now, she could make only slow headway against the seas, and before she got to her the men saw the *Monitor's* light disappear, and knew that she had gone down. The hawser having finally been cleared from the *Rhode Island's* wheel, she steamed around searching for the boat, sending up rockets and burning blue lights to show her position. When the day dawned nothing could be seen. After hailing a passing government vessel and telling them to search for the boat, the *Rhode Island* steamed with all speed for Fortress Monroe to report the loss.

When the survivors of the ill-fated vessel were mustered on the deck of the *Rhode Island*, four officers and twelve men were found missing, all of them probably buried in an iron coffin in a watery grave about fifty miles to the southward and eastward of Cape Hatteras Light.

The missing boat and crew of the *Monitor* were found by that vessel a week later safe in Beaufort, North Carolina. They had been picked up by a schooner and taken into that port. The officer in charge of the boat reported that in the early morning he had sighted a schooner standing toward them, and had hoisted a black silk handkerchief belonging to one of the crew on an oar as a signal of distress, but the people in the schooner, evidently thinking them pirates who had come out of some one of the inlets of the coast, turned tail and scudded away from them. A second schooner, coming along soon after, was more hospitable and took them aboard.

8

THE WRECK OF
A SLAVE SHIP

ANONYMOUS

*To the men who made their livings and fortunes from trading humans,
slaves were nothing more than cargo—valuable only to a point.*

The following extract of a letter from Philadelphia, dated November 11th, 1762, gives an account of the melancholy disaster that befel the *Phœnix*, Capt. M'Gacher, in lat. 37 deg. N. and lon. 72 deg. W. from London, bound to Potomac, in Maryland, from the coast of Africa, with 332 slaves on board.

"On Wednesday the 20th of October 1762, at six o'clock in the evening, came on a most violent gale of wind at south, with thunder and lightning, the sea running very high, when the ship sprung a leak, and we were obliged to lie-to under bare poles, the water gained on us with both pumps constantly working. 10 P. M. endeavored to put the ship before the wind to no purpose. At twelve the sand ballast having choked our pumps, and there being seven feet water in the hold, all the casks afloat, and the ballast shifted to leeward, cut away the rigging of the main and mizen masts, both of which went instantly close by the deck, and immediately after the foremast was carried away about twenty feet above. Hove overboard all our guns, upon which the ship righted a little. We were then under a necessity of letting all our slaves out of irons, to assist in pumping and baling.

"Thursday morning being moderate, having gained about three feet on the ship, we found every cask in the hold stove to pieces, so that we only saved a barrel of flour, 10 lbs. of bread, twenty-five gallons of wine, beer, and shrub, and twenty-five gallons of spirits. The seamen and slaves were employed all this day in pumping and baling; the pumps were frequently choked, and brought up great quantities of sand. We were obliged to hoist one of the pumps up, and put it down the quarter deck hatchway. A ship this day bore down upon us, and, though very near, and we making every signal of distress, she would not speak to us.

"On Friday, the men slaves being very sullen and unruly, having had no sustenance of any kind for forty-eight hours, except a dram, we put one half of the strongest of them in irons.

"On Saturday and Sunday, all hands night and day could scarce keep the ship clear, and were constantly under arms.

"On Monday morning, many of the slaves had got out of irons, and were attempting to break up the gratings; and the seamen not daring to go down in the hold to clear the pumps, we were obliged, for the preservation of our own lives, to kill fifty of the ringleaders and stoutest of them.

"It is impossible to describe the misery the poor slaves underwent, having had no fresh water for five days. Their dismal cries and shrieks, and most frightful looks, added a great deal to our misfortunes; four of them were found dead, and one drowned herself in the hold. This evening the water gained on us, and three seamen dropped down with fatigue and thirst, which could not be quenched, though wine, rum, and shrub were given them alternately. On Thursday morning the ship had gained, during the night, above a foot of water, and the seamen quite worn out, and many of them in despair. About ten in the fore-noon we saw a sail; about two she discovered us, and bore down; at five spoke to us, being the *King George*, of Londonderry, James Mackay, master; he immediately promised to take us on board, and hoisted out his yawl, it then blowing very fresh. The gale increasing, prevented him from saving any thing but the white people's lives, not even any of our clothes, or one slave, the boat being scarcely able to live in the sea the last trip she made. Capt. Mackay and some gentlemen, passengers he had on board, treated us with kindness and humanity."

9

THE *GENERAL SLOCUM* IN THE GATES OF HELL

J. S. OGILVIE

What began as a Sunday lark ended as one of the greatest human tragedies ever in New York City.

Nothing approaching the recent *General Slocum* disaster has happened in New York before. The exact number of the women and children who were burned to death and drowned by the burning of the pleasure steamer *General Slocum* will not be far from twelve hundred.

Nearly all of those who were burned and drowned were women and little children, members of the Sunday School of St. Mark's Lutheran Church, in Sixth street, who were on their annual excursion.

Between 1,400 and 1,500 people, so far as can be learned, started out on the *Slocum*. Nearly a third of them were babies. Try as best they could, the police and hospital authorities and the officers of the church could not find more than 300 or 400 survivors. But everybody believed that, when matters were straightened out, and all the hospitals began to give an accounting of the wounded they had taken in spontaneously, the list of those members of the excursion still living would be most happily lengthened. Many of the excursionists were children not attached to the church.

"How did such a thing happen?"

That was the question which was reiterated up and down the length and breadth of the city. People read of the captain who found at 110th street that his boat, with its precious cargo, was on fire and yet did not drive it to the shore until he was beyond 138th street, a mile and a half from the place where the cry of "Fire!" first reached his ears.

Captain William H. Van Schaick of the *Slocum* explained, as best he could, how such horrible disaster had come to a company under his care and direction. He is a man 61 years old, and has had long experience in commanding pleasure craft in the waters around New York.

Captain Van Schaick said that though he heard the alarm of fire early, he made up his mind at once that there was no certain place where she could be beached in shallow water south of North Brother Island. The tide was running up to the Sound with terrific velocity, and he was sure that he would lose time trying to turn his boat into a proper beaching place south of North Brother Island. He stuck to his post, although the flames scorched his clothing, until the boat was hard and fast ashore. Pilot Van Wart stayed with him.

Fishermen generally were divided as to the good judgment shown by Capt. Van Schaick in trying to go so far. The captain himself admitted that it was not until after the fire had been going some time that he realized its fierceness and its rapidity. Captain Van Schaick and pilots Van Wart and Weaver were arrested and were sent to the prison cells of Bellevue Hospital, for all of them were badly burned.

There was a compartment in the hold of the *General Slocum* known as the second cabin. It was forward, just aft the forecastle. In this room were kept the lamps and the oil for them, the gasolene and the brass-polishing liquids, and all the other inflammable supplies. It cannot be determined whether or not the fire started in this cabin.

But it was known that the flames were fed there to reach their greatest and most murderous intensity. From that cabin the fire swept back through the boat with a fierceness that no fire-fighting apparatus could hold in check.

There were scenes of horror on the *General Slocum* and on shore such as it would not be decent to set down on paper, even though any chronicler had the ability. It was a boatload of women and little children. For the last mile, when the steamer, spouting flames high into the air, was shooting swiftly out to the Sound with the tide, people on the shore and on other steamers could see the women and children fluttering over the sides into the water in scores.

The river is swift there at flood tide. The waves grab forward at one another with hungry white fingers. A strong man would have but little chance. The women and the children had no chance.

There have been heard such stories as often come out after a disaster—stories of cruel selfishness by members of the crew, of cold disregard of the *Slocum*'s distress signals and most evident need by pleasure and business craft in the harbor. In the end came the story that there had been looting of the bodies of the dead. Some of these things were more or less true.

But there was a glorious record of self-sacrifice and bravery to be set over against all that was evil or unmanly.

Of such were the bravery with which the old captain and his pilots stayed at their posts; the noble efforts of Policemen Kelk and Van Tassel, who were on the burning boat, to save the lives of those entrusted to their care; the beautiful recklessness of the women nurses and the convalescent patients from the hospitals on North Brother Island, risking their lives to dash into the water around the burning boat to pull out drowning children and women; the brave deeds of the men on the city's boats, the *Franklin Edson* and the *Massasoit*, and on the tugs *Theo* and *Wade*. Some day someone will fittingly dress out the deeds of that little man, Capt. Jack Wade, and his daredevil crew. For every one whose deeds were seen and mentally registered in the flying moments of horror and peril, there were hundreds of others in which the rescued were too much scared to appreciate what was being done for them, and the rescuers were too busy to take note for themselves.

Ambulances and patrol wagons from nearly every corner of the city were sent to points along The Bronx shore nearest the wreck. Physicians and nurses came by hundreds, not only from hospitals, public and private, in all the boroughs of the city, but singly, from their private offices, from as far away as Newark and Paterson.

Bodies were sent down to the Bellevue Morgue from North Brother Island as fast as they were recovered, until there was no more room there. Most of them were unidentified. At about 5 o'clock at night, when the tide was low, there was a sudden increase in the rapidity with which bodies were recovered. They were brought out of the water near where the *Slocum* had been grounded at the rate of about one a minute. A temporary morgue was established on the island. The systematizing of the work of identification was completed, and it is hoped that nearly all the recovered bodies may be recognized. Some of them were so badly burned that they will never be recognized. At night great silent crowds, thousands and thousands of people, stood in front of the church in Sixth street, in front of the morgue and the Alexander Avenue Police Station, and along the East River shore opposite

North Brother Island—wherever the bodies of the victims were laid or where news of them could be learned.

The *General Slocum*, which was built of wood, started around the Battery at about 7 o'clock on the morning of the fatal day. Her crew of twenty-seven was aboard. She reached the foot of Third street, in the East River, where there is a recreation pier, at about twenty minutes past 8 o'clock.

There were several hundred excursionists already on the pier when the *Slocum* arrived. There were mothers full of pride in their lusty German-American babies, and full of anxiety for fear some of them would fall overboard in their haste to get on board the *Slocum* before anybody else did. A band came and went to the afterdeck and began booming out melodies dear to the German and the East Side heart. The mothers and children kept pouring across the gang plank and scurrying for "good places" about the decks.

The Rev. G. C. F. Haas, and his assistant, the Rev. J. S. Schultz, stood on opposite sides of the gang plank and welcomed the mothers and the scholars. Policeman Kelk and Van Tassel, full of experience in the handling of Sunday School excursions, took posts on the off-shore side of the *General Slocum*, ready to dive after any towhead who by mischance should fall overboard. It was as fine a day for a picnic as ever was. The sunlight made the blue water seem as bright as though it lay anywhere but between the piers of the biggest city of this nation. The ugly factory walls were set off by masts and flags, and big boats and little boats seemed rather to be skittering over the river for their own amusement than for any purpose of sordid profit.

The excursion was late in starting. Lutherans are great folk for going to family picnics in big family parties. Greta and Wilhelmina and August's wife gather from the corners of Manhattan and Brooklyn and bring all their children, and combine their luncheons so that it shall be served to ten or fifteen hungry mouths in proper proportions. And if any one of the whole family circle was late, then all the rest went to Pastor Haas and besought him, by all that was dear and sweet, not to let the boat go until sister and her little ones came. Pastor Haas was good-natured, and it was well along toward 10 o'clock when the *Slocum* started, the band on the upper deck playing "Ein Feste Burg 1st Unser Gott."

The children tugged at their skirts, held down by their smiling mothers and big sisters and grandmothers, and cheered at the departing pier. There was not a chill in the air. There was not a cloud on the blue sky. Pastor Haas went up and down the decks, and the matrons loudly communicated their congratulations to him.

Hell Gate, where the tide was rushing out to the Sound with the utmost violence, was passed safely. There isn't a steamer captain in this harbor, no matter though he be as old as Capt. Van Schaick, who is not glad when he has passed through Hell Gate without a collision and without being slewed out of his course against its rocky sides.

Though Capt. Van Schaick did not know it, the steamer must even then have been on fire. Just back of the crew's quarters, up in the bow of the steamer under the main deck, is what is called the second cabin. On the *Slocum* this cabin has been used as a sort of storeroom. Spare hawsers and paint and oils were kept there. Gasolene was kept there, and it was there that Albert Payne, a negro steward, kept the ship's lamps when they were not in place, and cleaned and filled them. Payne, his face ashy with the horrors he had been through, swore that he had finished cleaning all the lamps before the boat left her dock early that morning, and that he had not been in the room, except to see that everything was all right. He swore that just before the boat left East Third Street the second cabin was all right.

Along the Astoria shore, where there are many yards for the building of small boats, the trouble was known sooner than it was on the steamer itself. As the *Slocum* passed Broadway, Astoria, John E. Cronan, a Dock Department employee, was struck with the gayety of the steamer, with her flags, her music and her load of hilarious children, and called to a companion:

"Look at the *Slocum*! Don't it make you hate to work when you see a crowd having as good a time as that?"

But a quarter of a mile further on, William Alloway, the captain of a dredge, saw a burst of smoke puff out from the lower deck of the *Slocum* just forward of the smokestacks. He let off four blasts of his dredge whistle. At the same moment other boats on each side of the river began to toot shrill warnings. Alloway and his men could see a scurrying on the decks of the *Slocum*. They wondered why Capt. Van Schaick didn't back his boat right into the Astoria shore.

From the best understanding of the situation which could be gained from those who were left alive when everything was over, it was quite a while after the *Slocum* was first found to be on fire that the seriousness of the situation was understood by all of her officers and crew. Very few of the passengers knew anything of the real danger they were in until the burning and drowning had begun.

Eddie Flanagan was the *Slocum*'s mate. On excursion steamers the safety and comfort of the passengers are delegated to the mate, while the captain is in the pilot house, as he always is, very properly, while the boat is in motion. To Flanagan there came a deckhand and Steward McGann. He caught Flanagan by the shoulder and said:

"Mate, there's a fire forward, and it's got a pretty good headway."

Flanagan jumped down through the dark space in the middle of the boat and turned the lever of the fire drill alarm. He sent McGann to warn Capt. Van Schaick. The crew was not enough to handle so many passengers. The fire crackled up through one deck after another, licking out far on the port side. There was a rush for the stern. Some of the children thought that the whole alarm was a joke, and laughed and pummeled one another as they ran.

The mothers didn't. They lumbered after, trying vainly to keep hold of some one garment on the bodies of each one of their youngsters.

Captain Van Schaick ran back from the pilot-house and saw that Flanagan had two lines of hose run from the steamer's fire-pumps toward the second cabin, and that the water was already spurting through them. The fire drill on the *Slocum* was always well done. It was held, without any requirement of law, once every week. But this fire was beyond any mere fire drill. It took Captain Van Schaick only a minute to see that he ought to get his passengers ashore as soon as he could, he determined on, the north shore of North Brother Island.

It takes time to read of all these things. It took almost no time at all for them to happen. The yells and screams of the few people who were caught on the decks below the hurricane deck forward were ringing horribly across the water. The roar and crackle of the oil-fed flames shut these screams off from the frightened mass of Sunday School people aft.

Kelk and Van Tassel had leaped into the crowds when the fire-gongs rang. It was due to them that more women and children were not caught forward of the fire. They herded the people back like sheep until nearly the whole company were huddled together on the broad afterdecks. The fire was eating its way back steadily. The people were getting more and more frightened. Mothers whose children had been separated from them in the rush were getting frantic, and dashing madly through the crowd. Confusion grew almost as fast as the fire at the other end of the boat was growing. Van Tassel took to the rail.

"Now, everybody keep quiet!" he shouted again and again, waving his big arms reassuringly at women who were grasping the rail and already leaning over and trying to make up their minds to jump.

Pastor Haas had found his wife and his twelve-year-old daughter Gertrude and had put them near the back of a companion way, where he was sure he could find them. He, too, tried to calm his people. He might as well have tried to calm the whirling tide that was bearing the burning steamer along to its end. They were fighting now. Mothers who had started side by side with an endless fund of sympathy for domestic difficulties were fighting like wild beasts.

Screams came from the water. A woman looked over and saw three children floating by on the starboard side. The head of one of them was covered with blood where a blade of the paddlewheel had wounded it. The woman screamed just once, so loud that for a moment all the other horrible sounds of the boat seemed hushed. She pointed a finger at the little bodies that were floating back from the forward decks.

"Frieda!" she screamed. "Meine Frieda!"

Before a hand could be raised to stop her, if indeed there was anyone there cool enough in that moment to raise a hand, the mother jumped on the seat and threw herself over the rail. She sank, whirling over and over in the swift current. So did the children. But other bodies came. As the flames worked upward and backward more and more people were driven to jump to escape being burned. Mercifully, the pilot-house, away forward and up in the air, was in a position which the flames found it hard to reach. The captain and his pilots were able to keep steering.

It seemed to be the captain's purpose as he came up past 130th street to try to find a berth on The Bronx side of the stream. There are a number of coal and wood yards along there and some factories. Fishermen said that he might well have carried out his plan. The land forces of the Fire Department could have reached him there. But he said that a tug warned him off, telling him that he would only be setting fire to the shore buildings, and would not be helping his people in the least, if he ran in there.

At any rate, the *General Slocum*, observed now by hundreds of horror-dazed people on both sides of the stream and on the islands, turned again toward North Brother.

Steamers and tugs from far down stream were making after her. The Department of Correction boat *Massasoit* was on the far side of the Brother islands. Her captain lay in wait for the *Slocum*, not knowing through what channel she would come. From downstream came the slim, white *Franklin Edson*, the Health Department boat.

Thence, too, came the sturdy little *Wade*, with her tough-talking, daredevil, great-hearted little captain, Jack Wade.

There came also the tugs *Theo* and *Easy Time*, tooting their whistles, headed for the burning steamer.

On board the *Slocum* horror was being piled on horror too fast for anyone to keep track of them. The fire, leaping now high above the steamer's framework and roaring with a smoky glare of red tongues up thirty feet over the tall brown smokestacks, had begun to scorch the edges of the compact mass of women and children who were crowding back out of its way at the rear end of the boat.

The greater number of these people by far were on The Bronx side of the decks. They seemed to feel, poor creatures, that small as their chance for rescue was, when it came it would come from the thickly populated shore rather than from the bleak, rocky, bare spaces on the islands on the starboard side. The *Slocum* was now opposite 138th street, heading partly across the river toward North Brother Island.

With a crack and echoing volley of screams that set on edge the teeth of men hardened to almost any form of death or evidence of pain, the port rail of the *Slocum*'s after-deck gave way and all the people near it slipped and slid, one over another, into the water. She had hardly gone 200 yards further on—indeed, by ones and threes and twos and sevens gaily dressed women and little tots all in white were seen whirling down from the deck into the racing tide—when worse came. The steamers and tugs in pursuit were catching up one woman here or a child there, but it was not much they could do. The tide was too swift, and there was too much work to be done ahead to warrant any delay over individuals.

There was a puff like a great cough down in the *Slocum*'s inwards. A red starry cloud of sparks and smoke and flames shot up and the greater part of the superstructure aft plunged forward into the flames. How many hundreds of lives were snuffed out in that one instant nobody will ever know. Outsiders could see writhing, crawling figures in the burning wreckage, slipping down further and further into the flames until they were gone. As bees cling along a branch when they are swarming, there was a thick clustering of women, all screaming, and boys and girls around the edges of so much of the superstructure as was still standing.

At the very back Kelk, the policeman, was standing, catching up some of the smallest children and hurling them out at the decks of the nearest following steamers. Mothers threw their children overboard and leaped after them. When the stanchions burned out and the superstructure fell families were separated.

Thus it happened to Dominie Haas. He had given up as hopeless any effort to get the people quiet, and had just found his wife and daughter. The crash came and he lost them. Now the big steamer, ablaze for more than two-thirds of her 250 feet of length, was rounding the point of North Brother Island. The flames were reaching out for the pilot-house. The door toward the fire was blackened here and there and the paint blisters were bursting with little puffs of fire. But the hundred nurses gathered eagerly on shore waiting a chance to help, saw old man Van Schaick and his pilots at their wheel, straining forward as though by their own physical force they could make the boat go faster.

The captain and Van Wart are both of scrawny, hollow-cheeked build. Both have sandy side-whiskers, cropped close. Van Wart is taller than the captain. Weaver, the other pilot, is of heavier build. They made a wonderful picture, the three of them.

Afterward, when the horrors were all over except the most ghastly horror of all—the piling up and labeling of the dead—men spoke of the picture. It was at no moment certain that the pilot-house would not shrivel up and vanish in a puff of smoke. If it did the *Slocum* would never get close enough to the shore to make it possible for help to be given to the passengers who were still living. And the two old men and the younger, with never a look backward, whirled their wheel and braced it, and with their teeth set close together and never a word kept their eyes fixed on the one little stretch of rocky beach where it was possible for a steamer as big as the *Slocum* to be beached accurately and safely.

They succeeded in the fight that they had been making all the way from the Sunken Meadows, where the *Seawanhaka* was beached years ago. Capt. Van Schaick was past the Sunken Meadows, he said yesterday, before he knew that he had a fire on his boat, and the tide was too strong to let him turn back to beach her there, even had there been any way of rescue out there in the middle of the river.

The only heartening incidents of the whole horrible half hour began happening as soon as the *Slocum*'s bottom scraped on the North Brother Island shore, about twenty-five feet from the sea wall.

The *Massasoit*, which was the closest boat behind the *Slocum* when she struck, drew so much water that it was impossible to get her bow within fifty feet of the *Slocum*.

It didn't make any difference to Carl Rappaport, her coxswain. He took a running jump forward over the bow and swam toward the burning steamer. Like a big red-headed St. Bernard he grabbed two babies and swam back to his own boat. Meantime the captain of the *Massasoit* was putting boats overboard as fast as he knew how. When these were out picking up people from the water wherever they could, Rappaport was floundering around helping from the water side.

The *Franklin Edson*, with her new clean coat of white and gilt paint, drew less water than the *Massasoit* and went right up to the *Slocum's* side so that people jumped from the burning decks and were dragged back to safety. For safety was not on the forward deck of the *Edson*. She needs a new coat of paint. Her forward windows were cracked by the heat and there are the marks of flame for the forward thirty feet of her superstructure.

Jack Wade, master and owner of his little tug, was pitching his life preservers over, turning loose his boats and pushing up so close to the burning decks that the hair on his brawny arms frizzled and his men, John McDonnell, Ruddy McCarrol, and Bob Brannigan, had their shirts burned off their backs. It wasn't worth while afterward to attempt to get this crew to tell how many lives it saved. They had been too busy to count.

Ruddy McCarrol was plain beaten out for the first time in his life. The effort which finished him had been getting a very heavy German woman over the side, single-handed. When she was aboard she began to scream. Ruddy laid himself out flat, face down along the rail, and was sure he was going to die, he was so exhausted.

All along the shore, as the burning steamboat had come along the stream on the breast of the tide, fire alarms had been rung. One alarm at the foot of 138th street was rung three times. There was nothing the firemen could do when they came except just one thing, which was done at once. The captain of the first company to arrive at the river's edge telephoned for the fireboat *Zophar Mills*. She came up the river, screaming, with a voice that outscreamed all the other whistles which were being blown in every factory and yard from which the blazing steamship could be seen.

The captain of the *Mills* saw that the *Slocum* was beached and that rescuers were more needed than pumpers of water. He ran into 138th street and took aboard Capt. Geoghegan and all the reserves of the Alexander Avenue Station and took them over the river to help in the work of picking people out of the water from rowboats and tugs. There is a big marble works opposite North Brother Island. The boss, when he saw the *Slocum*, knocked off all work and sent his 150 men across in any and every sort of craft that they could lay their hands on.

Meantime the hundred nurses and the tuberculosis patients were doing wonderful things. Delicate-looking young women, in the dainty white uniforms which nurses wear, ran down to the water's brink and waded in up to their necks and formed human chains, along which struggling, half-drowned refugees were passed. Miss O'Donnell, the assistant nurse in charge, went out and brought in seven dead people and eight living. Every other nurse in the place was doing nearly as well. Dr. Watson, the head of the hospital, was out in the water with them, cheering them on. Mary McCann, a 16-year-old ward helper, just over from Ireland swam out four times and each time brought a living child to the shore.

Even though relieved by these evidences—but one or two out of hundreds that were happening unrecorded—of the working of good and brave human hearts, the misery and the horror were going on almost undiminished. The great hulk was still burning like a furnace on top of the water. Living men and women were still rolling out from her decks. Hundreds sought shelter from the heat under the paddle-boxes, which seemed slow to burn. In there, among the wet paddle-blades, the rescue boats were filled again and again.

Long after every one had given up any idea that there was a human life in the forward part of the boat, except those of Capt. Van Schaick and his two pilots, there was a shout of surprise and agony on shore. A small boy—he seemed about six years old—climbed up to the flagstaff and began to make his way up as though to get away from the deck, which was burning under him. He climbed a little higher and a little higher with each jump of the tongues of flame from below until he was almost at the top. He was a sturdy-looking little chap, and each time he found he had not gone enough he would shake his yellow curls determinedly and work his way a few inches more. It was a brave fight, but he lost it. The flagstaff began to tremble, just as a boat was getting around in position to get at the child. The staff fell back into the floating furnace, and the boy with it.

As fast as dead and living were brought ashore the weaker of the convalescent patients took them and carried them up on the lawn. There was a constantly increasing number of physicians coming over from the mainland, some of them in rowboats. Every burnt woman or child who showed any signs of life was carried into the buildings.

The nurses' quarters and the doctors' quarters and the stables and every place that had a roof where cots could be erected was filled— except those in which there were contagious diseases.

The dead were laid out in long rows on the grass. The living walked or were carried by them. Heartrending recognitions were there: women throwing themselves on the bodies of their children; children catching at their mothers' hands and begging them to "wake up," and screaming inconsolably when they realized that there would be no waking up.

There was too much to be done at once for any list to be kept of those who were rescued. The Rev. Mr. Haas was pulled out of the water, into which he had fallen soon after the *Slocum* beached and found to be not very badly injured. But it was more than an hour before he could be found and identified.

One reason for the heavy loss of life ascribed by those who assisted in the work of rescue was the apparent inability of all the passengers of the *Slocum* to swim. Scores were drowned within a few steps of firm footing. Not a few were drowned who might have saved themselves by standing up. Capt. Van Schaick and his pilots and all the rest of his crew except Steward McGann and Chief Engineer Conklin swam ashore without much difficulty after they once got safely into the water away from the flames.

It is not known what happened to McGann. Other members of the crew were sure that when the divers got down into the wreck of the *Slocum* they would find that Chief Engineer Conklin would be found dead at his post, from which he might have escaped any time, had he wanted to abandon the passengers to their fate.

When the *Zophar Mills'* commander was satisfied that there was no more chance of saving any lives he ordered that the burning hulk be got out of the way. With the help of several of the other tugs she was yanked out into the stream and floated, ablaze from stem to stern, over to Hunt's Point, a mile away, where she grounded again and burned to the water's edge and sank. She lies now about half a mile from Hunt's Point on the Bronx side of the stream and about a mile north of North Brother Island.

She lies with her yellow smokestacks tilted over to the south and one of her big yellow paddle-boxes visible. For the rest there is an outline of charred timbers and nothing more.

On many of the bodies which were recovered were life preservers which seemed to have been perfectly worthless. Assistant District Attorney Garvan's attention was called to a collection of the *Slocum's* life preservers which had been made by Capt. Jack Wade. These life preservers were covered with such flimsy, rotten stuff that they could be ripped open by a scratch with one's thumbnail. They were filled with ground-up cork instead of with solid chunks which would retain their buoyancy.

The work of recovering bodies went on steadily from the time when all hope of saving more lives ended. Nearly a hundred policemen, assisted by men from all the hospitals and morgues, went out in small boats and waded out and worked from the shore and from the decks of the tugs with grappling-hooks, dragging up all that was left of victims of the disaster. The bodies of some of those who were burned were in an indescribably horrible condition.

In the rush and confusion there were many things which in the face of a disaster less appalling would have shocked the sensibilities of the most hardened man who witnessed them, such, for instance, as the sight witnessed on a trip on a tug across to North Brother Island—a rowboat, with two men at the oars, and a small boy, who was holding a line by which were towed the bodies of three women, dressed all three in flimsy white dresses. Nobody was to blame. The boat would have been swamped with the three bodies inside.

At 10:30 at night 415 corpses had been recovered and tagged at North Brother Island. Fifty had been recovered at other points. They included a dozen that had first been landed at Oak Point. More were coming in at the rate of twenty an hour.

The police of the harbor squad, assisted by volunteers, were wading and rowing about the shore picking them up with grappling-hooks. So numerous were the corpses that early in the evening the bodies were recovered at the rate of one a minute.

All the boats used by the police and other workers were equipped with lanterns. In addition lights were hung on poles that had been stuck in the mud along the shore of the island. The police boat Patrol stood by constantly with a big searchlight playing on the waters. The employees of the hospital rigged up temporary lines of incandescent lights along the lawn to aid those at work in tabulating and searching the bodies.

10

THE LOSS OF THE BONHOMME RICHARD

HUTCHINS HAPGOOD

To the daring John Paul Jones, his valiant ship was a living and heroic being and its loss was close to unbearable.

John Paul Jones was also compelled to treat with the other French captains, and several times modified his course in compliance with their demands. He had formed a daring design to lay Leith, on the coast of Scotland, and perhaps Edinburgh, under contribution, but first he had to argue the matter with his captains. Fanning says: "Jones displayed so artfully his arguments in favor of his plan that it was agreed pretty unanimously to put it in immediate execution."

Jones's art was manifested in this instance, according to his account, by showing the captains "a large heap of gold at the end of the prospect." During this enforced conference, however, the wind shifted, and the undertaking had to be given up. Fanning quaintly remarks: "All his [Jones's] vast projects of wealth and aggrandizement became at once a shadow that passeth away, never more to appear again!"

Jones, however, said that he would have succeeded, even at this late hour, if his plan had been followed, and showed a touch of the weak side of his character when he added: "Nothing prevented me from pursuing my design but the reproach that would have been cast upon my character, as a man of prudence, had the enterprise miscarried. It would have been said: 'Was he not forewarned by Captain Cottineau and others?'"

With his old ship, his motley squadron, and his insubordinate officers, Jones then cruised along the Yorkshire coast, destroyed or captured a number of vessels, and was preparing to end his voyage at the Texel, Holland, when chance threw in his way the opportunity which he so greatly embraced.

On the 23d of September the squadron was chasing a ship off Flamborough Head, when the Baltic fleet of merchantmen, for which Jones had been looking, hove in sight. The commodore hoisted the signal for a general chase. Landais, however, ignored the signal and went off by himself. The merchant ships, when they saw Jones's squadron bearing down upon them, made for the shore and escaped, protected by two ships of war, frigates, which stood out and made preparations to fight, in order to save their convoy.

These British ships of war were the *Serapis*, a new frigate of forty-four guns, and the *Countess of Scarborough*, twenty guns. The *Alliance*, at that time, which was late in the afternoon, was not in sight, and the little *Vengeance*, which had been sent to look for Landais, was also not available. There were, therefore, two ships on each side, and Jones ordered Captain Cottineau, of the *Pallas*, to look after the *Countess of Scarborough*, while he himself took care of the *Serapis*. Jones never lost his head in action, and yet he decided, with that "cool, determined bravery," of which Benjamin Franklin spoke, and with "that presence of mind which never deserted him" in action, recorded by Fanning, to engage a ship known by him to be the superior of the *Bonhomme Richard* in almost every respect.

It has been said of Jones by one who fought with him that only in battle was he absolutely at ease: only at times of comparative inaction, when he could not exert himself fully, was he restless and irritable. On this occasion he joyfully engaged a ship which threw a weight of metal superior to his by three to two, that sailed much faster, and was consequently at an advantage in manœuvring for position, and that had a crew equal to that of Jones in numbers, and far more disciplined and homogeneous. A battle resulted which for desperate fighting has never been excelled, and perhaps never equaled on the sea.

Jones crowded on all possible sail, and the *Bonhomme Richard* came within pistol shot of the *Serapis*. It was seven o'clock of a fine moonlight night. Captain Pearson, of the British ship, then hailed, and was answered with a whole broadside from the *Bonhomme Richard*, an unfriendly salute which was promptly returned by the British ship.

From the beginning the fight seemed to go against the *Bonhomme Richard*. There was hardly any stage of the three and a half hours' desperate combat when Jones might not, with perfect propriety, have surrendered. Hardly had the battle begun when two of the six old eighteen-pounders forming the battery of the lower gun-deck of the *Richard* exploded, killing the men working them and rendering the whole battery useless for the rest of the action. Captain Pearson, perceiving his advantage in speed and power of shot, attempted again and again to pass the bow of the *Richard* and rake her. Jones's whole effort, on the other hand, was to close with the *Serapis* and board, knowing that it was only a question of time when, in a broadside fight, the *Richard* would be sunk.

After the broadsiding had continued with unremitting fury for about three quarters of an hour, and several of the *Richard's* twelve-pounders also had been put out of action, Captain Pearson thought he saw an opportunity, the *Serapis* having veered and drawn ahead of the *Richard*, to luff athwart the latter's hawse and rake her.

But he attempted the manœuvre too soon, and perceiving that the two ships would be brought together if he persisted in his course, he put his helm alee, bringing the two vessels in a line; and the *Serapis* having lost her headway by this evolution, the *Richard* ran into her weather quarter. Jones was quick to make his first attempt to board, but he could not mass enough men at the point of contact to succeed, and the ships soon swung apart.

The *Richard*, even at this early stage of the action, was in a deplorable condition. Little of her starboard battery was left. Henry Gardner, a gunner during the action, stated in his account of the battle that, at this time, of the 140 odd officers and men stationed in the main gun-deck battery at the beginning, over eighty were killed or wounded. There were three or four feet of water in the hold, caused by the *Serapis's* eighteen-pound shot, which had repeatedly pierced the hull of the *Richard*.

It is no wonder that Captain Pearson, knowing that his enemy was hard put to it, thought, after the failure to board, that Jones was ready to surrender.

"Has your ship struck?" he called, and Jones made his famous reply:—

"I have not yet begun to fight."

That Jones really made some such reply, there is no doubt. Certainly, it was characteristic enough. Jones fought all his life, and yet when he died he had hardly begun the conflict, so many of his ambitious projects remained unrealized.

When the ships had swung apart, the broadsiding continued, increasingly to the advantage of the *Serapis*. Had not a lucky wind, favorable to the *Richard*, arisen at this point, doubtless her time above water would have been short. The veering and freshening breeze enabled the *Richard* to blanket the enemy's vessel, which consequently lost her headway, and another fortunate puff of wind brought the *Richard* in contact with the *Serapis* in such a way that the two vessels lay alongside one another, bow to stern, and stern to bow. Jones, with his own hand, helped to lash the two ships together. The anchor of the *Serapis* fortunately hooked the quarter of the *Richard*, thus binding the frigates still more firmly together.

During the critical time when Jones was bending every nerve to grapple with the *Serapis*, the *Alliance* made her first appearance, poured a broadside or two into the *Richard*, and disappeared. Of this remarkable deed Jones wrote to Dr. Franklin: "At last the *Alliance* appeared, and I now thought the battle at an end; but to my utter astonishment he discharged a broadside full into the stern of the *Bon Homme Richard*." It is probable that the *Serapis* also suffered from Landais's attack, but not so much as the *Richard*, which lay between the other two ships.

After the *Serapis* and the *Richard* had been well lashed together, there began a new phase of the battle, which had already lasted about an hour. There were only three guns left in action on the *Richard*, nine-pounders on the quarter-deck, and the ship was badly leaking. The eighteen-pounders of the enemy had riddled the gun-deck of the American ship, rendering her, below-decks, entirely untenable. The real fight from this time to the end was consequently above-decks.

Jones abandoned any attempt at great gun fire, except by the three small pieces on the quarter-deck, drew practically his entire remaining crew from below to the upper deck and the tops, and devoted his attention to sweeping the decks of the enemy by the musketry of his French marines from the quarter and poop decks, and of the American sailors in the tops. The crew of the *Serapis*, on the other hand, were forced mainly to take refuge in their well-protected lower decks, from which they continued to fire their great guns into the already riddled hull and lower decks of the *Richard*.

After the juncture of the vessels Captain Pearson made several desperate attempts to cut the anchor loose, hoping in that way to become free again of the *Richard*, in which case he knew that the battle was his. Jones, of course, was equally determined to defend the anchor fastenings. He personally directed the fire of his French marines against the British in their repeated attempts to sever the two ships, to such good purpose that not a single British sailor reached the coveted goal. So determined was Jones on this important point that he took loaded muskets from the hands of his French marines and shot down several of the British with his own hand.

The captain of the French marines, who rendered at this important stage of the action such good service, had been wounded early in the battle, and the succeeding lieutenants had also been either killed or disabled. The marines had been greatly diminished in numbers and were much disheartened at the time Jones took personal command of them. Nathaniel Fanning vividly narrates the manner in which Jones handled these Frenchmen: "I could distinctly hear, amid the crashing of the musketry, the great voice of the commodore, cheering the French marines in their own tongue, uttering such imprecations upon the enemy as I never before or since heard in French or any other language, exhorting them to take good aim, pointing out objects for their fire, and frequently giving them direct example by taking their loaded muskets from their hands into his and firing himself. In fact, toward the very last, he had about him a group of half a dozen marines who did nothing but load their firelocks and hand them to the commodore, who fired them from his own shoulder, standing on the quarter-deck rail by the main topmast backstay."

A French sailor, Pierre Gerard, who has left a memoir of the battle, tells how his countrymen responded to Jones's presence: "Commodore Jones sprang among the shaking marines on the quarter-deck like a tiger among calves. They responded instantly to him. In an instant they were filled with courage! The indomitable spirit, the unconquerable courage of the commodore penetrated every soul, and every one who saw his example or heard his voice became as much a hero as himself!"

Both vessels were at this time, and later, on fire in various places. Captain Pearson says in his official report that the *Serapis* was on fire no less than ten or twelve times. Half the men on both ships had been killed or disabled. The leak in the *Richard*'s hold grew steadily worse, and the mainmast of the *Serapis* was about to go by the board. The *Alliance* again appeared and, paying no heed to Jones's signal to lay the *Serapis* alongside, raked both vessels for a few minutes indiscriminately, went serenely on her way, and brought her inglorious and inexplicable part in the action to a close.

Captain Pearson had, for a moment, towards the end of the action, a ray of hope. A gunner on the *Richard*, thinking the ship was actually sinking, called for quarter, but Jones stunned him with the butt end of a pistol, and replied to Pearson, who had again hailed to know if the *Richard* had struck, to quote his own report, "in the most determined negative." About the same time, the master at arms, also believing the ship to be sinking, opened the hatches and released nearly two hundred British prisoners, taken in the various prizes of the cruise.

Nothing, apparently, could be more desperate than the situation of Paul Jones then. His guns useless, his ship sinking and on fire, half of his crew dead or disabled, the *Alliance* firing into him, a portion of his crew panic-stricken, and two hundred British prisoners at large on the ship! But with Lieutenant Richard Dale to help him, he boldly ordered the prisoners to man the pumps, and continued the fight with undiminished energy. Soon after occurred the event which practically decided the battle in his favor.

He had given orders to drop hand grenades from the tops of the *Richard* down through the enemy's main hatch. It was by this means that the *Serapis* had been so often set on fire. Now at an opportune moment, a hand grenade fell among a pile of cartridges strung out on the deck of the *Serapis* and caused a terrible explosion, killing many men. This seemed to reduce materially the fighting appetite of the British, and soon after a party of seamen from the *Richard*, with the dashing John Mayrant at their head, boarded the *Serapis*, and met with little resistance. Captain Pearson thereupon struck his colors, and the victory which marked the zenith of Jones's career, and upon which all else in his life merely served as commentary, was scored.

Captain Pearson, in his court-martial, which was a formality in the British navy in case of defeat, explained Jones's victory in a nutshell: "It was clearly apparent," he said, "that the American ship was dominated by a commanding will of the most unalterable resolution," and again, "the extraordinary and unheard-of desperate stubbornness of my adversary had so depressed the spirits of my people that, when more than two hundred had been slain or disabled out of 317 all told, I could not urge the remnant to further resistance."

The capture of the British ship, which took place about half-past ten at night, came none too soon, for the old *Bonhomme Richard* was sinking. The flames were extinguished by combined efforts of crew and prisoners by ten o'clock the next morning, but with seven feet of water, constantly increasing in the hold, it was then apparent that it was impossible to keep the old vessel afloat, and men, prisoners, and powder were transferred to the *Serapis*.

On the morning of the 25th Jones obtained, "with inexpressible grief," as he said, "the last glimpse of the *Bonhomme Richard*," as she went down.

The desperate battle fought in the bright moonlight was witnessed by many persons in Scarborough and on Flamborough Head, and they spread the alarming tidings throughout England. In a letter to Robert Morris, written soon after, Jones said, of the cruise in general: "We alarmed their coasts prodigiously from Cape Clear round to Hull; and had I not been concerned with sons of interest I could have done much."

With his two new prizes (for the *Countess of Scarborough* had after a short action struck to the greatly superior *Pallas*) Jones set off for the Texel, with a most dilapidated crew and fleet. The *Alliance*, well called a "Comet" by the editor of the Janette-Taylor collection of Jones's papers, disappeared again after the battle. Landais, whose conduct was described by Jones as being that of "either a fool, a madman, or a villain," was afterwards dismissed the service, but not until he had cut up other extraordinary pranks. He now went off with his swift and uninjured frigate to the Texel, leaving Jones, laden down with prisoners and wounded, unassisted.

Of the *Richard*'s crew of 323, 67 men had been killed, leaving 106 wounded and 150 others to be accommodated on the injured *Serapis*. Then there were 211 English prisoners on the *Richard* at the beginning of the action; and of the 332 (including 8 sick men and 7 non-combatants) men composing the crew of the *Serapis*, there were 245 left to be cared for—134 wounded, 87 having been killed. There were, consequently, only 150 well men to look after 562 wounded and prisoners.

Some of the latter were afterwards transferred to the *Pallas*, but altogether it was an unwieldy fleet which slowly sailed for the Texel, at which neutral port Jones arrived October 3, none too soon, for as he entered the roads, an English squadron, consisting of a sixty-four ship of the line and three heavy frigates, which had been looking for him, hove in sight.

The effect of the cruise was very great. The English people, alarmed and incensed, never forgot it. Never before had one of their ships of war been conquered by a vessel of greatly inferior force. Their coasts, deemed impregnable, were again invaded by the man whom they called, in the blindness of their rage, pirate and renegade. Professor Houghton, a serious-minded historian, writing of Jones said: "His moral character can be summed up in one word—detestable."

English comment on Paul Jones may be summed up truthfully in one word,—envenomed.

Jones's exploits, moreover, greatly increased the prestige of young America, and made of himself a still greater hero at home and particularly in France. For the rest of his life, indeed, Jones, in France especially, where spectacles are peculiarly appreciated, was the man on horseback, and he enjoyed the position intensely. Fanning narrates how Jones, while at Amsterdam, soon after his arrival in the Texel, "was treated as a conqueror. This so elated him with pride, that he had the vanity to go into the State House, mount the balcony or piazza, and show himself in the front thereof, to the populace and people of distinction then walking on the public parade."

11

THE BURNING OF
THE *PHILADELPHIA*

HENRY CABOT LODGE AND
THEODORE ROOSEVELT

A daring plan and a resolute crew announced to the world that the young America was not going to take it anymore.

It is difficult to conceive that there ever was a time when the United States paid a money tribute to anybody. It is even more difficult to imagine the United States paying blackmail to a set of small piratical tribes on the coast of Africa. Yet this is precisely what we once did with the Barbary powers, as they were called the States of Morocco, Tunis, Tripoli, and Algiers, lying along the northern coast of Africa.

The only excuse to be made for such action was that we merely followed the example of Christendom. The civilized people of the world were then in the habit of paying sums of money to these miserable pirates, in order to secure immunity for their merchant vessels in the Mediterranean. For this purpose Congress appropriated money, and treaties were made by the President and ratified by the Senate.

On one occasion, at least, Congress actually revoked the authorization of some new ships for the navy, and appropriated more money than was required to build the men-of-war in order to buy off the Barbary powers. The fund for this disgraceful purpose was known as the "Mediterranean fund," and was intrusted to the Secretary of State to be disbursed by him in his discretion.

After we had our brush with France, however, in 1798, and after Truxtun's brilliant victory over the French frigate *L'Insurgente* in the following year, it occurred to our government that perhaps there was a more direct as well as a more manly way of dealing with the Barbary pirates than by feebly paying them tribute, and in 1801 a small squadron, under Commodore Dale, proceeded to the Mediterranean.

At the same time events occurred which showed strikingly the absurdity as well as the weakness of this policy of paying blackmail to pirates. The Bashaw of Tripoli, complaining that we had given more money to some of the Algerian ministers than we had to him, and also that we had presented Algiers with a frigate, declared war upon us, and cut down the flag-staff in front of the residence of the American consul. At the same time, and for the same reason, Morocco and Tunis began to grumble at the treatment which they had received.

The fact was that, with nations as with individuals, when the payment of blackmail is once begun there is no end to it. The appearance, however, of our little squadron in the Mediterranean showed at once the superiority of a policy of force over one of cowardly submission. Morocco and Tunis immediately stopped their grumbling and came to terms with the United States, and this left us free to deal with Tripoli.

Commodore Dale had sailed before the declaration of war by Tripoli was known, and he was therefore hampered by his orders, which permitted him only to protect our commerce, and which forbade actual hostilities. Nevertheless, even under these limited orders, the *Enterprise*, of twelve guns, commanded by Lieutenant Sterrett, fought an action with the Tripolitan ship *Tripoli*, of fourteen guns. The engagement lasted three hours, when the *Tripoli* struck, having lost her mizzenmast, and with twenty of her crew killed and thirty wounded. Sterrett, having no orders to make captures, threw all the guns and ammunition of the Tripoli overboard, cut away her remaining masts, and left her with only one spar and a single sail to drift back to Tripoli, as a hint to the Bashaw of the new American policy.

In 1803 the command of our fleet in the Mediterranean was taken by Commodore Preble, who had just succeeded in forcing satisfaction from Morocco for an attack made upon our merchantmen by a vessel from Tangier. He also proclaimed a blockade of Tripoli and was preparing to enforce it when the news reached him that the frigate *Philadelphia*, forty-four guns, commanded by Captain Bainbridge, and one of the best ships in our navy, had gone upon a reef in the harbor of Tripoli, while pursuing a vessel there, and had been surrounded and captured, with all her crew, by the Tripolitan gunboats, when she was entirely helpless either to fight or sail.

This was a very serious blow to our navy and to our operations against Tripoli. It not only weakened our forces, but it was also a great help to the enemy. The Tripolitans got the *Philadelphia* off the rocks, towed her into the harbor, and anchored her close under the guns of their forts. They also replaced her batteries, and prepared to make her ready for sea, where she would have been a most formidable danger to our shipping.

Under these circumstances Stephen Decatur, a young lieutenant in command of the *Enterprise*, offered to Commodore Preble to go into the harbor and destroy the *Philadelphia*. Some delay ensued, as our squadron was driven by severe gales from the Tripolitan coast; but at last, in January, 1804, Preble gave orders to Decatur to undertake the work for which he had volunteered.

A small vessel known as a ketch had been recently captured from the Tripolitans by Decatur, and this prize was now named the *Intrepid*, and assigned to him for the work he had in hand. He took seventy men from his own ship, the *Enterprise*, and put them on the *Intrepid*, and then, accompanied by Lieutenant Stewart in the *Siren*, who was to support him, he set sail for Tripoli. He and his crew were very much cramped as well as badly fed on the little vessel which had been given to them, but they succeeded, nevertheless, in reaching Tripoli in safety, accompanied by the *Siren*.

For nearly a week they were unable to approach the harbor, owing to severe gales which threatened the loss of their vessel; but on February 16 the weather moderated and Decatur determined to go in. It is well to recall, briefly, the extreme peril of the attack which he was about to make. The *Philadelphia*, with forty guns mounted, double-shotted, and ready for firing, and manned by a full complement of men, was moored within half a gunshot of the Bashaw's castle, the mole and crown batteries, and within range of ten other batteries, mounting, altogether, one hundred and fifteen guns.

Some Tripolitan cruisers, two galleys, and nineteen gunboats also lay between the *Philadelphia* and the shore. Into the midst of this powerful armament Decatur had to go with his little vessel of sixty tons, carrying four small guns and having a crew of seventy-five men.

The Americans, however, were entirely undismayed by the odds against them, and at seven o'clock Decatur went into the harbor between the reef and shoal which formed its mouth. He steered on steadily toward the *Philadelphia*, the breeze getting constantly lighter, and by half-past nine was within two hundred yards of the frigate. As they approached Decatur stood at the helm with the pilot, only two or three men showing on deck and the rest of the crew lying hidden under the bulwarks. In this way he drifted to within nearly twenty yards of the *Philadelphia*. The suspicions of the Tripolitans, however, were not aroused, and when they hailed the *Intrepid*, the pilot answered that they had lost their anchors in a gale, and asked that they might run a warp to the frigate and ride by her.

While the talk went on the *Intrepid*'s boat shoved off with the rope, and pulling to the fore-chains of the *Philadelphia*, made the line fast. A few of the crew then began to haul on the lines, and thus the *Intrepid* was drawn gradually toward the frigate.

The suspicions of the Tripolitans were now at last awakened. They raised the cry of "Americanos!" and ordered off the *Intrepid*, but it was too late. As the vessels came in contact, Decatur sprang up the main chains of the *Philadelphia*, calling out the order to board. He was rapidly followed by his officers and men, and as they swarmed over the rails and came upon the deck, the Tripolitan crew gathered, panic-stricken, in a confused mass on the forecastle.

Decatur waited a moment until his men were behind him, and then, placing himself at their head, drew his sword and rushed upon the Tripolitans. There was a very short struggle, and the Tripolitans, crowded together, terrified and surprised, were cut down or driven overboard. In five minutes the ship was cleared of the enemy.

Decatur would have liked to have taken the *Philadelphia* out of the harbor, but that was impossible. He therefore gave orders to burn the ship, and his men, who had been thoroughly instructed in what they were to do, dispersed into all parts of the frigate with the combustibles which had been prepared, and in a few minutes, so well and quickly was the work done, the flames broke out in all parts of the *Philadelphia.*

As soon as this was effected the order was given to return to the *Intrepid.* Without confusion the men obeyed. It was a moment of great danger, for fire was breaking out on all sides, and the *Intrepid* herself, filled as she was with powder and combustibles, was in great peril of sudden destruction. The rapidity of Decatur's movements, however, saved everything. The cables were cut, the sweeps got out, and the *Intrepid* drew rapidly away from the burning frigate.

It was a magnificent sight as the flames burst out over the *Philadelphia* and ran rapidly and fiercely up the masts and rigging. As her guns became heated they were discharged, one battery pouring its shots into the town. Finally the cables parted, and then the *Philadelphia,* a mass of flames, drifted across the harbor, and blew up. Meantime the batteries of the shipping and the castle had been turned upon the *Intrepid,* but although the shot struck all around her, she escaped successfully with only one shot through her mainsail, and, joining the *Siren,* bore away.

This successful attack was carried through by the cool courage of Decatur and the admirable discipline of his men. The hazard was very great, the odds were very heavy, and everything depended on the nerve with which the attack was made and the completeness of the surprise. Nothing miscarried, and no success could have been more complete. Nelson, at that time in the Mediterranean, and the best judge of a naval exploit as well as the greatest naval commander who has ever lived, pronounced it "the most bold and daring act of the age."

We meet no single feat exactly like it in our own naval history, brilliant as that has been, until we come to Cushing's destruction of the

Albemarle in the war of the rebellion. In the years that have elapsed, and among the great events that have occurred since that time, Decatur's burning of the *Philadelphia* has been well-nigh forgotten; but it is one of those feats of arms which illustrate the high courage of American seamen, and which ought always to be remembered.

12

THE LOSS OF
THE BRIG *TYRELL*

*For a crewman of a coastwise schooner, a leak in the hull was only the
beginning.*

The following, which is a circumstantial account given by T. Purnell, chief mate of the brig *Tyrell*, Arthur Cochlan, commander, and
the only person among the whole crew who had the good fortune to
escape.

On Saturday, June 29th, 1759, they sailed from New York to Sandy
Hook, and there came to an anchor, waiting for the captain's coming down with a new boat, and some other articles. Accordingly he
came on board early the succeeding morning, and the boat cleared,
hoisted in, stowed and lashed. At eight o'clock, A. M. they weighed
anchor, sailed out of Sandy Hook, and the same day at noon, took

their departure from the High Land Never Sunk, and proceeded on their passage to Antigua. As soon as they made sail, the captain ordered the boat to be cast loose, in order that she might be painted, with the oars, rudder and tiller, which job, he (Captain Cochlan) undertook to do himself.

At four P. M. they found the vessel made a little more water, than usual; but as it did not cause much additional labour at the pump, nothing was thought of it. At eight, the leak did not seem to increase. At twelve it began to blow very hard in squalls, which caused the vessel to lie down very much, whereby it was apprehended she wanted more ballast. Thereupon the captain came on deck, being the starboard watch, and close reefed both top-sails.

At four A. M. the weather moderated—let out both reefs:—at eight it became still more moderate, and they made more sail, and set top-gallant-sails; the weather was still thick and hazy. There was no further observation taken at present, except that the vessel made more water. The captain was now chiefly employed in painting the boat, oars, rudder and tiller.

On Monday, June 30, at four P. M. the wind was at E. N. E. freshened very much, and blew so very hard, as occasioned the brig to lie along in such a manner as caused general alarm. The captain was now earnestly intreated to put for New York, or steer for the Capes of Virginia. At eight, took in top-gallant-sail, and close reefed both top-sails, still making more water. Afterwards the weather became still more moderate and fair, and they made more sail.

July 1, at four A. M. it began to blow in squalls very hard, took in one reef in each top-sail, and continued so until eight A. M. the weather being still thick and hazy.—No observation.

The next day she made still more water, but as every watch pumped it out, this was little regarded. At four P. M. took second reef in each top-sail,—close reefed both, and sent down top-gallant-yard; the gale still increasing.

At four A. M. the wind got round to N. and there was no appearance of its abating. At eight, the captain well satisfied that she was very crank and ought to have had more ballast, agreed to make for Bacon Island Road, in North Carolina; and in the very act of wearing her, a sudden gust of wind laid her down on her beam-end, and she never rose again!

At this time Mr. Purnell was lying in the cabin, with his clothes on, not having pulled them off since they left land.—Having been rolled out of his bed (on his chest,) with great difficulty he reached the round-house door; the first salutation he met with was from the step-ladder that went from the quarter-deck to the poop, which knocked him against the companion, (a lucky circumstance for those below, as, by laying the ladder against the companion, it served both him and the rest of the people who were in the steerage, as a conveyance to windward); having transported the two after guns forward to bring her more by the head, in order to make her hold a better wind; thus they got through the aftermost gun-port on the quarter-deck, and being all on her broadside, every moveable rolled to leeward, and as the vessel overset, so did the boat, and turned bottom upwards, her lashings being cast loose, by order of the captain, and having no other prospect of saving their lives but by the boat, Purnell, with two others, and the cabin-boy (who were excellent swimmers) plunged into the water, and with difficulty righted her, when she was brim full, and washing with the water's edge. They then made fast the end of the main-sheet to the ring in her stern-post, and those who were in the fore-chains sent down the end of the boom-tackle, to which they made fast the boat's painter, and by which they lifted her a little out of the water, so that she swam about two or three inches free, but almost full.

They then put the cabin-boy into her, and gave him a bucket that happened to float by, and he bailed away as quick as he could, and soon after another person got in with another bucket, and in a short time got all the water out of her.—They then put two long oars that were stowed in the larboard-quarter of the *Tyrell* into the boat, and pulled or rowed right to windward; for, as the wreck drifted, she made a dreadful appearance in the water, and Mr. Purnell and two of the people put off from the wreck, in search of the oars, rudder and tiller.

After a long while they succeeded in picking them all up, one after another. They then returned to their wretched companions, who were all overjoyed to see them, having given them up for lost. By this time night drew on very fast. While they were rowing in the boat, some small quantity of white biscuit (Mr. Purnell supposed about half a peck,) floated in a small cask, out of the round house; but before it came to hand, it was so soaked with salt water, that it was almost in a fluid state: and about double the quantity of common ship-biscuit likewise floated, which was in like manner soaked. This was all the provision that they had; not a drop of fresh water could they get; neither could the carpenter get at any of his tools to scuttle her sides, for, could this have been accomplished, they might have saved plenty of provisions and water.

By this time it was almost dark; having got one compass, it was determined to quit the wreck, and take their chance in the boat, which was nineteen feet six inches long, and six feet four inches broad; Mr. Purnell supposes it was now about nine o'clock; it was very dark.

They had run about 360 miles by their dead reckoning, on a S. E. by E. course. The number in the boat was 17 in all; the boat was very deep, and little hopes were entertained of either seeing land or surviving long. The wind got round to westward, which was the course they wanted to steer; but it began to blow and rain so very hard, that they were obliged to keep before the wind and sea, in order to preserve her above water. Soon after they had put off from the wreck the boat shipped two heavy seas, one after another, so that they were obliged to keep her before the wind and sea; for had she shipped another sea, she certainly would have swamped with them.

By sunrise the next morning, July 3, they judged that they had been running E. S. E. which was contrary to their wishes. The wind dying away, the weather became very moderate. The compass which they had saved proved of no utility, one of the people having trod upon, and broken it; it was accordingly thrown overboard. They now proposed to make a sail of some frocks and trowsers, but they had got neither needles nor sewing twine, one of the people however, had a needle in his knife, and another several fishing lines in his pockets, which were unlaid by some, and others were employed in ripping the frocks and trowsers.

By sunset they had provided a tolerable lug-sail; having split one of the boat's thwarts, (which was of yellow deal,) with a very large knife, which one of the crew had in his pocket, they made a yard and lashed it together by the strands of the fore-top-gallant-halyards, that were thrown into the boat promiscuously.—They also made a mast of one of the long oars, and set their sails, with sheets and tacks made out of the top-gallant-halyards. Their only guide was the North star. They had a tolerable good breeze all night; and the whole of the next day, July 4, the weather continued very moderate, and the people were in as good spirits as their dreadful situation would admit.

July 5, the wind and weather continued much the same, and they knew by the North star that they were standing in for the land. The next day Mr. Purnell observed some of the men drinking salt water, and seeming rather fatigued.—At this time they imagined the wind was got round to the southward, and they steered, as they thought by the North star, to the northwest quarter; but on the 7th, they found the wind had got back to the northward, and blew very fresh. They got their oars out the greatest part of the night, and the next day the wind still dying away, the people laboured alternately at the oars, without distinction. About noon the wind sprung up so that they laid in their oars, and, as they thought, steered about N. N. W. and continued so until about eight or nine in the morning of July 9, when they all thought they were upon soundings, by the coldness of the water.— They were, in general, in very good spirits. The weather continued still thick and hazy, and by the North star, they found that they had been steering about N. by W.

July 10.—The people had drank so much salt water, that it came from them as clear as it was before they drank it; and Mr. Purnell perceived that the second mate had lost a considerable share of his strength and spirits; and also, at noon, that the carpenter was delirious, his malady increasing every hour; about dusk he had almost overset the boat, by attempting to throw himself overboard, and otherwise behaving quite violent.

As his strength, however, failed him, he became more manageable, and they got him to lie down in the middle of the boat, among some of the people. Mr. Purnell drank once a little salt water, but could not relish it; he preferred his own urine, which he drank occasionally as he made it. Soon after sunset the second mate lost his speech. Mr. Purnell desired him to lean his head on him; he died, without a groan or struggle, on the 11th of July, being the 9th day they were in the boat. In a few minutes after, the carpenter expired almost in a similar manner.

These melancholy scenes rendered the situation of the survivors more dreadful; it is impossible to describe their feelings. Despair became general; every man imagined his own dissolution was near.

They all now went to prayers; some prayed in the Welch language, some in Irish, and others in English; then, after a little deliberation, they stripped the two dead men, and hove them overboard.

The weather being now very mild, and almost calm, they turned to, cleaned the boat, and resolved to make their sail larger out of the frocks and trowsers of the two deceased men. Purnell got the captain to lie down with the rest of the people, the boatswain and one man excepted, who assisted him in making the sail larger, which they had completed by six or seven o'clock in the afternoon, having made a shroud out of the boat's painter, which served as a shifting back-stay.— Purnell also fixed his red flannel waistcoat at the mast-head, as a signal the most likely to be seen.

Soon after this some of them observed a sloop at a great distance, coming, as they thought, from the land. This roused every man's spirits; they got out their oars, at which they laboured alternately, exerting all their remaining strength to come up with her; but night coming on, and the sloop getting a fresh breeze of wind, they lost sight of her, which occasioned a general consternation; however, the appearance of the North star, which they kept on their starboard-bow, gave them hopes that they stood in for land.

This night one William Wathing died; he was 64 years of age, and had been to sea 50 years; quite worn out with fatigue and hunger, he earnestly prayed, to the last moment, for a drop of water to cool his tongue. Early the next morning Hugh Williams also died, and in the course of the day another of the crew: entirely exhausted,—they both expired without a groan.

Early in the morning of July 13, it began to blow very fresh, and increased so much, that they were obliged to furl their sail, and keep the boat before the wind and sea, which drove them off soundings. In the evening their gunner died. The weather now becoming moderate and the wind in the S. W. quarter, they made sail, not one being able to row or pull an oar at any rate; they ran all this night with a fine breeze.

The next morning (July 14) two more of the crew died, and in the evening they also lost the same number. They found they were on soundings again, and concluded the wind had got round to the N. W. quarter. They stood in for the land all this night, and early on July 15 two others died; the deceased were thrown overboard as soon as their breath had departed. The weather was now thick and hazy, and they were still certain that they were on soundings.

The cabin-boy was seldom required to do any thing, and as his intellects, at this time, were very good, and his understanding clear, it was the opinion of Mr. Purnell that he would survive them all, but he prudently kept his thoughts to himself. The captain seemed likewise tolerably well, and to have kept up his spirits. On account of the haziness of the weather, they could not so well know how they steered in the day time as at night; for, whenever the North star appeared, they endeavored to keep it on their starboard bow, by which means they were certain of making the land some time or other. In the evening two more of the crew died, also, before sunset, one Thomas Philpot, an old experienced seaman, and very strong; he departed rather convulsed; having latterly lost the power of articulation, his meaning could not be comprehended. He was a native of Belfast, Ireland, and had no family. The survivors found it a difficult task to heave his body overboard, as he was a very corpulent man.

About six or seven the next morning, July 16, they stood in for the land, according to the best of their judgment, the weather still thick and hazy. Purnell now prevailed upon the captain and boatswain of the boat to lie down in the fore-part of the boat, to bring her more by the head, in order to make her hold a better wind. In the evening the cabin-boy, who lately appeared so well, breathed his last, leaving behind, the captain, the boatswain and Mr. Purnell.

The next morning, July 17, Mr. Purnell asked his two companions if they thought they could eat any of the boy's flesh; and having expressed an inclination to try, and the body being quite cold, he cut the inside of his thigh, a little above his knee, and gave a piece to the captain and boatswain, reserving a small piece for himself; but so weak were their stomachs that none of them could swallow a morsel of it, the body was therefore thrown overboard.

Early in the morning of the 18th, Mr. Purnell found both of his companions dead and cold! Thus destitute, he began to think of his own dissolution; though feeble, his understanding was still clear, and his spirits as good as his forlorn situation could possibly admit. By the colour and coldness of the water, he knew he was not far from land, and still maintained hopes of making it. The weather continued very foggy. He lay to all this night, which was very dark, with the boat's head to the northward.

In the morning of the 19th, it began to rain; it cleared up in the afternoon, and the wind died away; still Mr. Purnell was convinced he was on soundings.

On the 20th, in the afternoon, he thought he saw land, and stood in for it; but night coming on, and it being now very dark, he lay to, fearing he might get on some rocks and shoals.

July 21, the weather was very fine all the morning, but in the afternoon it became thick and hazy. Mr. Purnell's spirits still remained good, but his strength was almost exhausted; he still drank his own water occasionally.

On the 22d he saw some barnacles on the boat's rudder, very similar to the spawn of an oyster, which filled him with greater hopes of being near land. He unshipped the rudder, and scraping them off with his knife, found they were of a salt fishy substance, and eat them; he was now so weak, the boat having a great motion, that he found it a difficult task to ship the rudder.

At sunrise, July 23, he became so sure that he saw land, that his spirits were considerably raised. In the middle of this day he got up, leaned his back against the mast, and received succour from the sun, having previously contrived to steer the boat in this position. The next day he saw, at a very great distance, some kind of a sail, which he judged was coming from the land, which he soon lost sight of. In the middle of the day he got up, and received warmth from the sun as before. He stood on all night for the land.

Very early in the morning of the 25th, after drinking his morning draught, to his inexpressible joy he saw, while the sun was rising, a sail, and when the sun was up, found she was a two-mast vessel. He was, however, considerably perplexed, not knowing what to do, as she was a great distance astern and to the leeward. In order to watch her motions better, he tacked about. Soon after this he perceived she was standing on her starboard tack, which had been the same he had been standing on for many hours. He saw she approached him very fast, and he lay to for some time, till he believed she was within two miles of the boat, but still to leeward; therefore he thought it best to steer larger, when he found she was a top-sail schooner, nearing him very fast.—He continued to edge down towards her, until he had brought her about two points under his lee-bow, having it in his power to spring his luff, or bear away. By this time she was within half a mile, and he saw some of her people standing forwards on her deck and waiving for him to come under their lee-bow.

At the distance of about 200 yards they hove the schooner up in the wind, and kept her so until Purnell got alongside, when they threw him a rope, still keeping the schooner in the wind. They now interrogated him very closely; by the manner the boat and oars were painted, they imagined she belonged to a man of war, and that they had run away with her from some of his Majesty's ships at Halifax, consequently that they would be liable to some punishment if they took him up; they also thought, as the captain and boatswain were lying dead in the boat, they might expose themselves to some contagious disorder. Thus they kept Purnell in suspense for some time. They told him they had made the land that morning from the mast-head, and that they were running along shore for Marblehead, to which place they belonged, and where they expected to be the next morning. At last they told him he might come on board; which as he said, he could not without assistance, the captain ordered two of his men to help him.—They conducted him aft on the quarter deck, where they left him resting on the companion.

They were now for casting the boat adrift, but Mr. Purnell told them she was not above a month old, built at New York, and if they would hoist her in, it would pay them well for their trouble. To this they agreed, and having thrown the two corpses overboard, and taken out the clothes that were left by the deceased, they hoisted her in and made sail.

Being now on board, Purnell asked for a little water, Captain Castleman (for that was his name) ordered one of his sons, (having two on board) to fetch him some; when he came with the water, his father looked to see how much he was bringing him, and thinking it too much, threw some of it away, and desired him to give the remainder, which he drank being the first fresh water he had tasted for 23 days. As he leaned all this time against the companion, he became very cold, and begged to go below; the captain ordered two men to help him down to the cabin, where they left him sitting on the cabin-deck, leaning upon the lockers, all hands being now engaged in hoisting in and securing the boat.

This done, all hands went down to the cabin to breakfast, except the man at the helm. They made some soup for Purnell, which he thought very good, but at present he could eat very little, and in consequence of his late draughts, he had broke out in many parts of his body, so that he was in great pain whenever he stirred. They made a bed for him out of an old sail, and behaved very attentive. While they were at breakfast a squall of wind came on, which called them all upon deck; during their absence, Purnell took up a stone bottle, and without smelling or tasting it, but thinking it was rum, took a hearty draught of it, and found it to be sweet oil; having placed it where he found it, he lay down.

They still ran along shore with the land in sight, and were in great hopes of getting into port that night, but the wind dying away, they did not get in till nine o'clock the next night. All this time Purnell remained like a child; some one was always with him, to give him whatever he wished to eat or drink.

As soon as they came to anchor, Captain Castleman went on shore, and returned on board the next morning with the owner, John Picket, Esq. Soon after they got Purnell into a boat, and carried him on shore; but he was still so very feeble, that he was obliged to be supported by two men. Mr. Picket took a very genteel lodging for him, and hired a nurse to attend him; he was immediately put to bed, and afterwards provided with a change of clothes.

In the course of the day he was visited by every doctor in the town, who all gave him hopes of recovering, but told him it would be some time, for the stronger the constitution, the longer (they said) it took to recover its lost strength. Though treated with the utmost tenderness and humanity, it was three weeks before he was able to come down stairs. He stayed in Marblehead two months, during which he lived very comfortably, and gradually recovered his strength. The brig's boat and oars were sold for 95 dollars, which paid all his expenses, and procured him a passage to Boston. The nails of his fingers and toes withered away almost to nothing, and did not begin to grow for many months after.

13

THE LAST CRUISE OF THE *SAGINAW*

GEORGE H. READ

One might think that the crew of a U.S. Navy ship stranded on a South Pacific island were delighted by their misfortune. But they would be dead wrong.

During the winter of 1869–70 the United States Steamer *Saginaw* was being repaired at the Mare Island Navy Yard, and her officers and crew were recuperating after a cruise on the west coast of Mexico,—a trying one for all hands on board as well as for the vessel itself.

The *Alta-Californian* of San Francisco published the following soon after our return from the Mexican coast. It is all that need be said of the cruise. We were all very glad to have it behind us and forget it:

"The *Saginaw*, lately returned from the Mexican coast, had a pretty severe experience during her short cruise. At Manzanillo she contracted the coast fever, a form of remittent, and at one time had twenty-five cases, but a single death, however, occurring.

"On the way up, most of the time under sail, the machinery being disabled, the voyage was so prolonged that when she arrived at San Francisco there was not a half-day's allowance of provisions on board and for many days the officers had been on 'ship's grub.'"

Our repairs and refitting were but preliminary to another (and the last) departure of the *Saginaw* from her native land. Our captain, Lieutenant-Commander Montgomery Sicard, had received orders to proceed to the Midway Islands, *via* Honolulu, and to comply with instructions that will appear later in these pages. (I should explain here that the commanding officer of a single vessel is usually addressed as "Captain," whatever his real rank may be, and I shall use that term throughout my narrative.)

In a northwesterly direction from the Sandwich Islands there stretches for over a thousand miles a succession of coral reefs and shoals, with here and there a sandy islet thrown up by the winds and waves. They are mostly bare of vegetation beyond a stunted growth of bushes. These islets are called "atolls" by geographers, and their foundations are created by the mysterious "polyps" or coral insects.

These atolls abound in the Pacific Ocean, and rising but a few feet above the surface, surrounded by uncertain and uncharted currents, are the dread of navigators.

Near the centre of the North Pacific and near the western end of the chain of atolls above mentioned, are two small sand islands in the usual lagoon, with a coral reef enclosing both. They were discovered by an American captain, N.C. Brooks, of the Hawaiian bark *Gambia*, and by him reported; were subsequently visited by the United States Steamer *Lackawanna* and surveyed for charting.

No importance other than the danger to navigation was at that time attached to these mere sandbanks. Now, however, the trans-Pacific railroads, girdling the continent and making valuable so many hitherto insignificant places, have cast their influence three thousand miles across the waters to these obscure islets. The expected increase of commerce between the United States and the Orient has induced the Pacific Mail Steamship Company to look for a halfway station as a coaling-depot, and these, the Midway Islands, are expected to answer the purpose when the proposed improvements are made.

To do the work of deepening a now shallow channel through the reef, a contract has been awarded to an experienced submarine engineer and the *Saginaw* has been brought into service to transport men and material. Our captain is to superintend and to report monthly on the progress made. Thus, with the voyages out and return, coupled with the several trips between the Midways and Honolulu, we have the prospect of a year's deep-water cruising to our credit.

February 22, 1870. Once more separated from home and friends, with the Golden Gate dissolving astern in a California fog (than which none can be more dense). Old Neptune gives us a boisterous welcome to his dominions, and the howling of wind through the rigging, with the rolling and pitching of the ship as we steam out to sea, where we meet the full force of a stiff "southeaster," remind us that we are once more his subjects.

On the fourteenth day out we heard the welcome cry of "Land ho!" at sunrise from the masthead. It proved to be the island of Molokai, and the next day, March 9, we passed into the harbor of Honolulu on the island of Oahu. We found that our arrival was expected, and the ship was soon surrounded by canoes of natives, while crowds of people were on the wharves.

After six days spent in refitting and obtaining fresh food and ship-stores, we took up our westward course with memories of pleasant and hospitable treatment, both officially and socially, from the native and foreign people. Nothing happened outside of the usual routine of sea life until March 24, when we sighted the Midway Islands, and at 8 P.M. were anchored in Welles's Harbor, so called, although there is barely room in it to swing the ship. The island is a desolate-looking place—the eastern end of it covered with brown albatross and a few seal apparently asleep on the beach. We can see the white sand drifting about with the wind like snow. The next day a schooner arrived with the contractor's supplies and lumber for a dwelling and a scow, the latter to be used by the divers in their outside work. There also arrived, towards night, a strong gale. It blew so hard that with both anchors down the engines had to be worked constantly to prevent drifting either on the island or the reef.

During the month of April work both afloat and ashore was steadily pushed. The contractor's house was set up and the divers' scow completed and launched. In addition, a thorough survey of the entire reef and bar was completed.

Our several trips between the Midways and Honolulu need but brief mention. They were slow and monotonous, being made mostly under sail. The *Saginaw* was not built for that purpose. On one occasion, on account of head winds, we made but twenty miles on our course in two days.

The last return to the Midways came on October 12, and the appropriation of $50,000 having been expended, our captain proceeded to carry out his orders directing him to take on board the contractor's workmen with their tools and stores and transport them to San Francisco.

We found the shore party all well and looking forward with pleasure to the closing day of their contract. They certainly have had the monotonous and irksome end of the business, although we have not been able to derive much pleasure from our sailings to and fro.

A brief résumé of the work performed during their seven months' imprisonment I have compiled from the journal of Passed Assistant Engineer Blye, who remained upon the island during our absences.

Their first attempt at dislodging the coral rock on the bar was made by the diver with two canisters of powder, and about five tons of rock were dislodged and well broken up. Thereafter the work was intermittently carried on, as weather permitted. During September and October there were frequent strong gales from the west, and on such occasions the mouth of the harbor, being on that side, was dangerous to approach.

After toiling laboriously and constantly for six months, using large quantities of powder and fuse, the result now is a passage through the bar fifteen feet in width and four hundred feet in length, whereas one hundred and seventy feet in width is estimated as essential. A proper completion would call for a much larger appropriation.

During the month of April the thermometer ranged from 68 degrees at sunrise to 86 degrees at noon and 80 degrees at sundown. The prevailing winds during the summer months were the northeast trades, varying from northeast to east southeast.

A cause of much annoyance has been the drifting of sand during high winds, when it flies like driven snow, cutting the face and hands. (This was so great an annoyance that on our first trip to Honolulu I purchased for each person a pair of goggles to protect the eyes.)

Taking into consideration the dangers of navigation in a neighborhood abounding with these coral reefs, the fact that they are visible but a short distance only in clear weather, and that an entrance to the lagoon could only be made in a smooth sea, it really seems a questionable undertaking to attempt the formation of an anchorage here for the large steamers of the Pacific Mail Company.

When the westerly gales blow, the mouth of the lagoon being, as in most coral islands, on that side, the sea breaks heavily all over the lagoon and no work can be done. On one occasion the workmen were returning to the island from the entrance to the channel when one of these gales came on and, as one of them told me, "It was a mighty big conundrum at one time whether we would ever reach the shore."

THE WRECK

With the homeward-bound pennant flying from the mainmast head and with the contractor's working party on board, we sailed from the Midway Islands on Friday, October 29, at 4 P.M. for San Francisco. We had dragged high up on the beach the scow from which the divers had worked, secured the house doors, and taken a last look at the blinding sand with thankful hearts for leaving it.

As Doctor Frank, our surgeon, and myself were walking down the beach to the last boat off to the ship, there occurred an incident which I will relate here for psychological students.

He remarked, as we loitered around the landing, that he felt greatly depressed without being able to define any cause for it and that he could not rid himself of the impression that some misfortune was impending. I tried to cheer him up; told him that the "blues" were on him, when he ought to be rejoicing instead; that we had a fair wind and a smooth sea to start us on a speedy return to the old friends in San Francisco. It was in vain, however; he expressed a firm belief that we should meet with some disaster on our voyage and I dropped the subject with a "pooh pooh."

As soon as we reached the open sea, the captain ordered the ship headed to the westward and the pressure of steam to be reduced, as with topsails set we sailed along to a light easterly breeze. It was his intention, he stated, to come within sight of Ocean Island about daylight and to verify its location by steaming around it before heading away for San Francisco.

It should be noted that it is in the direct line of a naval commander's duty, when he is in the neighborhood of such dangers to navigation, to confirm by observation their position on the charts as well as to rescue any unfortunate persons that fate may have cast away upon them. Our own subsequent situation gives proof of the wisdom of such a regulation.

Ocean Island is about fifty miles to the westward of the Midway Islands, is of similar formation, and is the last one (so far as our chart shows) in the chain of ocean dangers that I have referred to as extending more than a thousand miles to the westward from the Sandwich Islands. It was on this reef that the British ship *Gledstanes* was wrecked in 1837, and the American ship *Parker* in September, 1842, the crew of the latter vessel remaining there until May, 1843, when they were taken off.

The vessel was wrecked July 9, 1837, at midnight. One of the crew only was lost, he having jumped overboard in a state of intoxication. Captain Brown remained on the island over five months, when, with his chief mate and eight seamen, he embarked for these islands in a schooner which had been constructed from the fragments of the wreck. The other officers and men, who remained on the island several months longer, endured great suffering and were finally brought off in a vessel sent for them by H.B.M. Consul.

Captain Brown gave the following description of the island. "The island is in latitude 28° 22' North, and longitude 178° 30' West, and is about three miles in circumference. It is composed of broken coral and shells and is covered near the shore by low bushes. In the season it abounds with sea birds and at times there are considerable numbers of hair seals. The highest part of the island is not more than ten feet above sea level and the only fresh water is what drains through the sand after the heavy rains."

Charles Darwin has the following to say concerning Ocean Island, which he characterizes as a true "atoll," as distinguished from "barrier" and "fringing" reefs, which are generally formed near the shores of higher land:

"I have in vain consulted the works of Cook, Vancouver, La Peyrouse, and Lisiansky for any satisfactory account of the small islands and reefs which lie scattered in a northwest line prolonged from the Sandwich group and hence have left them uncolored, with one exception, for I am indebted to Mr. F.D. Bennett for informing me of an atoll-formed reef in latitude 28° 22', longitude 178° 30' West, on which the *Gledstanes* was wrecked in 1837. It is apparently of large size and extends in a northwest and southeast line; very few inlets have been formed on it. The lagoon seems to be shallow; at least the deepest part which was surveyed was only three fathoms."

Mr. Couthony describes this island under the name of Ocean Island. Considerable doubts should be entertained regarding the nature of a reef of this kind with a very shallow lagoon, and standing far from any other atoll, on account of the possibility of a crater or flat bank of rock lying at the proper depth beneath the surface of the sea, thus affording a foundation for a ring-formed coral reef.

The evening following the departure passed quietly in our wardroom quarters and in fact all over the ship. Officers and men were more than usually fatigued after the preparations for sea both on shore and on board. There was none of the general hilarity accompanying a homeward cruise. There was also a prevailing dread of a long and tedious journey of over three thousand miles, mostly to be made under sail, and we all knew the tendency of the old *Saginaw* in a head wind to make "eight points to leeward," or, as a landlubber would say, to go sideways. We occupied ourselves in stowing and securing our movables, and after the bugle sounded "Out lights" at 9 P.M. the steady tramp of the lookouts and their half-hour hail of "All's well" were all that disturbed the quiet of the night.

The night was dark, but a few stars were occasionally visible between the passing clouds. The sea continued smooth and the ship on an even keel. When I turned in at ten o'clock I had the comforting thought that by the same time to-morrow night we should be heading for San Francisco. We were making about three knots an hour, which would bring Ocean Island in sight about early dawn, so that there would be plenty of time to circumnavigate the reef and get a good offing on our course before dark.

How sadly, alas! our intentions were frustrated and how fully our surgeon's premonitions were fulfilled! My pen falters at the attempt to describe the events of the next few hours. I was suddenly awakened about three o'clock in the morning by an unusual commotion on deck; the hurried tramping of feet and confusion of sounds. In the midst of it I distinguished the captain's voice sounding in sharp contrast to his usual moderate tone, ordering the taking in of the topsails and immediately after the cutting away of the topsail halliards. Until the latter order was given I imagined the approach of a rain squall, a frequent occurrence formerly, but I knew now that some greater emergency existed, and so I hastily and partly dressed myself sufficiently to go on deck.

Just before I reached the top of the wardroom ladder I felt the ship strike something and supposed we were in collision with another vessel. The shock was an easy one at first, but was followed immediately by others of increasing force, and, as my feet touched the deck, by two severe shocks that caused the ship to tremble in every timber. The long easy swell that had been lifting us gently along in the open sea was now transformed into heavy breakers as it reached and swept over the coral reef, each wave lifting and dropping with a frightful thud the quaking ship. It seemed at each fall as though her masts and smokestack would jump from their holdings and go by the board. To a landsman or even a professional seaman who has never experienced the sensation it would be impossible to convey a realizing sense of the feelings aroused by our sudden misfortune.

There is a something even in the air akin to the terror of an earthquake shock—a condition unnatural and uncanny. The good ship that for years has safely sailed the seas or anchored in ports with a free keel, fulfilling in all respects the destiny marked out for her at her birth, suddenly and without warning enters upon her death-struggle with the rocks and appeals for help. There is no wonder that brave men—men having withstood the shock of battle and endured the hardships of the fiercest storms—should feel their nerves shaken from their first glance at the situation.

The captain had immediately followed his orders, to take in the sails that were forging us on towards the reef, by an order to back engines. Alas! the steam was too low to give more than a few turns to the wheels, and they could not overcome the momentum of the ship. In less than an hour of the fierce pounding the jagged rock broke through the hull and tore up the engine and fire room floor; the water rushed in and reached the fires; the doom of our good ship was now apparent and sealed.

I hastily returned to my stateroom, secured more clothing, together with some of the ship's papers, then ascended to the hurricane deck to await developments or to stand by to do rescue work as ordered. I had participated in the past in drills that are called in Navy Regulations "abandoned ship." In these drills every one on board is supposed to leave the vessel and take station as assigned in one of the ship's boats. I had only taken part in these drills during calm weather at sea, and thought it a pretty sight to see all the boats completely equipped and lying off in view of the deserted vessel. Here, however, no programme could help us. Our captain's judgment and quickness of decision must control events as they develop.

The night was clear and starlit, but we could see nothing of any land. Perhaps we had struck on some uncharted reef, and while strenuously employed in getting the boats over the side opposite the sea we waited anxiously for daylight. The scene was one for a lifelong remembrance and is beyond my power adequately and calmly to describe.

There was at first some confusion, but the stern and composed attitude of the captain and his sharp, clear orders soon brought every one to his senses, and order was restored.

One of the most reassuring things to me at this time was the sight of our colored wardroom steward in double irons for some offense, sitting on a hatch of the hurricane deck, whistling "Way down upon the Suwanee River." He seemed to me far from realizing the gravity of the situation, or else to possess great courage. At any rate, it diverted my thoughts of danger into other channels. He said the key to the irons could not be found. The irons were soon severed, however, with a chisel and hammer, and he went below to aid the men with his knowledge of the stowage of the officers' provender. His confinement was never renewed, for he did good work in the rescue of food.

A few of the more frightened ones had at first, either through a misunderstanding or otherwise, rushed to our largest boat—the launch—hanging at the starboard quarter and partly lowered it before the act was noticed. A large combing sea came along and tore it from their hold, smashing it against the side of the ship and then carrying its remnants away with its tackles and all its fittings. This was a great loss, we felt, if we should have to take to the boats, for we did not know at that time where we were.

The same wave also carried off one of the crew, a member of the Marine Guard, who had been on the bulwarks; and whisking him seaward, returned him miraculously around the stern of the ship to the reef, where his struggles and cries attracted the notice of others. He was hauled over the lee side, somewhat bruised and water-soaked, but, judging from his remarks, apparently not realizing his wonderful escape from death.

As the night wore on, the wind increased and also the size of the breakers. The ship, which had first struck the reef "bows on," was gradually swung around until she was at first broadside to the reef, and then further until the after part, to which we were clinging, was lifted over the jagged edge of the perpendicular wall of rock. She was finally twisted around until the bow hung directly to seaward, with the middle of the hull at the edge. Thus the ship "seesawed" from stem to stern with each coming wave for an hour or more and until the forward part broke away with a loud crash and disappeared in the deep water outside. Our anchors, that had been "let go," apparently never touched bottom until the bow went with them.

All that was left of our good ship now heeled over towards the inner side of the reef, the smokestack soon went by the board and the mainmast was made to follow it by simply cutting away the starboard or seaward shrouds. Over this mast we could pass to the reef, however, and there was comparative quiet in the waters under our lee. This helped us in passing across whatever we could save from the wreck, and in this manner went three of our boats, the captain's gig, one of the cutters, and the dinghy, without much damage to them. We also secured in this way an iron lifeboat belonging to the contractor.

As the first gray streaks of dawn showed us a small strip of terra firma in the smooth water of the lagoon and not far from the reef, many a sigh of relief was heard, and our efforts were redoubled to provide some means of prolonging existence there. At any rate, we knew now where we were and could at least imagine a possible relief and plan measures to secure it.

Although the sea had robbed us of the larger part of our provisions, in the forward hold there were still some of the most important stowed within the fragment we were clinging to, which contained the bread and clothing storerooms. With daylight our task was made easier.

A line was formed across the reef and everything rescued was passed over the side and from hand to hand to the boats in the lagoon, for transfer to the island. Thus we stood waist-deep in the water, feet and ankles lacerated and bleeding, stumbling about the sharp and uneven coral rock, until five in the afternoon, and yet our spirits, which had been low in the dark, were so encouraged by a sight of a small portion of dry land and at least a temporary escape from a watery grave that now and then a jest or a laugh would pass along the line with some article that suggested a future meal.

At five o'clock in the afternoon the order was given to abandon the wreck (which was done while hoping that it would hold together until to-morrow), and as the sun went down on the "lone barren isle," all hands were "piped" by the boatswain's whistle to supper.

A half-teacup of water, half a cake of hardtack, and a small piece of boiled pork constituted our evening meal, to which was added a piece of boiled mutton that had been intended for the wardroom table.

After this frugal meal all hands were mustered upon the beach to listen to a prayer of thankfulness for our deliverance and then to a few sensible and well-timed remarks from the captain enjoining discipline, good nature, and economy of food under our trying circumstances. He told us that by the Navy Regulations he was instructed, as our commanding officer, to keep up, in such sad conditions as we were thrown into, the organization and discipline of the Service so far as applicable; that he would in the event of our rescue (which we should all hope for and look forward to) be held responsible for the proper administration of law and order; that officers and crew should fare alike on our scanty store of food, and that with care we should probably make out, with the help of seal meat and birds, a reduced ration for some little time. He would detail our several duties to-morrow. Then we were dismissed to seek "tired nature's sweet restorer" as best we could.

With fourteen hours of severe labor, tired, wet, and hungry, we were yet glad enough to sink to rest amid the bushes with but the sky for a canopy and a hummock of sand for a pillow. In my own case sleep was hard to win. For a long time I lay watching the stars and speculating upon the prospects of release from our island prison. Life seemed to reach dimly uncertain into the future, with shadow pictures intervening of famished men and bereaved families.

I could hear the waves within a few rods of our resting-places— there was no music in them now—lapping the beach in their restlessness, and now and then an angry roar from the outside reef, as though the sea was in rage over its failure to reach us. I realized that for more than a thousand miles the sea stretched away in every direction before meeting inhabited shores and for treble that distance to our native land; that our island was but a small dot in the vast Pacific—a dot so small that few maps give it recognition. Truly it was a dismal outlook that "tired nature" finally dispelled and that sleep transformed into oblivion; for I went to sleep finally while recalling old stories of family gatherings where was always placed a vacant chair for the loved absent one should he ever return.

ON THE ISLAND

Sunday, October 30. No pretensions to the official observance of the Sabbath were made to-day. We always had religious services on board the ship when the weather permitted on Sunday, but to-day every effort has been made to further the safety of our condition.

The captain, executive officer, and many of the crew went off early to the wreck in order to make further search for supplies and equipment. The wreck appears from the island to be about as we left it, for the wind has been light and the sea calm during the night.

I remained on shore with a few men to assist in sorting out and making a list of the articles rescued yesterday and to assemble them in the best place suitable for their preservation. We spread out in the sun the bread, bags of flour, and other dry foodstuffs, even to the smallest fragments, and it was early apparent that unless much more food is secured we shall be compelled to live upon a greatly reduced ration and that our main source of food will be the seal and brown albatross (or "goonies," as they are commonly called). Both of these seem plentiful and are easily captured.

The seal succumb quickly to a blow upon the head, a fact we discovered early in our first visit to the Midway Islands. One of the boat's crew, when pushing off from the beach, carelessly and without intent to kill, struck a near-by seal on the head with an oar, and the next morning it was found dead, apparently not having moved from the spot. Its mate had found it and was nosing it about, while moaning in a most humanlike voice.

These seal are quite different from the Alaska fur seal, of such great value for their fur. These have a short lustreless hair, and their principal value is in the oil that is extracted by the few seal hunters who seek them. They frequently exceed two hundred pounds in weight, and are savage fighters if one can judge by the many scars found upon them. We never thought, when, a few months ago, we amused ourselves on the verandas of the Cliff House at San Francisco in watching their disporting about Seal Rock, that we should make such a close acquaintance with them.

The "goonies" also are easy to capture, although they are large and strong and a blow from the wing would break a man's limb. I measured one of them from tip to tip of wing, and it was over seven feet. They are, however, very awkward on their feet, and, having a double-jointed wing (that is, a joint in it like an elbow) can only rise from the ground when the wind is in their faces. Owing to this fact one only needs to get to the windward of them with a club and look out for the wings. We should like to add some of their eggs to our bill of fare, but dare not for fear of driving the birds away. I imagine it would take but a few of the eggs, if eatable, to go around, for I saw one at the Midways that was as large as those of the ostrich.

Fresh water will, however, apparently be our greatest cause for anxiety; for we have secured but a small supply, considering our number—ninety-three. A few breakers or kegs only, that were stowed in the boats, were secured. Rain, of course, we count upon; but to conserve our scanty supply until it comes is most necessary. To-day several wells have been dug in various parts of the island, but the water found in them is near the surface and is too brackish for any use.

The old timbers of a former wreck, probably of the *Gledstanes*,— the "bones" as sailors call them,—lie near on the beach and look as though they would yield us fuel for a long time. Our fire, which was started last evening by a match that Mr. Bailey, the chief diver, had for- tunately kept dry, has been constantly going for lack of more lighting material.

Evening. The reef party returned at sundown, reporting a strenuous day on the wreck. We all had a supper of "scouse" (a dish of pork, potato, and hard tack), and before sleeping the camp site was laid out, the sails and awnings which had come on shore temporarily set up, to our greater comfort. Besides the sails and awnings, more food supplies were captured from the after storeroom and a particularly fortunate prize secured in a small portable boiler that had been lashed to the afterdeck. This had been used by the contractor's party in hoisting to the scow the blasted coral from the reef, at Midway Islands.

There were also in one of the wheelhouses of the wreck some distilling-coils, which the engineer's force with our chief engineer suc- cessfully rescued after hard labor, for the sea was washing through the wheelhouse with terrible force. The boiler, suspended between two boats, was successfully landed on the beach, and we are greatly encouraged at the promise of fresh water to-morrow. We secured a barrel, also, partly filled with sperm oil, and a lantern in good condi- tion. These two articles insure us a supply of lighting material for the cooking-fire, which can now be put out at night and much fuel saved. Considerable clothing was secured from the officers' staterooms, and I was fortunate enough to find some of mine rolled up in one of the large wet bundles; and a few soaked mattresses and blankets were also brought in. The carpenter's chest, too, came ashore intact, and altogether we feel our situation greatly improved.

Mr. Talbot tells me that they are literally "stripping" the wreck, and nothing movable will be left on it if the weather will but hold good long enough. No one stops to question the utility of an article found adrift; it is seized hastily and thrown out on the reef to be transported later to the island. Pieces of rigging, boxes of tinned coffee, canned goods, tools, crockery, sails, awnings, etc., all come to the beach in a promiscuous mass to be sorted out later.

Monday, October 31. Still at work on the wreck. Boiler set up on the beach and connected with the distilling-coils by a piece of canvas hose. The inner end of the coils was joined to a length of our pilot-house speaking-tube as a return to the beach. By this arrangement the steam passed under the cooler water of the lagoon and was condensed as it returned to a bucket on the beach. Great joy was expressed at the first sight of the little stream and a great fear was lifted from our thoughts. At supper we had a cup of coffee to finish the quarter-ration of food, which was made into a scouse as before. The hard tack needed in making the scouse, however, will soon be exhausted, for, excepting a small quantity saved in tins, it is spoiling rapidly.

So to-day I opened a bag of flour to ascertain if we were to have any breadstuff. I found to my glad surprise that, with the exception of about an inch on the outside, it was sweet and sound. The sea water had protected it with a crust. A barrel of beans was also found to be in good condition; so that our pile of foodstuff under the sentry's charge begins to loom high for our safety for some time to come.

Tuesday, November 1. The crew was formed into several messes to-day, and also into watches. Each mess was provided with a tent, that for our mess (the wardroom) being made from the *Saginaw*'s quarter-deck awning. Such of our dry goods and bedding as had been rescued were removed to them, and our little camp begins to take on the appearance of comfort.

The duties of every member of the ship's company have been so arranged that it is hoped and expected that no one will have much time to brood over our situation or the future.

Wednesday, November 2. The bad weather we have feared has arrived. It came on suddenly this morning from the southeast with a high wind and a heavy rainfall, and before we had been able firmly to secure the tents. After strenuous exertion, however, we saved them from being blown over, but were wet to the skin when they were finally safe in place.

Fortunately the wreck on the reef has been thoroughly explored and there is very little material there now that could be of use to us, unless it may be the timbers themselves, to help us in building a seaworthy boat should it be necessary to do so in a final effort to get away. The idea of sending a boat to the Sandwich Islands for relief has been already revolving in our minds, and to-day was revealed by an order from the captain to the senior officers. After a consultation singly with us, he has directed each one to file with him an opinion on the feasibility and necessity of doing so—each written opinion to be without knowledge of the others.

It is probable that the hulk will be considerably broken up before the wind and sea go down, for one can see it rise and fall with the breakers, and occasionally a piece is detached and floated across the reef into the lagoon. As soon as it is safe to launch the boats, the work of securing these pieces will be started.

The boats are now resting at the highest part of the island in the centre of the camp, for even with the protecting reef the sea in the lagoon has been so rough that combers have reached within a few feet of our tents. As I write my journal we are a wet and sad party of unfortunates.

Our captain and his boat's crew must be having an experience worse than ours, however. They left this morning in the cutter for the sand spit near and to the west of us, to collect driftwood, and are "marooned" there in the storm. They can be seen, with the glasses, huddled together beneath the upturned boat. They do not, however, seem to be in imminent danger, and have made no signals of distress; so we expect them to return as soon as the sea abates.

Thursday, November 3. It has been still too rough to-day to launch the boats for work in the lagoon. We have, however, busied ourselves in erecting a storehouse for the better preservation of our food supplies, and to-night have them safely under cover. Last night the rats robbed us of a box of macaroni, and, therefore, we have put our storehouse on posts and two feet above the ground with inverted pans upon the posts.

We made the acquaintance of the rats last night in our tent when a noisy fight over a piece of candle disturbed our sleep. We had seen a few of them before, but did not suppose them to be so very numerous—as on first thought there seemed to be so very little for them to eat. We now found them to have good lungs and appetites, however, and a good deal of thrashing around with boots, etc., was necessary to expel them. We discussed them before we went to sleep again in the light of a future food supply,—an addition to our one-quarter ration,—and the opinion was general that should the seal and gooney desert us the rats would become more valuable. At any rate, they would thrive on the refuse of the food we had now.

The captain returned this morning from his expedition and gives a sad story of their luck. They had to literally bury themselves to the neck in the sand and lie under the boat to prevent being drenched by the rain. During the height of the storm they had one streak of good luck. They found some companions that the rough sea had induced to seek the shelter of the lagoon and beach. They were large sea turtles, and he and his crew turned them on their backs to prevent their escape. To-day we have them added to our food-supply and they are very welcome, notwithstanding the sad plight of their captors when they returned.

We have also added to our fresh water a supply of about fifty gallons caught in the rainstorm of yesterday, and doled out an extra cupful to each person.

Friday, November 4. The sea is rolling in huge breakers on the reef to-day, enveloping the wreck in spray, and we are constantly expecting to see the last of the *Saginaw* as a hulk. Several pieces can be seen adrift in the lagoon, and the hurricane deck is probably among them. The boats were launched and the mainmast towed to the landing, where it was anchored. It is the intention to have it set up near our camp and to use it for a lookout station as well as a means of flying a distress signal in case a passing vessel should be sighted. However, we do not pin much faith to the idea of rescue from passing ships, for the presence of these coral reefs constitutes such a menace to navigation that they are avoided. Vessels generally pass far to the north or south of them.

Saturday, November 5. The gig was carried well up on the beach to-day and set in a cradle, to be prepared for a voyage to the Sandwich Islands. It is the intention to raise her sides a few inches, to construct a light deck over all, and to fit her with two masts and sails. (Part of the sails were saved with the boat.) In the deck there are to be four square small hatches (with covers in case of bad weather), in which the men can sit and row when the wind is too light or contrary for sailing. From this it may be seen that the perilous trip has been decided upon by the captain. I have no doubt he feels the responsibility which he assumes, and I have great faith in his judgment. Our opinions were handed in to him yesterday, but of course we do not know what their influence has been, but it must be evident to him that all hands—officers and men alike—are loyally co-operating with him in our trying situation.

We learn that Lieutenant Talbot volunteered the day after the wreck to make the attempt and that several of the crew have also asked to go with him. In fact, so many of the men have volunteered that it will be necessary to take the pick of those most likely to stand the exposure, for although we have seen that such a trip was made in the case of the *Gledstanes*, it must be remembered that they took five months to build a seaworthy vessel, while our brave boys will go in a practically open boat.

Sunday, November 6. We were mustered for divine service to-day, and it being the first Sunday of the month the roll was called and each man answered "Here" as his name was called. After that prayers were read by the captain and an extra cup of water served out from the quantity caught during the recent gale. Work was suspended so far as possible, but the lagoon being so quiet it was thought necessary to launch two of the boats and tow in some of the floating timbers. We were overjoyed thus to receive and haul up free of the water a large fragment of the old hurricane deck. We can imagine some value in almost any piece of timber, but in this particular we are confident of securing much material for the building of our future boat, it being of three inch thick narrow planking. We believe we can make one and a half inch stuff from it by rigging up a staging and converting our one bucksaw into a jigsaw with a man above and one below. The black-smith believes that he can extract a good supply of nails, and in many ways it is evident that we are not going to wait supinely for the relief we hope for from our brave comrades' voyage.

To-day we killed our first goonies and had some for supper. They were very tough and "fishy," and Solomon Graves, once the *Saginaw*'s cabin cook, but now "King of the Galley" on Ocean Island, says that he cooked them all day. Only a portion of the bird could be masticated. However, it was voted superior to seal, the latter being so tough that Graves has to parboil it overnight and fry it in the morning. The hard tack is exhausted, but so much of the flour has been found good that we are to have a tablespoonful every other day and the same quantity of beans on the alternate days as substitutes for the hard tack. A cup of coffee or tea every day for the morning meal. Supper we have at five.

We had a luxury after supper. There are nine of us in the wardroom mess who smoke, and each of us was generously supplied with a cigar by Passed Assistant Engineer Blye, whose chest was rescued the second day; it contained a box of five hundred Manila cigars.

Monday, November 7. The mainmast is ready to raise to-morrow. An excavation has been made at the highest point of the island, near the captain's tent, and the mast rolled up to it with the rope guys ready to hold it upright. The carpenter's gang have been busy all day in sorting out material for the gig's deck and for raising her sides eight inches.

While the weather is fine, there seems to be a considerable swell at sea from the late storm, and the wreck is gradually, as it were, melting away. To-day a piece of the hull floated towards us and a boat was sent after it. When it reached the beach I recognized the remains of my stateroom, with twisted bolts protruding from the edge where it had been wrenched away from the rest of the hull. I viewed mournfully the remnant of my long-time home and reflected how it had once been my protection and that now fate had turned me out of its shelter.

Many of the hopes that were bred within its wooden walls have been shattered by its destruction, and I thought it would be appropriate to bury it on the beach with an epitaph above it showing the simple words "Lights out" which I had so often heard at its door when the ship's corporal made his nightly rounds at the "turning-in" hour. However, it was valuable even in its ruin for building and burning material. Besides, we are not ready yet to think of anything like a funeral.

Tuesday, November 8. I am writing my journal this evening with feelings of cheer and strengthened hopes, for although the fore part of the day was full of gloomy forebodings it has ended eventfully and happily. Our task to-day, as I have said, was to set up the mainmast, and the work was begun immediately after our breakfast. All hands were strenuously employed until noon. First, the mast was rolled into position so that the foot would be exactly over the centre of the hole dug yesterday. Then a small derrick was made to support the mast nearly in balance. With tackles and ropes then adjusted, as all good sailors know how to do, the heel was lowered slowly and the top elevated by the guys, until the mast stood on its foot and was secured upright. It was dinner-time when we considered it safe to leave, and we were glad when it was finally in place, for the work took about all the strength we had.

What was our dismay while we were at dinner to hear the snap of rope and the crash of the falling mast. Everybody rushed to the spot, and it was discovered that one of the guys had parted and that the sand had not been firm enough to hold the mast erect. Luckily the mast was not injured, and the captain said calmly, as though it was an everyday occurrence, "Well, men, we must do it again."

While we were standing about the hole and the captain was directing preparations for another effort, one of the men, noticing the water at the bottom, scooped some of it up in a shovel and raised it to his lips. I shall never forget his expression as he swallowed it. His eyes snapped, his face went white, and broadened almost into a grin, and he seemed for an instant to hold his breath. Then his color came back, and with a wild shout of gladness he exclaimed so that all could hear, "Boys—fresh water, by G——."

And so it proved,—soft and pure,—although within twenty feet of the salt water at the beach. Examination showed that there was quite a "pocket" of this filtered rainwater, and that the point where we had excavated was evidently where the island had originally commenced to form on solid ground. We noticed, too, during the afternoon that the water in it rises and falls with the tide of the ocean in the lagoon without mixing. This was explained by one of the officers, who had before seen such conditions, as due to the difference in density of the two waters, and the fact that the small rise and fall of the tide, which is only about twelve inches here, does not create an inrush and outgo sufficiently strong to force a mixture. However, we are greatly rejoiced over the "blessing in disguise" our falling mast has proved to be, and although the supply is probably moderate and dependent on the rains, we shall be able to dispense with the boiler, which has begun to give trouble from rust and leakage.

Wednesday. Blye and I went inland among the bushes and killed twelve boobies for supper to-morrow. Breakfast, pork scouse and cup of water. Provisions got wet from leak in storehouse last night; took tea, coffee, and wet bread out to dry. Several showers during the day. Mr. Talbot went over to the sand spit and brought back driftwood and four large turtles. Supper, salt beef and two dough-balls from mouldy flour.

Thursday, 10th. Breakfast, salt beef and flour-balls. Getting up ship's mainmast for flagstaff and lookout. One boat off to the wreck. Several rain squalls during day, and unable to dry out stores. Supper on boobies and flour-balls.

Friday, 11th. Breakfast, turtle steak and a tablespoonful of mashed potatoes. The mast was again raised to-day and care taken to prevent a repetition of Tuesday's accident. Stronger guys were led to heavy, deep-driven stakes. A topmast was added and a rope ladder to the crosstrees. Work on the gig progressing fast—nearly decked over. Supper, turtle, eight goonies, potatoes, and cup of tea.

Saturday, 12th. Breakfast on fish, turtle soup, and mashed potatoes. Supper, seal meat and tablespoonful of mashed beans. The fish from the reef are voted no good. They are brilliantly colored but strong in taste, and are said by the captain to be similar to the "parrot fish" that is found among our West India coral reefs. Solomon Graves says that the parrot fish is poisonous, so it is decided to leave them out of our bill of fare. Should it become necessary to augment our ration it will, no doubt, be done by adding the *rats*, and for myself I believe they will improve it.

Sunday, November 13. Ship breaking up rapidly and boats out to pick up driftwood. Had prayers (read by Captain S.) at 3 P.M., and he addressed us with remarks as to necessity in our situation of working on Sabbath. Thousands of rats about. Put extra night watch on storehouse, for fear of further depredations.

Monday, 14th. Same diet as yesterday. Aired all clothing. Work on gig pushing, and we expect to get her off this week. Every one writing letters to send in her.

Tuesday, 15th. Diet, goonies and turtle, with last of potatoes. The gig was launched and provisions sent down from storehouse. Had a long talk with Talbot. He realizes danger of trip, but is brave and confident; gave him my revolver.

Wednesday, 16th. Cup of tea, 7 A.M. and breakfast as usual at 10; turtle and gooney; Heavy sea on reef, and ship fast disappearing, boats out picking up driftwood. Had to take the condenser and all wood high up on the beach. Wind shifted suddenly from north to southeast. Gave Talbot two hundred dollars in gold coin for possible expenses.

Thursday, November 17. Blowing hard from north. Tea at 7 A.M. The gig anchored off shore. Mr. Bailey and I fixed up the well where fresh water was found when mast fell; good-by to the old condenser. "The little cherub that sits up aloft" doing good work for us all.

THE SAILING OF THE GIG

Friday, November 18. The weather has been fine since the breaking up of the storm of the second.

As to work, every one has had his duties portioned out to him, and there is no doubt of the captain's wisdom in providing thus an antidote to homesickness or brooding. Faces are—some of them—getting "peaked," and quite a number of the party have been ill from lack of power to digest the seal meat; but there are no complaints, we all fare alike. Medicines are not to hand, but a day or two of abstinence and quiet generally brings one around again. In the evenings, when we gather around the smoking lamp after supper, there are frequent discussions over our situation and prospects.

They are, however, mostly sanguine in tone, and it is not uncommon to hear the expression "when we get home." No one *seems* to have given up his hope of eventual relief. It has been very noticeable, too, at such times that no matter where the conversation begins it invariably swings around, before the word is passed to "douse the glim," to those things of which we are so completely deprived—to narratives of pleasant gatherings—stories of banquets and festival occasions where toothsome delicacies were provided. It would seem as though these reminiscences were given us as a foil to melancholy, and they travel along with us into our dreams.

Upon one point we are all agreed, that we are very fortunate in being wrecked in so agreeable a climate, where heavy clothing is unnecessary. The temperature has been, aside from the storm we had soon after the landing, between seventy and seventy-five degrees during the day and around fifty degrees at night. We are very sensible of the discomforts that would be ours if tumbled upon some of the islands of the northern ocean in winter.

The moonlit nights have been grand, and calculated to foster romance in a sailor's thoughts were the surroundings appropriate. As it is, the little cheer we extract from them is in the fact that we see the same shining face that is illuminating the home of our loved ones.

Often in my corner of the tent, Mr. Foss and I pass what would be a weary hour otherwise, over a game of chess, the pieces for which he has fashioned from gooney bones and blocks of wood.

Mr. Main has made a wonderful nautical instrument—a sextant—from the face of the *Saginaw*'s steam gauge, together with some broken bits of a stateroom mirror and scraps of zinc. Its minute and finely drawn scale was made upon the zinc with a cambric needle, and the completed instrument is the result of great skill and patience. Mr. Talbot has tested it and pronounces it sufficiently accurate for navigating purposes.

Another officer has made a duplicate of the official chart of this part of the Pacific, and still another has copied all the Nautical Almanac tables necessary for navigation.

I have been directed by the captain to make a selection from the best-preserved supplies in the storehouse most suitable for boat service, and calculate that Talbot will have the equivalent of thirty-five days' provender at one-half rations, although many of the articles are not in the regular ration tables.

This morning the boat was surrounded by many men and carried bodily into water that was deep enough to float her. There she was anchored and the stores carried out to her. Mr. Butterworth, standing waist deep in the water, put on the last finishing touches while she was afloat by screwing to the gunwales the rowlocks for use in calm weather.

There was expended from store-book the following articles: ten breakers (a small keg) of water, five days' rations of hard tack sealed in tin, ten days of the same in canvas bags, two dozen small tins of preserved meat, five tins (five pounds each) of dessicated potato, two tins of cooked beans, three tins of boiled wheaten grits, one ham, six tins of preserved oysters, ten pounds of dried beef, twelve tins of lima beans, about five pounds of butter, one gallon of molasses, twelve pounds of white sugar, four pounds of tea and five pounds of coffee. A small tin cooking apparatus for burning oil was also improvised and furnished.

I had intended putting on board twenty-five pounds of boiled rice in sealed tins, but discovered one of the tins to be swollen just before the provisions were started off. Hastily the tins were opened and the rice found unfit for use. The dessicated potatoes were at once served out in place of the rice, the cans scalded and again sealed.

With the navigating instruments and the clothing of the voyagers on board, the boat was pronounced ready and we went to dinner. There was little conversation during the meal. The impending departure of our shipmates hung like a pall of gloom over us at the last and was too thought-absorbing for speech. Talbot seemed to be the most unconcerned of all, but as I watched him I felt that the brave fellow was assuming it to encourage the rest of us. I had a long friendly talk with him, last evening, during which he seemed thoroughly to estimate the risk he was to take, and entrusted to me his will to be forwarded to his parents in Kentucky in case he should not survive the journey.

All hands have been given permission to send letters by the boat, so all papers, together with a bill of exchange for two hundred pounds sterling, which by order of the captain I have given to Talbot, have been sealed air tight in a tin case. I sent the following letter to my home in Philadelphia, which I will insert here, as it partially represents the state of affairs:—

"You will of course be surprised to receive a letter from this desert island, but it now has a population of ninety-three men, the *Saginaw*'s crew. In short, we were wrecked on the coral reef surrounding it, and the *Saginaw* is no more. We left Midway Islands on the evening of Friday, October 28, and the next morning at three o'clock found ourselves thumping on the reef. We stayed by the ship until daylight, when we got out three boats and all the provisions we possibly could. We also saved the safe, part of the ship's books, about one fourth of my clothing, and my watch. If you could see me now you would hardly recognize me: a pair of boots almost large enough for two feet in one, ragged trousers, an old felt hat, and no coat—I keep that for evenings when it is cool. I have my best uniform saved, having rescued it to come ashore in. We had to wade about two hundred feet on the reef, and I stood in water about one half of the day helping to pass provisions to the boats; then went ashore and spread them on the beach to dry.

"We have been living on very short allowance, being thankful for a spoonful of beans, a small piece of meat twice a day, with a cup of tea or coffee in the morning. I am indeed thankful that no lives were lost, and hope to see you all in three months' time. The gig has been decked over and is to start for Honolulu, to-morrow or next day, for relief.

"Ocean Island is similar in formation to Midway, but is larger and the coral reef is farther from the land.

"We had for breakfast this morning some of the brown albatross or "goonies," as they call them. We shall not want for meat for some time, as there is an abundance of fish, seal and turtle, but the flour, rice, and hard bread will not last more than two and one half months.

"I hope this will reach you before you get anxious about us, for if the gig should not be successful we may have to stay here until the middle of March. I shall send this in her to be mailed from Honolulu. Our executive officer and four men go in her, and a perilous trip it will be, for she is only twenty feet long and the distance is over a thousand miles. Look us up on the map.

"Most of our sails were saved and we are comparatively comfortable in good tents. I am well but hungry. We have dug wells, but found no fresh water. However, we are getting some from a condenser fitted by our chief engineer. Altogether we have more conveniences than might be expected and are in good health generally. I should like to write to friends, but space in the boat is scarce and everybody is writing."

The hour set for the boat's departure (four o'clock) arrived and we were all mustered upon the beach. Prayers were read by the captain, after which final farewells were said and the brave men who were to peril their lives for us waded off to the gig and climbed on board. They quickly stepped the little masts, spread the miniature sails, raised their anchor, and slowly gaining headway stood off for the western channel through the reef. With full hearts and with many in tears, we gave them three rousing cheers and a tiger, which were responded to with spirit, and we watched them until the boat faded from sight on the horizon to the northward.

As I write this by the dim light of a candle the mental excitement due from the parting with our shipmates seems still to pervade the tent and no one is thinking of turning in.

Mr. Bailey, the foreman of the contractor's party, came into the tent soon after we had gathered for the evening. He had in his hand a small book and on his face a smile as he passed it around, showing each one an open page of the book; when he reached me I saw it was a pocket Bible opened at the fifty-first chapter of Isaiah, where Mr. B.'s finger rested under the words, "The isles shall wait upon me and on my arm shall they trust." He did not speak until I had read, and then said he had opened the Bible by chance, as was his habit every evening. Poor Bailey! We all feel very sorry for him. He is a fine character, well advanced in years; and having by economy accumulated considerable money, had bought himself a home, before coming out, to which he was intending to retire when this contract was completed.

By invitation from the captain I accompanied him in walking around the entire island, avoiding, however, the extreme point to the westward, where albatross were nesting. He talked but little, and I saw that his eyes often turned to the spot where the gig had disappeared from view. As we separated in front of his little tent he said with a voice full of pathos to me, "Good-night, Paymaster; God grant that we see them again."

I find that I have so far omitted to give the personnel of Talbot's crew. As stated before there were many volunteers, but the surgeon was ordered to select from a list given him four of the most vigorous and sturdy of the applicants and report their names to the captain. There was considerable rivalry among them. In fact I was accidentally a witness to a hard-fought wrestling-match between two of the crew who sought the honor of going and risking their lives. The defeated one, I was told, was to waive his claim in favor of the victor.

The following letter, which has gone in the boat from our captain to the Admiral of the Pacific fleet, gives the personnel of the boat's crew and other information.

Ocean Island, Pacific Ocean,
November 16, 1870.
Rear Admiral John A. Winslow,
Commanding Pacific Fleet.
Sir:—I have the honor to recommend that the attention of the Department be particularly called to the fine conduct of Lieu-

tenant J.G. Talbot. The day after the wreck of the *Saginaw*, Lieutenant Talbot came to me and volunteered to take one of the ship's boats to Honolulu in order to bring back relief for the officers and crew of the vessel. He has been most zealous and spirited through this whole affair and of the greatest assistance to me.

His boat (by the usual route at this season) will probably have to sail and pull some fifteen hundred miles, and I think some recognition of his handsome conduct would be proper.

The names of the crew are as follows:—Lieutenant J.G. Talbot; Coxswain William Halford; Quartermaster Peter Francis; Seaman John Andrews; Seaman James Muir. The last two are contractor's men and were specially enlisted by me from Mr. Townsend's party for one month. They were men of such fine qualities and endurance that I thought it proper to let them go.

The enlistment was made with the express understanding between myself and them that it did not interfere with their previous contract with Mr. Townsend.

I am very respectfully,

Your obedient servant,

Montgomery Sicard,

Lieut.-Comd'r-commanding.

WAITING

Thursday, November 24. Thanksgiving Day—at home; the noble bird, roast turkey, has not graced our tarpaulin-covered table. He has been replaced by a tough section of albatross. Nor was there any expression of thanks at the mess table until one of the officers, having finished the extra cup of coffee served in honor of the day, said, "Say, fellows, let's be thankful that we are alive, well and still with hope."

Last evening about nine o'clock we were given another flurry of excitement over expected relief. The storehouse sentry reported a light to the eastward and in a "jiffy" our tent was empty. Sure enough, there was a bright light close to the horizon which, as we watched, appeared to grow larger and nearer. The captain was called, and I joined him with Mr. Cogswell (our new executive officer since Talbot left) in front of his tent. After watching the light for a few minutes, the captain turned to us and said, "Gentlemen, it is only a star rising and the atmosphere is very clear. Better turn in again"; and he entered the tent.

Sunday, November 27. Last Sunday and to-day we have had divine service led by the captain reading the prayers of the Episcopal ritual.

(*Note.*—I find nothing but the Thanksgiving note in my journal after the departure of the gig until November 27, other than official entries of receipts and expenditures of food,—the receipt of seals and albatross killed by Mr. Blye and his detail of men; the expenditure being the same with the daily allowance of flour or beans and the coffee for the noon meal.)

Work has been steadily pushed on the schooner. The keel has been hewed out of the *Saginaw's* late topmast and is blocked up on the beach. We are ripping the old deck planks in two with our old bucksaw and one handsaw, and while it is slow work we can see our boat planking ahead of us when the frame is ready. The schooner is to be forty feet long, of centre-board, flat-bottomed type, and the captain has settled upon her shape and dimensions after experimenting with a small model in company with the contractor's carpenter, who has had experience in boat-building.

This morning about sunrise the camp was roused to excitement by the loud cry of "Sail ho!" I found on joining the crowd at the landing that the captain had ordered a boat launched and her crew were already pulling away in a northerly direction.

I could see nothing from the crow's nest at the masthead, but the statement of one of the crew that he had seen a sail was positive; and the camp was full of a nervous expectancy until nine o'clock, when the boat returned with the disappointing news that the alleged sail was only a large white rock on the north end of the reef that had reflected the sun's rays. As the sun rose to a greater angle the reflection disappeared. An order was at once given out that no one should again alarm the camp before permission from the captain was obtained.

Sunday, December 25. Christmas Day!! Merry Christmas at home, but dreary enough here! Still the salutation was passed around in a half-hearted manner. It is the first day since the wreck that depression of spirit has been so contagious and camp-wide. The religious services, as we stood in the sand bareheaded (some barefooted also), hardly seemed to fit our situation, and the voice of the captain was subdued and occasionally tremulous. I had donned my best uniform coat, which had come ashore when the wreck was stripped, and tried also to put on a cheerful face. No use; I could not keep up the deceit, and I slipped out of line before the service was ended, to change back to the blue sailor shirt and working clothes. I felt that I had been "putting on airs." It has been my first really blue day, for the pictures in my mind of the Christmas festivities at home but emphasized the desolation of the life here.

Strangely enough, Dr. Frank has seemed to a certain extent to be more cheerful than usual. It seems queer that he, pessimist as he appeared to me when he predicted disaster before we sailed from the Midway Islands, should now be the optimist and attempt to dispel our gloom. Some expert in psychical research may be able to discern, as I cannot, why the doctor's belief in Talbot's success should now have influence enough to change my melancholy into a firmer hope than ever.

We borrowed the chart from the captain and followed in pure imagination the course of the gig; and when we folded it, the doctor said that he believed Talbot had arrived at the end of his journey and we should be relieved. Talbot has now been away thirty-seven days, and our several estimates of the time he would consume have been between thirty and forty.

Every afternoon, when work is suspended for the day and we have repaired to the tent, the expression of Talbot's whereabouts is the first note of discussion; as though it had not been in our minds all the long weary day of work.

As the possible failure of Talbot's brave effort begins to enter our calculations, the greater is the exertion to provide in the near future another avenue of escape. So, with gradually weakened strength, owing to lack of sustaining food, the labor we find arduous and exhausting; I, being included in the carpenter's gang on the schooner, realize that fact thoroughly. Yesterday the captain and myself made another circuit of the island, and both were glad to rest on the return to the camp.

The captain has ordered the cutter to be also fitted for a voyage to the Midway Islands. There he intends to have a sign erected stating, briefly, our situation; to serve in case the Navy Department should send (as we expect it will) a searching vessel for us. Twice every day I have climbed the rope ladder on the mast and searched with anxious eyes through my rescued opera glasses the shipless horizon; sometimes with such a strain of nerves and hope that phantom vessels plague my vision. The loneliness and solitude of the vast expanse of water surrounding us is beyond expression. Truly, it is the desert of the Pacific Ocean, and more dangerous than that upon the land, for there are no trails or guide-posts for the weary traveler when the sky is obscured. One might easily fancy that beyond the line of the horizon there exists only infinite space. As the Prince of the Happy Valley observes in "Rasselas," after an ocean voyage, "There is no variety but the difference between rest and motion."

I do not remember the cry of "Sail ho!" during all of our cruising between the Hawaiian and Midway Islands save in the vicinity of the former.

The rats are more in evidence of late. At first small and timid, they are now growing larger and bolder; running about and over us in the tents during the night. We are getting quite accustomed to their visits, however, and, rolling ourselves in blankets or whatever covering we have, pay small attention to them. If we stay here, though, our attention will become more acute; for they begin to loom up in importance as a food supply.

The seal, on the contrary, are growing less in numbers, although great care has been taken not to frighten them away. Also, we have not lately attempted fishing on the reef, for fear of reducing their food. We have been prevented from trying the eggs of the albatross, that their nesting may continue without interruption. They will probably leave, too, when the hatching season is over and the young have been taught to fly.

So far as our present ration is concerned, with the exception of beans, flour, and coffee from which our small daily issue is made, we are situated as though no provisions had been rescued from the wreck; for the captain has wisely ordered that all the rest must be held intact to provision the schooner. So, with all the nerve we can muster, the work on the schooner is being pushed. To-day the frame stands ready for the planking, and the captain thinks that in another week her mast can be ready for stepping.

Last Thursday we had our second most violent wind and rainstorm. It came with hurricane force from the eastward, and the tremendous sea crossed the reef and reached our beach with considerable energy left in it. Our schooner that is to be, with her frame almost completed, was perilously near the waves, and all hands were called. We turned out in the storm and carried her bodily higher up on the beach and breathed more at ease when we saw the seas diminish with the dying wind.

Mr. Blye has been, to-day, our Santa Claus, and with several others I have received a Christmas present of great value. As before noted, there came on shore from the wreck when it was being stripped a box of Manila cigars, and it has been supposed that they were all distributed by the generous owner and had been smoked. To-day, however, Mr. Blye discovered that three of them lay in the bottom of his chest, and to be impartial he divided them into three parts each and doled them out. My present was thankfully and cheerfully accepted, and while I am writing my journal, is passing off in wreaths of hope above my head.

Mr. Bailey and myself have for several days been having the joint use of an old clay pipe he had saved, and we have been trying to smoke the dried leaves and bark of the bushes around us. It is a failure with me. Now much has been said by learned men *for* as well as *against* the use of tobacco, but I do not hesitate to testify to its great value in conditions such as ours. It has been a cheering companion to our thoughts in solitude, and a comfort in depression of spirits. I have even seen one man offer his only coat for a piece of plug about the size of a silver dollar.

Sunday, January 1, 1871. New Year's Day—"Happy New Year"! I think no one but the marine sentry at the storehouse saw the birth of the new year or cared to see the new year come in. For myself I hope there will be no more holidays to chronicle here except it may be the one that liberates us from these surroundings. They have—the three we have had here—aroused too many sombre reflections in contrasting those of the past with the present.

Talbot has now been away forty-three days and it seems almost beyond probability that he should have reached the Sandwich Islands before the food was exhausted. There is a lingering hope, however, that some delay in starting relief for us may have occurred or that he may have reached some island other than Oahu, where Honolulu is situated, and that communication with Oahu may be limited. We are "threshing out" the whole situation to-night in earnest discussion between the sanguine and non-sanguine members of the mess.

RESCUED

Tuesday, January 3. At midnight. It is near an impossibility sanely and calmly to write up my journal to-night—my nerves are shaken and my pencil falters. I have climbed into the storehouse to get away from the commotion in the tent and all over the camp. No one can possibly sleep, for I can see through a rent in the canvas men dancing around a huge fire on the highest point of the island, and hear them cheering and singing while feeding the fire with timbers that we have been regarding as worth their weight in coin. To a looker-on the entire camp would seem to have gone crazy. I will tell what I can now and the rest some other time.

At half-past three this afternoon I was working on the schooner near Mr. Mitchell, one of the carpenters of the contractor's party. I was handing him a nail when I noticed his eyes steadily fixed on some point seaward. He paid no attention to me, and his continued gaze induced me to turn my eyes in the same direction to find what was so attractive as to cause his ignoring me. I saw then, too, something that held my gaze. Far off to the northeast and close to the horizon there was something like a shadow that had not been there when I had last visited the lookout. It appeared as a faintly outlined cloud, and as we both watched with idle tools in our hands it seemed to grow in size and density. Very soon he spoke in a low voice, as though not wishing to give a false alarm: "Paymaster, I believe that is the smoke of a steamer," and after another look, "I am sure of it"; and then arose a shout that all could hear, "Sail ho!"

The order concerning alarms was forgotten in his excitement, but as the captain stood near and his face beamed with his own joy, no notice was taken of the violation. He directed me at once to visit the lookout, and I did so, rapidly securing my glasses. By the time I reached the top of the mast I could see that the shadow we had watched was developing into a long and well-marked line of smoke and that a steamer was headed to the westward in front of it. I notified the eager, inquiring crowd at the foot of the mast and still kept my glasses trained on the steamer until her smokestack came into view. She was not heading directly for us, and I cannot describe the anxiety with which I watched to see if she was going to pass by,—my heart was thumping so that one could hear it. I could not believe she would fail to see our signal of distress that waved above me, and pass on to leave us stricken with despair.

When she arrived at a point nearly to the north of us, I saw her change her course until her masts were in line, and then I shouted the fact to those below, for it was evident she was bound for Ocean Island.

The long dreary suspense was over; our relief was near, and I slid down the Jacob's ladder, pale and speechless. The few moments of tense watchfulness had seemed to me like hours of suspense, and it is slight wonder that it took some time to recover my speech. When I did so I acquainted the captain with all I had seen. By the time I had completed my statement the steamer was in view from the ground, and then I witnessed such a scene as will never be forgotten.

Rough-looking men—many of them having faced the shocks of storm and battle—all of them having passed through our recent misfortunes without a murmur of complaint—were embracing each other with tears of joy running down their cheeks, while laughing, singing, and dancing.

I was at once ordered to break into our supplies and issue the best meal to all hands that I could concoct. This I certainly did with haste, and after our supper of boiled salt pork, flour, and beans, finished off with a cup of coffee, I felt as I might after a Delmonico dinner. It was a much-interrupted meal, however, for some one or more were continually rushing out of the tent and returning to report to the rest the movements of the steamer. By the time we had finished supper she was very near and was recognized as the *Kilauea*, a vessel belonging to the King of the Sandwich Islands. She came within half a mile of the reef where the *Saginaw* was wrecked and dipped her flag and then slowly steamed away in a southerly direction. This manœuvre we understood, for, as it was getting late in the day, our rescuers were evidently intending to return to-morrow and avoid the danger of a night near the reef. Our captain has ordered a fire to be kept in good blazing order throughout the night as a beacon.

Thursday, January 5. On board the *Kilauea* (pronounced Kilaway) at sea. It was next to impossible yesterday to make any entries in my journal, and even this evening I have been compelled to ask Captain Long for the temporary use of his stateroom, owing to the tumult in the cabin and on deck; because I wish to record events while they are fresh in my memory. So much excitement and so many incidents were crowded in during the time we were rapidly collecting our effects and embarking on the *Kilauea* that it is difficult to note them in order.

The *Kilauea* appeared at daybreak and anchored near the west entrance of the lagoon, and very soon after her captain came to our landing-place in a whaleboat. I recognized in him an old Honolulu friend,—Captain Thomas Long, a retired whaling captain, and as he stepped from his boat, we gave him three rousing cheers while we stood at attention near the fringe of bushes around the camp. Captain Sicard went down the beach alone to receive him, and after a cordial greeting, they conferred together for a few minutes. Together they came towards us apparently in sober thought, and Captain Sicard held up his hand as a signal for silence. He uncovered his head and said, in a tremulous voice, "Men, I have the great sorrow to announce to you that we have been saved at a great sacrifice. Lieutenant Talbot and three of the gig's crew are dead. The particulars you will learn later; at present, Captain Long is anxious for us to remove to the *Kilauea* as quickly as possible."

He bowed his head and a low murmur of grief passed along our line. From a cheering, happy crowd we were as in an instant changed to one of mourning. All the dreary waiting days we have passed seemed to fade into insignificance in the face of this great sorrow.

Captain Long inquired if anything was needed immediately, stating that a generous supply of food and clothing had been rushed on board the *Kilauea* in Honolulu, and that she had started to sea eight hours after he had been notified of her mission. One of the officers told him that the thing that would best supply a long-felt want was tobacco; so the *Kilauea*'s boat was at once dispatched to the steamer for a box of it, which when opened on the beach was greedily appropriated.

I went off to the *Kilauea* in the first of the embarking boats, taking the ship's safe and papers that had been stored at the head of my mattress in the tent; therefore did not see the final disposition of articles left on the island; but they suddenly lost all interest to me and, beyond the fact that our water supply was labeled with a sign for future unfortunates, I know but little. The captain tells me that Captain Long demurred at the length of time it would take to bring off most of the government property, saying that his duty to us and to his vessel made it necessary to get away from this dangerous neighborhood at the earliest possible moment; the rescue of life and not property was his object in coming to us. So our food supply and many articles of equipment were collected and stored at the highest point of the island.

When I reached the *Kilauea* I was served with a good meal, of which I ate sparingly; and, having deposited the safe in a near corner of the cabin, "turned in" on a near berth, boots and all, sleeping through all the turmoil made when the others came off. And so we sailed away at dusk to the eastward, turning our backs on the desolate home where we had suffered for sixty-seven days.

I have learned that a fast-sailing schooner, *Kona*, was dispatched on Saturday evening under charter by the American Minister, eight hours after the arrival of Halford. Our consul and vice-consul, with other friends, however, prevailed upon the United States Minister, Mr. Pierce, to accept the offer of the *Kilauea* by the King; urging as a reason that there was no certainty of our being in a condition to await the slow progress of a sailing-vessel; that there might be sickness and even starvation in our party. The *Kilauea* was hastily coaled and sailed on Monday.

(*Note.* The *Kona* was sighted in the offing as we were leaving Ocean Island, and running down to her Captain Long ordered her back to Honolulu.)

On the way to Honolulu, while sitting in the pilot house of the *Kilauea*, I overheard a conversation on deck between two of the *Saginaw*'s men concerning the superstition connected with sailing on Friday. "What better proof," said one of them, "would you have of its being an unlucky day than in the case of the *Saginaw*? She sailed from the Midway Islands on a Friday, and two days afterward she lay a total wreck among the breakers of Ocean Island. The gig that went for help also started on Friday, and what was the result? Four out of the five brave boys who manned her came to an untimely end—how Halford escaped is a mystery to me; but I guess he'll think twice before venturing on another voyage on that day of the week." I said to myself that I would think twice, too, unless I was starting under orders.

THE FATE OF THE GIG

Honolulu, January 28, 1871. Perhaps some reader may deem the story of the *Saginaw*'s last cruise complete. I cannot, however, consider it so while lacking the sorrowful story of our comrades' voyage in the gig, with its fatal ending as told by Halford, the sole survivor. Nor would it be less than ingratitude to pass unnoticed the fact of our hearty reception when we arrived here on the fourteenth, well fed and well clothed through the generous exertions of our friends. The King, his Cabinet, and most of the population were on the wharves as the *Kilauea* steamed into the harbor. The cheers and hat-waving were but the prelude to a most cordial and affectionate greeting when we landed in the midst of the throng.

Several of the officers were at once seized upon and taken to the homes of their old-time friends. When I could elude the crowd I was whisked away in a carriage to the Nuuanu Valley home of Mr. John Paty, and there rested in luxury and comfort until to-day, when we are to sail on the steamer *Moses Taylor*.

On Thursday our captain and several officers were received in audience by the King, and in acknowledgment of the great kindness shown us, the following address was presented.

Our captain said:—

In behalf of the rear admiral commanding the Pacific fleet, I desire to thank your Majesty for the most courteous offer of the steamer *Kilauea* to go to the assistance of the shipwrecked crew of the United States Ship *Saginaw* on Ocean Island. It was a most welcome and opportune relief to the company of United States officers and seamen there in distress; a proof of your Majesty's friendly feeling toward our Navy. I am sure your Majesty's kind and humane intentions were most efficiently carried out by the very capable and intelligent officer with his officers and crew sent in command of the *Kilauea*. I must ask your Majesty, also, to accept my thanks and those of my officers and men for the sympathy shown us in our probable distress; for the personal interest taken by you in the speedy dispatch of the *Kilauea*. Your Majesty's Minister of the Interior, also, manifested the strongest interest in our relief; to his energetic and efficient efforts was it due that your intentions were so promptly carried into effect.

At Ocean Island we recognized your Majesty's ship as soon as she appeared on the horizon. Our feelings of gratitude may perhaps be imagined, but can only be thoroughly appreciated by those who have been placed in a similar situation. On our arrival in port we were welcomed with the most warm-hearted cordiality, and since have received abundant proofs of the kind feelings of the Hawaiian people.

One officer and four men belonging to my vessel bravely and generously volunteered on a long sea voyage in a small boat for the relief of their shipmates. These finally, with one exception, made sacrifice of their lives upon the shores of the island of Kauai. Your Majesty's subjects on that island received the survivor of the boat's crew with great kindness and hospitality. They were most solicitous to recover the remains of my officer and his men, and to inter them in a suitable and Christian manner. I desire again to return thanks for all that has been done for the *Saginaw*'s officers and crew.

His Majesty replied to the captain as follows:—

Captain—I am pleased to see you here to-day and congratulate you and the officers and crew of the late United States Ship *Saginaw* upon the delivery from their unpleasant position upon a desolate island. I am glad that my Government has been enabled to render you assistance. The officers of your Service in this ocean have always shown themselves prompt to go to the assistance of distressed men of all nations, and I have lately had a proof of their prompt humanity in the offer of Captain Truxton, of the ship *Jamestown*, to assist some of my subjects in the Micronesian Islands, and in the efficient aid which he rendered them. Such interchanges tend to promote personal and national friendship.

I sympathize with you, Captain, for the loss of your ship—a misfortune always keenly felt by a sensitive officer, however unavoidable it may have been. I sympathize with you for the loss of the gallant officer and men who, after a long voyage in an open boat, met their death on the shores of Kauai. Such examples of devotion to duty are a rich legacy to all men. Permit me, Captain, to express a hope that you and your officers who have shared with you your service in this ocean for some time past and your peril in the late shipwreck may live to attain the highest honors in your profession.

On Saturday last there was held a sale by a local auctioneer of such articles belonging to the Navy Department as we were able to bring away from Ocean Island. Among them was included the gig which Halford brought from the island of Kauai. We were surprised to learn later that the boat had been bid in by a syndicate of our friends for presentation to us as a souvenir. It has been accepted and we are considering plans for its future preservation. I went down to the dock yesterday to see it prepared for shipment, and its sad story was almost told in the scars upon it. Its bow was bound with iron straps and a large gap in the starboard side was covered with canvas. Its wounds seemed almost as making a mute appeal for sympathy, and expressed the struggle it had gone through.

HALFORD'S STORY

When we left Ocean Island, November 18th, we ran to the north to latitude 32°, there took the westerly winds and ran east to, as Mr. Talbot supposed, the longitude of Kauai (Kowee), but it proved ultimately that we were not within a degree of that longitude. We then stood south. Five days out we lost all light and fire and had no means of making either—no dry tinder or wood, although we had flint and steel. About five or six days before making Kauai we succeeded in getting a light with a glass taken from an opera glass. We suffered much from wet, cold, and want of food. The ten days' ration of bread in a canvas bag was mostly spoiled; the two tins of cooked beans could not be eaten, causing dysentery, as did also the boiled wheat; the gallon of molasses leaked out, and the sugar, tea, and coffee were spoiled by wetting. To the dessicated potato, five five-pound tins of which were given us at the last moment before sailing, we attributed the preservation of our lives from starvation. For the last week it was all we had, mixed with a little fresh water.

We had heavy weather while running to the eastward; hove to with the sea anchor twice, the last time lost it. We then made another drag from three oars, which was also lost. Then we made still another from two oars and a square of sail by crossing them. That lasted for three turns of bad weather; but the third time it broke adrift and all was lost.

Mr. Talbot was ill with diarrhœa for seven or eight days, but got better, although he continued to suffer much from fatigue and hardship. He was somewhat cheerful the whole passage. Muir and Andrews were sick for two or three weeks. Francis was always well.

We did not make land within a week of what we expected. The first land we saw was Kawaihua Rock, at the southern end of Niihau (Neehow) Island, on Friday morning, December 16th. We stood north by east, with the island in sight all day. During that night and Saturday stood northeast by north, and on Saturday night headed east and south southeast.

Sunday morning the wind allowed us to head southeast with the island of Kauai in sight, and Sunday night we were off the Bay of Halalea on the north coast. We then hove to with head to the northwest, the wind having hauled to the westward. We laid thus until eleven P.M. It being my watch on deck, I called Mr. Talbot and told him that the night was clear and I could see the entrance to Halalea Harbor. He ordered the boat to be kept away and steered for the entrance. As we came near the entrance it clouded up and became dark, so we hove to again with head to the northwest. At one A.M. I called my relief. Andrews and Francis came on deck, as did also Mr. Talbot. After I went below the boat was again kept away toward the land for a short time and again hove to. At a little past two A.M. Sunday morning she was kept away again for the third time. I remained below until I felt from the boat's motion that she was getting into shoal water.

Then I awoke Muir and told him it was time we went on deck. He did not go, but I did. Just as I got to the cockpit a sea broke aboard abaft. Mr. Talbot ordered to bring the boat by the wind. I hauled aft the main sheet with Francis at the helm and the boat came up into wind. Just then another breaker broke on board and capsized the boat. Andrews and Francis were washed away and were never afterwards seen. Muir was still below, and did not get clear until the boat was righted, when he gave symptoms of insanity. Before the boat was righted by the sea Mr. Talbot was clinging to the bilge of the boat and I called him to go to the stern and there get up on the bottom. While he was attempting to do so he was washed off and sank. He was heavily clothed and much exhausted. He made no cry. I succeeded in getting on to the bottom and stripped myself of my clothes. Just then the sea came and righted the boat.

It was then that Muir put his head up the cockpit, when I assisted him on deck. Soon afterward another breaker came and again upset the boat; she going over twice, the last time coming upright and headed on to the breakers. We then found her to be inside of the large breakers, and we drifted toward the shore at a place called Kalihi Kai, about five miles from Hanalei. I landed with the water breast-high and took with me a tin case of dispatches and letters. On board there was a tin box with its cover broken containing navigation books, charts, etc., also Captain Sicard's instructions to Lieutenant Talbot, with others, among which were Muir's and Andrews's discharge papers; they having been shipped November 15th for one month. (They belong to the contractors, in whose employ they were previous to that time.) This box also contained Francis's and my transfer papers and accounts destined for the Mare Island Navy Yard. This box with everything not lashed fell into the water when we were first upset.

I landed about three A.M., but saw no one until daybreak, when, seeing some huts, I went to them and got assistance to get the boat onto the beach. I had previously, by making five trips to the boat, succeeded in bringing ashore the long tin case first mentioned, the chronometer, opera glasses, barometer, one ship's compass, boat's binnacle compass, and had also assisted Muir to the shore. He was still insane, saying but little and that incoherently. He groaned a great deal.

I was now much exhausted and laid myself down to rest until sunrise, when I looked for Muir and found him gone from the place I left him. Soon after I found him surrounded by several natives, but he was dead and very black in the face.

During the day I got some food and clothing from the natives—one of them called Peter. After resting myself Peter and I went on horseback over to Hanalei to Sheriff Wilcox and Mr. Burt. Then we returned with the sheriff and coroner to Kalihi Kai, where an inquest was held over the bodies of Lieutenant Talbot and Muir, the former having drifted ashore just before I left Kalihi Kai for Hanalei. Mr. Talbot's forehead was bruised and blackened, apparently from having struck the boat or wreckage.

After the inquest the two bodies were taken to Hanalei, put into coffins and buried the next day in one grave at a place where a seaman belonging to the U.S.S. *Lackawanna* was buried in 1867. Funeral services were performed by Mr. Kenny by reading the Episcopal burial service, and the two Misses Johnson (daughters of an American missionary) singing.

Before I left Hanalei for Honolulu it was reported by a half-white who had been left to watch the shore at Kalihi Kai that Andrews's body had come ashore and had been taken care of.

Captain Dudoit, the schooner *Wainona*, offered to bring me direct to Honolulu, leaving his return freight at Wainiea for another trip. I accepted the same through Mr. Bent, and we sailed for Honolulu on the evening of Tuesday, December 20, and arrived at Honolulu at eleven A.M., December 24, bringing with me the effects saved as aforementioned. I went, on landing, immediately to the United States Consul's office, where I saw him and the Minister President and told to them my story.

(*Note.* The reader may remember the incident I related as occurring at the time we were provisioning the gig; the discovery that the boiled rice had fermented and the hasty substitution of the dessicated potatoes. Halford was emphatic to me in the assertion that the potato was the preserver of their lives and that mixed with water it constituted their only food during the last week of their sufferings. The dessicated potato was at that time a part of the Navy ration. It was also called "evaporated," and was prepared by thoroughly drying the potato and coarsely grinding it. In appearance it resembles a very coarse meal.)

Halford has told me of several remarkable incidents which happened during the voyage of the gig and which, although not considered essential in his official statement, would be lifelong memories to him.

Of one of these he says—and I give his own words: "We were scudding before a gale of wind under a reefed square sail. A nasty sea was running at the time. I was standing in the after hatch steering; had the reeving string of the cover that was nailed around the combings drawn tight under my armpits to keep out the sea as it washed over the boat, when I felt a shock. The boat almost capsized, but the next sea lifted her over. I looked astern and saw a great log forty or fifty feet long and four or five feet in diameter, water-logged and just awash. We had jumped clean over it. It was a case of touch and go with us."

Of another incident he says: "One night I had relieved Peter Francis at the tiller and he had crawled forward on deck. Somehow or other he got overboard; luckily we had a strong fishing-line trailing astern all the voyage, but never got as much as a bite until it caught Francis and we got him on board again. It was a bright moonlight night."

Of another happening he says: "Then, when our provisions had run out entirely, a large bird came and landed on the boat and looked at me as I stood at the tiller. The other four at this time were very weak from want of food and from dysentery; they were more dead than alive. I caught the bird, tore off the feathers, cut it up in five pieces, and we all had a good meal. It was raw, but it tasted good. About thirty-six hours after this, just at break of day, as I was sitting at the tiller, I felt something strike my cheek. It was a little flying-fish. I caught it, and soon a school of them came skipping along, several dropping on deck. I captured five or six of them and they gave us the last meal we had on the gig: for at daylight I saw land—Tahoora or Kaula Rock."

Our captain has made the following report to the Secretary of the Navy, which adds to and confirms the story of the lone survivor of the gig:—

Honolulu, Hawaiian Islands,
January 18, 1871.
Sir:—I forward herewith the brief report called for by regulation of the death of Lieutenant J.G. Talbot (and also three of the crew of the United States Steamer *Saginaw*) at the island of Kauai (Hawaiian Group).

I feel that something more is due to these devoted and gallant friends, who so nobly risked their lives to save those of their shipmates, and I beg leave to report the following facts regarding their voyage from Ocean Island and its melancholy conclusion.

The boat (which had been the *Saginaw*'s gig and was a whale-boat of very fine model) was prepared for the voyage with the greatest care. She was raised on the gunwale eight inches, decked over, and had new sails, etc.

The boat left Ocean Island November 18, 1870. The route indicated by me to Lieutenant Talbot was to steer to the northward "by the wind" until he got to the latitude of about 32 degrees north, and then to make his way to the eastward until he could "lay" the Hawaiian Islands with the northeast trade winds. He seems to have followed about that route. The boat lost her sea anchor and oars in a gale of wind and a good deal of her provision was spoiled by salt water. The navigation instruments, too, were of but little use, on account of the lively motions of the boat. When she was supposed to be in the longitude of Kauai she was really about one and one half degrees to the westward; thus, instead of the island of Kauai she finally sighted the rock Kauhulaua (the southwestern point of land in the group) and beat up from thence to the island of Kauai. She was hove off the entrance of Hanalei Bay during part of the night of Monday, December 19th, and in attempting to run into the Bay about 2.30 A.M. she got suddenly into the breakers (which here made a considerable distance from the shore) and capsized.

I enclose herewith a copy of the deposition of William Halford, coxswain, the only survivor of this gallant crew; his narrative being the one from which all accounts are taken. I have not seen him, personally, as he left here before my arrival.

Peter Francis, quartermaster, and John Andrews, coxswain, were washed overboard at once and disappeared. Lieutenant Talbot was washed off the boat, and when she capsized he clung to the bottom and tried to climb up on it, going to the stern for that purpose; the boat gave a plunge and Halford thinks that the boat's gunwale or stern must have struck Mr. Talbot in the forehead as he let go his hold and went down.

James Muir was below when the boat struck the breakers, and does not appear to have come out of her until she had rolled over once. He must have suffered some injury in the boat, as he appears to have been out of his mind and his face turned black immediately after his death. As will be seen by Halford's statement, Muir reached shore, but died of exhaustion on the way to the native huts.

The body of John Andrews did not come on shore until about December 20th. All clothes had been stripped from it. The body of Peter Francis has never been recovered.

The bodies are buried side by side at Hanalei (Kauai). The service was read over them in a proper manner. Suitable gravestones will be erected over them by subscription of the officers and crew of the *Saginaw*.

As soon as we had gotten on Ocean Island after the *Saginaw*'s wreck, Lieutenant Talbot volunteered to take this boat to Honolulu, and the rest volunteered as soon as it was known that men might perhaps be wanted for such service.

Mr. Talbot was a very zealous and spirited officer. I had observed his excellent qualities from the time of his joining the *Saginaw* (September 23, 1870) in Honolulu. During the wreck and afterwards he rendered me the greatest assistance and service by his fine bearing, his cheerfulness, and devotion to duty. His boat was evidently commanded with the greatest intelligence, fortitude, and gallantry and with the most admirable devotion. May the Service always be able to find such men in the time of need.

The men were fine specimens of seamen—cool and brave, with great endurance and excellent physical strength. They were, undoubtedly, those best qualified in the whole party on Ocean Island to perform such a service. Both Lieutenant Talbot and his men had very firm confidence in their boat and looked forward with cheerfulness to the voyage. Such men should be the pride of the Navy, and the news of their death cast a deep gloom over the otherwise cheerful feelings with which the *Kilauea* was welcomed at Ocean Island.

I do not know that I sufficiently express my deep sense of their devotion and gallantry; words seem to fail me in that respect.

Previous to the sailing of the boat from Ocean Island I had enlisted John Andrews and James Muir as seamen for one month. Since I have ascertained their fate I have ordered them to be rated as petty officers (in ratings allowed to most of the "fourth rates"), as I have thought that all the crew of that boat should have stood on equal footing as regards the amount they might be entitled to in case of disaster, as they all incurred the same risk.

Andrews and Muir belonged to the party of Mr. G.W. Townsend (the contractor at Midway Islands), and it was made a condition, by them, of their enlistment that it should not interfere with their contract with Mr. Townsend. It was intended as the security of their families against the risk incurred while performing the great service for the shipwrecked party. I have forwarded their enlistment papers to the Bureau of Equipment and Recruiting.

I am very respectfully,

Your obedient Servant,

Montgomery Sicard,

Lieut. Comdr. U.S.N. Comd'g.

Hon. George M. Robeson,

Secretary of the Navy.

IN GOD'S COUNTRY AGAIN

San Francisco, February 8, 1871. After a pleasant voyage in the *Moses Taylor* we are again, all hands,—minus our gallant comrades,—on American soil, and the cruise of the *Saginaw* is officially closed. The officers have taken up quarters on shore, and the crew temporarily transferred to the U.S. Steamer *Saranac* for discharge or detail as their period of enlistment may require. The gig came with us and will be temporarily stored until it is decided as to her future. We have started a subscription for a suitable memorial to the gig's heroes, and the other ships of the squadron have generously offered their help. The most approved plan seems to be a marble tablet on the walls of the chapel at the Naval Academy, and the captain has made a sketch of one as it would appear there.

14

BARK *KATHLEEN* SUNK BY A WHALE

THOMAS JENKINS

A New Bedford whaling ship, an angry whale, and tale that seemed to be the stuff of fiction. But it wasn't.

Rammed and Sunk by an Infuriated
Bull Whale—*New York Journal.*
The most thrilling episode ever known in the history of the American Whale Fisheries has just occurred.

It is full of the mystery and thrill and terror of the deep sea. It is even more wonderful than any of the stories told by Mr. Frank T. Bullen, author of the famous "Cruise of the Cachalot."

The bark *Kathleen* sailed from New Bedford, Mass., October 22, 1901, for a whaling voyage in the South Atlantic.

The *Kathleen* was about 195 tons and with outfits was valued at $20,000, being partially insured by her several owners. She also had on board at the time of the accident a small quantity of oil taken since leaving port.

The *Kathleen* had always been called a "lucky ship" and had made many good voyages.

She was built for the merchant service at Philadelphia in 1844, and after a year in the trade, was purchased by Captain James Slocum and fitted as a whaler. Her first master in the whaling industry was Captain William Allen, and she had in her day made many a good voyage. Among her masters have been Captain Charles Childs, Captain Daniel W. Gifford and Captain Samuel R. Howland. She had been almost entirely built over only a few years ago, and just before being fitted for a cruise to St. Helena in 1899, where she loaded oil, was thoroughly overhauled.

Last year, it will be remembered, the *Kathleen* arrived in port in a disabled condition. This was on Sept. 28th, 1901, when she was commanded by Captain Fred H. Smith. For three days that month on the 6th, 7th and 8th, while southeast of Barbados, she was on her beam ends and at the mercy of the sea. The crew lived on the quarter deck at the time, not daring to go below. In fitting her up for the last cruise she was newly sparred.

THE CAPTAIN'S STORY

Having been requested to give an account of the sinking of the Bark *Kathleen* by a whale I will do the best I can, though I think that those who have read the papers know as much or more about it than I do.

We sailed from New Bedford the 22d October, 1901, and with the exception of three weeks of the worst weather I have ever had on leaving home, everything went fairly well till we arrived out on the 12-40 ground.

The day we arrived there we raised a large whale and chased him most all day but could not seem to get any aim of him. We lost the run of him at last in a rain squall.

A few days after, the 17th of March, 1902, was one of the finest whaling days I have ever seen, smooth water and a clear sky. When they were going up to mast head I told them to look sharp for some one was going to raise a whale before night.

We steered different courses during the fore-noon and at 1 p.m. the man aloft raised a white water which proved to be sperm whales, and there was a lot of them, some heading one way, some another.

When we got within a mile of them we lowered four boats, and soon after Mr. Nichols, the first mate, struck a whale, the other whales went to leeward and I followed them with the ship till I was sure the boats saw them.

Mr. Nichols then had his whale dead about one mile to windward, so I came to wind on the port tack, but it took us some time to get up to the mate, as we could not carry any foretopsail or flying jibs as the topmast had given out.

I stood on the port tack a while and then tacked. When we got braced up the dead whale was one point off the lee bow. I saw we were going to fetch him all right. Mr. Nichols had wafted his whale and was chasing some more. By that time, about 3 p.m., the lookout called out that the three boats to leeward were all fast. Of course we were all glad to hear that. I ran the ship alongside of the dead whale and after darting at him two or three times managed to get fast and get him alongside. Just then it was reported that the boats to leeward were out of sight. That worried me some so I told the cooper to get the fluke chain on the whale and I would go aloft and see if I could see the boats.

At this time Mr. Nichols had given up chasing and was coming on board. I got up to the topmast crosstrees and sat down. I then heard a whale spout off the weather beam and glancing that way, saw sure enough a large whale not more than five hundred feet from us, coming directly for the ship.

Mr. Nichols was then alongside, just going to hoist his boat. I told him there was a whale, a big fellow, trying to get alongside and to go and help him along and he did help him along. He took him head and head and did not get fast. I don't know why. He certainly was near enough, the boatsteerer said too near, and did not have a chance to swing his iron.

Instead of that whale going down or going to windward as they most always do, he kept coming directly for the ship, only much faster than he was coming before he was darted at. When he got within thirty feet of the ship he saw or heard something and tried to go under the ship but he was so near and was coming so fast he did not have room enough to get clear of her.

He struck the ship forward of the mizzen rigging and about five or six feet under water. It shook the ship considerably when he struck her, then he tried to come up and he raised the stern up some two or three feet so when she came down her counters made a big splash. The whale came up on the other side of the ship and laid there and rolled, did not seem to know what to do. I asked the cooper if he thought the whale had hurt the ship any and he said he did not think so for he had not heard anything crack.

Mr. Nichols was still trying to get to the whale when I thought we had no business fooling with that whale any more that day as the other three boats were out of sight and fast to whales and night coming on, so I told him to come alongside. "What for?" asked Mr. Nichols, "the whale is laying there." I said, "Never mind the whale but come alongside and hoist the boat up as soon as you can." He did so and I told him to get his glasses and come up to masthead and see if he could see the boats. His eyes were younger than mine and he soon raised them. Just at this time one of the men went to the forecastle to get some dry clothes and he found the floor covered with water. He cried out and then I knew the ship must have quite a hole in her. I immediately ordered flags set at all three mastheads, a signal for all boats to come on board under any and all circumstances.

Mr. Viera was then not more than a mile and a half from the ship and I knew he could not but help seeing the flags, but it was no use, he would not let go that whale he was fast to. If he had only come to the ship they could have got some more water and bread. I set two gangs at work right away, one getting water and the other getting bread. The cask of bread was between decks and three men staid with that cask till the water came in and floated the cask away from them.

I then went to the cabin and found Mrs. Jenkins reading. She did not know that there was anything the matter with the ship. I told her the ship was sinking and to get some warm clothing as soon as she could but not to try to save anything else. Well, the first thing she did was to go for the parrot and take him on deck. Then she got a jacket and an old shawl.

By that time it was time to take to the boat, which we did without any confusion whatever.

There were twenty-one of us in the boat and with the water and bread and some old clothes she was pretty near the water, so deep that the water came over the centre board, so that some of us had to keep bailing all the time, while the rest were paddling down to the boat that was still laying by the whale.

The ship rolled over to windward five minutes after we got clear of her. Well, we got to Mr. Viera at last and divided the men and give him his share of bread and water. Then it was dark and very necessary that we should find the other boats, for I knew they did not see the ship capsize and they would be looking for her for a day or so with no water to drink. Well, we set our sails and steered as near as we could where we thought the boats ought to be and about nine o'clock we raised them.

They were very much surprised to hear that the *Kathleen* was gone. I gave them some bread and water and divided the men up again, so three boats had ten men each and one boat nine men. I told them all to keep in sight of me and that I would keep a lantern burning all night. We then started for the island of Barbados, distant 1,060 miles. It was a beautiful moonlight night with a smooth sea. When morning came there was not a boat to be seen so I came to the wind and laid with the sheet slacked off over an hour and raised a boat to windward steering for us. It was the third mate and he wanted some water. The water we gave him the night before was all salt. Well, we divided with him again and again started on our journey with five gallons of water. I told the third mate to keep up with me if he could but I should not stop for him or any one else again. About nine o'clock a.m. some one said he saw something off the port bow. We all looked and made it out to be smoke from a steamer and soon saw she was coming right for us, so we knew we were saved.

When she got near we saw she had a whale boat on her davits. They had picked up our second mate an hour before and he had told the captain that there were three other boats adrift and one of them had the captain and wife on board, so he was steaming around with two men at the masthead with glasses looking for us. We got alongside and she was way out of water. I asked Mrs. Jenkins if she could get up on a rope ladder they had put over the side and she said yes, she could get up if it was twice as high and she was not long in getting on deck.

Captain Dalton met us and welcomed us on board of the *Borderer* of Glasgow. He was very kind to us and did everything possible for us for the nine days we were on board his steamer, gave up his room to Mrs. Jenkins and myself even.

In nine days we were landed at Pernambuco and from there we came to Philadelphia on steamer *Pydna*, Captain Crossley.

We found friends everywhere we went; even in Philadelphia I had telegrams asking me to telegraph them if I needed any assistance. We arrived at New Bedford in due time and even Mr. Wing, (the agent of the Bark *Kathleen*), met me smilingly and seemed glad to see me. Everything seemed to work our way after the accident. When we were leaving the *Borderer* Capt. Dalton gave me thirty dollars in American bills, all he had with him.

He told me to take it and if I felt able when I got home to send the amount to his wife in England. It seems that Capt. Dalton had been running down this way for some years and having met head currents decided *this* trip to make a passage three or four degrees to the eastward to see if he couldn't get out of it.

Owing to this fact we were picked up as we were.

As we had not seen a sail of any description for some time we might have been days in our boat before seeing any vessel.

The other boat containing one of the mates and 9 seamen landed safely at the Barbados after being in the boat 9 days with but 5 gallons of water and a little ship bread.

LOSS OF THE SHIPS *ANN ALEXANDER* AND *ESSEX*

Cases of whales rushing head on are very rare. One instance which will be remembered by some of the older residents of the city was in

1851, when the ship *Ann Alexander* was sunk in the Pacific ocean by a maddened whale.

In the Whaleman's Shipping List of Nov. 4, 1851, is a very full account of that occurrence. The story, which is substantially as follows, first appeared in the *Panama Herald*, as told by Captain John S. Deblois, follows:

The ship *Ann Alexander* sailed from New Bedford, June 1st, 1850, for a cruise in the South Pacific. Having taken 500 barrels of sperm oil in the Atlantic, Captain Deblois proceeded on the voyage to the Pacific.

On the 20th of August, 1851, while cruising on the "Off Shore grounds," at 9 o'clock in the morning, whales were discovered, and at noon of the same day succeeded in making fast to one.

The mate's boat made fast to the whale, which ran with the boat for some time, and then suddenly turning about rushed at the boat with open jaws, crushing the little craft into splinters. Captain Deblois rescued the boat's crew.

Later the waist boat was lowered from the ship and another attack made upon the leviathan. The mate again in charge of the attacking boat experienced another smashup, for in the battle the whale again turned on the boat's crew and crushed the second boat. The crew was saved and all hands returned to the ship, which proceeded after the whale.

The ship passed on by him, and immediately after it was discovered that the whale was making for the ship. As he came up near her they hauled on the wind and suffered the monster to pass her.

After he had fairly passed they kept off to overtake and attack him again. When the ship had reached within about 50 rods of him the crew discovered that the whale had settled down deep below the surface of the water, and as it was near sundown, it was decided to give up the pursuit.

The ship was moving about five knots, and while Captain Deblois stood at the rail he suddenly saw the whale rushing at the ship at the rate of 15 knots. In an instant the monster struck the ship with tremendous violence, shaking her from stem to stern. She quivered under the violence of the shock as if she had struck upon a rock.

The whale struck the ship about two feet from the keel, abreast the foremast, knocking a great hole entirely through her bottom, through which the water roared and rushed in impetuously. The anchors and cables were thrown overboard, as she had a large quantity of pig iron aboard. The ship sank rapidly, all effort to keep her afloat proving futile.

Captain Deblois ordered all hands to take to the boats and was the last to leave the ship, doing so by jumping from the vessel into the sea and swimming to the nearest boat. The ship was on her beam end, her topgallant yards under water.

They hung around in the vicinity of the *Ann Alexander* all that night, and the next day the captain boarded his vessel and cutting away the masts she righted, when they succeeded in getting stores from her hold, with which to supply their boats, should it become necessary to make a boat voyage to land.

On August 22 ship *Nantucket*, Captain Gibbs, cruising in that vicinity, discovered the imperiled sailors and taking them in charge landed them at Paita, September 15th. The *Ann Alexander* was hopelessly wrecked and left to her fate on August 23.

Five months after this disaster this pugnacious whale was captured by the *Rebecca Simms* of this port. Two of the *Ann Alexander*'s harpoons were found in him and his head had sustained serious injuries, pieces of the ship's timbers being imbedded in it. The whale yielded 70 to 80 barrels of oil.

The only other known case of a like nature occurred to the ship *Essex* of Nantucket, commanded by Captain George Pollard, Jr.

She sailed from Nantucket, August 12, 1819, for a cruise in the Pacific ocean. On the morning of November 20, 1819, latitude 0.40 south and longitude 119 west, whales were discovered and all three boats lowered in pursuit.

The mate's boat soon struck a whale, but a blow of the animal's tail opening a bad hole in the boat, the crew was obliged to cut from him.

In the meantime, the captain's and second mate's boats had fastened to another whale, and the mate, heading the ship for the other boats, set about overhauling his boat preparatory to lowering again.

While doing this he saw a large sperm whale break water about 20 rods from the ship. The whale disappeared, but immediately came up again about a ship's length off, and made directly for the vessel, going at a velocity of about three miles an hour, and the *Essex* was advancing at about the same rate of speed.

Scarcely had the mate ordered the boy at the helm to put it hard up, when the whale, with greatly accelerated speed, struck the ship with his head just forward of the forechains.

The ship brought up suddenly and violently and trembled like a leaf. The whale passed under the vessel, scraping her keel as he went, came up on the leeward side, and lay apparently stunned for a moment.

The vessel began to settle at the head with the whale 100 yards off thrashing the water violently with his tail and opening and closing his jaws with great fury.

While the mate was thinking of getting the two extra boats clear, as the vessel had begun to settle rapidly, the cry was started by a sailor: "Here he is; he is making for us again!"

The whale came down for the ship with twice his ordinary speed and a line of foam about a rod in width, made with his tail, which he continually thrashed from side to side, marked his coming.

The whale crashed into the bows of the *Essex*, staving them completely in directly under the cathead. The whale after the second assault passed under the ship and out of sight to the leeward.

The crew were in a fix, in mid-ocean, a thousand miles from the nearest land and nothing but the frail whaleboat to save them.

The lashings of the spare boat were cut and she was launched with the ship falling on her beam ends. The ship hung together for three days. Provisions were taken from her and the whaleboats strengthened.

The boats started for the coast of Chile or Peru and after a hard time they landed at Ducies island. Unable to find subsistence there they again started, Dec. 27th, after leaving three of their number, of their own desire, and commenced to make the perilous voyage to the island of Juan Fernandez.

Many of the boats' crew died and the recital states that the flesh of a dead comrade was eaten by members of the mate's boat.

On Feb. 17th the surviving crew of the mate's boat were picked up by brig *Indian*. Captain Pollard and Charles Ramsdale, the sole survivors of the captain's boat, were picked up Feb. 23d by a Nantucket whaler, and the third boat was never heard from.

15

WRECKED, STRANDED, AND CAPTURED

HORACE HOLDEN

A young New Hampshire lad thought life at sea would provide relief from the hard work at home.

I was born in the town of Hillsborough, in the state of New Hampshire, on the 21st of July, 1810. My father's name was Phineas Holden. My parents were in moderate circumstances, and derived their chief support from a small farm. From the time to which my earliest recollections extend, until I was about ten years of age, our little circle, consisting of our parents, their three sons and two daughters, enjoyed a large share of the pleasures of a New England home. We were all accustomed to labor, but our exertions to secure a respectable maintenance were richly rewarded by each other's approving smiles, and by that contentment, without which blessings, however great or numerous, are bestowed upon us in vain.

But, in early life, and in the midst of our enjoyments, we were called upon to experience a loss which nothing on earth can supply. My father, after a painful sickness of long continuance, died, and left us with no other earthly protector than our affectionate mother; who, had her ability and means been adequate to our support, or equal to her maternal fondness and anxiety, would have saved us from every hardship, and supplied all our reasonable desires. But, having no means of support except our own industry, we were at that tender age thrown upon the world, and compelled to provide for ourselves as Providence might best enable us. I labored at different occupations until the age of twenty-one; when, finding myself unable, by reason of an impaired constitution, to do more than provide for myself, and feeling desirous to contribute my share towards the maintenance of our surviving parent, I resolved upon making the experiment of a voyage at sea.

I accordingly left the place of my nativity, sundered the many ties that bound me to home and friends, and, in July, 1831, entered on board the ship *Mentor*, at the port of New Bedford, Massachusetts, for a whaling voyage to the Indian ocean. The ship was owned by William R. Rodman, Esquire, an eminent merchant of that place, to whose benevolence, since my return home, I acknowledge myself to be deeply indebted. We sailed on the day of my enlistment; and I soon found myself upon the bosom of the great deep, and at the mercy of an element to which I had been but little accustomed.

After leaving port, nothing remarkable occurred during the first part of our voyage. Having succeeded in obtaining a small quantity of oil, we touched at Fayal, one of the Azores, or Western islands, to leave the oil and replenish our stores. We left Fayal on the following day. Our course was down the Cape de Verd islands; and, without any accident worth relating, we passed round the cape of Good Hope, through the straits of Madagascar, and found ourselves in the Indian ocean.

We continued to cruise among the small islands for some time; but being unsuccessful in the object of our voyage, it was deemed advisable to make for Java. We ran the whole length of the island of Java, passing through the straits of Sandal-Wood Island, to the island of Timor, and touched at the port of Coupang, where we remained about five days, took in wood and water, and replenished our small stores. After leaving that place we attempted to pass through the straits of Timor, with a view of gaining the Pacific ocean; but owing to adverse winds, and the strong currents setting against us, we were compelled to abandon the undertaking; and accordingly altered our course. We intended to have touched at Ternate, the principal of the Moluccas or Spice islands; but we passed it, running down the island of Morty, (or Mortay) to its furthermost point. Seeing no port at which we could stop, we altered our course, intending to make for some of the Ladrone islands, which we knew to be in possession of the Spanish.

I must here observe, that soon after leaving the island of Mortay, there came on a violent storm, which lasted the whole of three days and nights. During all this time we were unable to take an observation. This led to the melancholy disaster, which was the commencement of misfortunes and sufferings, too great to be adequately conceived of by any but those who experienced them. The violence of the storm compelled us to take in all the sails except the top-sail, (which was close reefed,) foresail, and foretop-mast stay-sail.

We were sailing in this manner, not apprehending danger, when, about eleven o'clock at night, on the 21st of May, 1832, just at the time of relieving the watch, the ship struck with great violence upon what we afterwards found to be the coral reef extending to the northward and eastward of the Pelew islands. The ship ran directly upon the rocks, and struck three times in quick succession, the waves dashing over and around us with tremendous violence.

At this awful moment I was in my berth, in the steerage. When the ship struck the third time, so great was the shock that I was thrown from my berth against the opposite side of the steerage; but, soon recovering myself, I rushed upon deck. There all was confusion, horror and dismay. The ship, immediately after striking the third time, swung round so as to bring her starboard side to the windward, and was in a moment thrown upon her beam ends. While in this awful condition, with the waves continually breaking over us, threatening to overwhelm us in a watery grave, or dash us in pieces against the rocks, the captain came upon deck, and inquired of the second mate, "Where are we?" The reply was, "I don't know, but I think there is land to leeward." There was no time for deliberation; it seemed that the immediate destruction of the ship was inevitable.

In the midst of this confusion I heard the mate give orders for lowering the larboard quarter boat. His directions were immediately complied with, and ten of the crew threw themselves into it, thinking it more safe thus to commit themselves to the mercy of the waves, than to remain on board with the prospect of a certain and speedy termination of their existence. But there are reasons which force upon the mind the painful conviction, that their departure from the ship at that time proved fatal to them all. As the oars were fastened to the sides of the boat, some one asked for a knife or hatchet, with which to cut them loose. The request was complied with; and, quitting their hold upon the ship, they parted from us, and we never saw them more!

As some doubts have existed in the minds of those interested in the fate of our shipmates who took to the boat in the manner just described, it is deemed advisable here to state my reasons for entertaining the opinion above expressed. Far would it be from me to desire to extinguish any well-founded hopes of their having survived; but a knowledge of the following facts renders it too certain, that they must all have perished, soon after their departure from the ship. The next morning the remains of a boat in every respect similar to that in which they embarked, were distinctly seen on the rocks, at the distance of about fifty yards from the ship, bottom up, and with her sides stove in. The water being clear and shallow, we could see that she was held there by a harpoon and lance, which constituted a part of the fishing implements, or crafts, in the boat when she left.

These were apparently stuck into the crevices of the coral rock (of which the whole reef is composed) either by accident or design; and the presumption is, that she became fast in that place, and that the waves swept that portion of our companions in suffering into a watery grave. But this, though a melancholy subject of reflection, is not without some circumstances of consolation; for, admitting that they thus met their fate, they were saved from that extremity of suffering which some of the ship's crew were destined to experience. Were such a death, or the pains of captivity endured by my associates and myself, to be the only alternatives, I have doubted whether I should not prefer the former. To be far from kindred and friends, among a people but one grade above the most ferocious beasts, sick at heart, and deprived of necessary food, stripped of our clothing, and subjected to unheard-of severities,—to endure all this, was to purchase a continuance of life at a dear rate.

Soon after the departure of the first boat, the captain, thinking it impossible for the ship to hold together till morning, ordered his own boat to be let down. This could be effected only by the united exertions of the whole of the remaining part of the crew. Some of the men, and myself among the rest, had resolved upon remaining on the ship to the last; and, considering it impossible for a boat to live, we earnestly expostulated with the captain, for the purpose of persuading him not to hazard the experiment. But he seemed to think it best to make it, and with great earnestness entreated the men to assist him in lowering his boat.

As this was a time when but little attention could be paid to the distinctions usually kept up on board, I suggested that it might be well to cut away the masts, believing that this would relieve the ship, and cause her to lie easier upon the rock. This was the more necessary on account of her position being such as to render it next to impossible to let down the boat. The proposal was acceded to; and, seizing an axe, I assisted in cutting away the masts and rigging. This, to some extent, had the desired effect; and we were enabled, at length, by great exertion, to lower the boat. The captain, Charles C. Bouket, William Sedon, and William Jones, immediately placed themselves in it, and commenced preparing to leave us. In compliance with his request, a rope was fastened round the waist of the captain, so that should the boat be destroyed, as there was reason to apprehend she would be, there might be some chance of rescuing him from the waves.

They were furnished with the necessary nautical instruments, log-book, a bag of clothing, a small quantity of bread in a tin tureen, and a keg of water. The boat was at this time suspended by her falls, and, with a view of letting themselves down, the captain stood in the stern, and Bouket in the forward part of the boat, both having hold of the falls. Sedon still held on by the boat's lashing. Jones had nothing in his hands. At this conjuncture, a tremendous sea broke into the boat, and dashed it in pieces;—so entire was the destruction, that not a fragment was afterwards seen. Jones was soon after seen floating in the water apparently dead. Sedon, in consequence of having hold of the boat's fastenings, saved himself by climbing into the ship. Bouket, being an expert swimmer, on finding himself in the sea, swam round to the leeward side of the ship, caught hold of some part of the rigging, and thus escaped.

The captain was drifted away to the distance of nearly one hundred and fifty yards. It was with the utmost difficulty that we retained our hold on the rope which had been fastened to him; but at length we succeeded in drawing him in. On hearing his cries for assistance, forgetting our own danger, we redoubled our exertions, and soon drew him on board. He was much exhausted, but fortunately had received no fatal injury.

After the failure of this attempt, and having in so short a time lost one half our number, it was agreed upon, after due consultation to remain upon the wreck till daylight should reveal to us more fully our situation. In this state of suspense and suffering, we clung to the rigging, and with much difficulty kept ourselves from being washed away. Our situation and prospects during that awful night were such, that no ray of hope was permitted to penetrate the dreary prospect around us; our thoughts and feelings, wrought up to the highest degree of excitement by the horrors of our situation, continually visited the homes we had quitted,—probably forever,—and offered up prayers for the dear friends we had left behind. Every succeeding wave that dashed over us threatened to sweep us into an untried eternity; and while we impatiently awaited approaching day, we committed our spirits to Him who alone could control the raging elements.

At daybreak, we discovered that a part of the reef, apparently about three miles off to the leeward, was dry; and this, though but of small consequence, afforded us some comfort. In a short time we discovered land at the distance of twenty or thirty miles, in an eastwardly direction. This, though we were ignorant of the character of the inhabitants—if indeed it should turn out to be the residence of human beings—presented to our minds the possibility of escape; and without any delay we prepared, as well as we could, to abandon the vessel. There remained but one boat, and that was in a poor condition for conveying us, eleven in number, so great a distance. But, as no choice was left us, the boat was soon prepared; and when the sun was about two hours high, we had completed our arrangements. We took into the boat one small chest of bread, some water, a quantity of wearing apparel, a canister of gunpowder, one musket, a brace of pistols, three cutlasses, and a tinder-box. In this frail bark, and with these poor means of subsistence and defence, with little to rely upon but the mercy of Providence, we took leave of the ship; not without feelings of deep sorrow, and with small hopes of improving our forlorn condition.

On leaving the ship we steered directly for the reef above mentioned, and without much difficulty landed and drew up our boat. This proved to be, as we had previously conjectured, a part of the reef upon which we had been wrecked; and we soon ascertained that the portion of the rock above water was but about sixteen rods long, and quite narrow, but sufficiently large to afford us a secure footing for the little time we had to stay upon it. It was our first, and almost our only object, to remain here until we could render our arrangements more perfect, and either put to sea with less hazard, or make our passage to the land, which was still distinctly visible.

As yet but little time had been afforded us for calm reflection; and it was now a question of serious importance, whether it would be most prudent to encounter the billows in the crazy boat which was our chief dependence, upon the open sea, with our scanty means of subsistence, or to throw ourselves into the hands, and upon the mercy of whatever race of beings might chance to inhabit the island. In favor of the former plan it was suggested that we might be seen, and taken up by some vessel cruising in those seas, and thus saved from captivity or death among a barbarous people; and, on the other hand, it was maintained, that a chance among the savages of those islands would be preferable to the risk of going to sea in a boat which was in all respects unseaworthy, and with only a few pounds of bread, and but little water, for our subsistence.

COMFORTS AND CONCERNS

Happily, by the goodness of the all-wise Disposer of events, the unfortunate can avail themselves of a thousand sources of comfort, which, by those in prosperous circumstances, are either overlooked or neglected. We were upon a barren rock, in the midst of a waste of waters, far from kindred and friends, and the abodes of civilized man; the ship which had been our home, and on board of which we had embarked with high hopes, lay within sight, a useless wreck; still we were enabled to enjoy a moment of relief, if not of actual pleasure, derived from an event, which, though trifling in itself, is worthy of being recorded.

We succeeded in taking an eel, a few crabs, and a small quantity of snails. Having our fire-works with us, we collected a sufficient number of sticks, with a few pieces of drift-wood which had lodged upon the rock, to make a fire; with this we cooked our fish and snails; and, with a small allowance of bread, we made what we then thought a sumptuous repast! After we had finished our meal, we began to prepare for the night. We erected a tent with some of our clothes and pieces of canvas, at a little distance from the boat; and, when night came on, a part of our number kept watch, and the rest soon lost all consciousness of their misfortunes in sleep. About midnight those who had watched took their turn at resting; and in the morning we found ourselves considerably refreshed; though an increased activity of our minds served only to bring home a more vivid picture of the horrors of the previous night, and of our present condition.

Providence, it would seem, had ordained that we should not long remain undetermined as to the course to be adopted; for before sunrise we discovered a canoe within a short distance of us, containing twenty-two of the inhabitants of the neighboring island. They approached to within pistol-shot of where we stood, and there lay on their oars for some time, looking at us, and manifesting no small degree of fear. Thinking it best to be on friendly terms with them, we attached a shirt to one of our oars, and hoisted it as a token of a wish, on our part, to regard and treat them as friends. This had the desired effect; and they immediately rowed up to the rock. Manifesting great pleasure, they left their canoe and rushed towards the place where the principal part of our boat's crew were standing, bringing with them cocoa-nuts, and a small quantity of bread made of the cocoa-nut boiled in a liquor extracted from the trunk of the tree.

At that time, I was standing near the tent, at a little distance from my companions, and was an anxious spectator of the scene. Their appearance excited my astonishment, and I was filled with horror by the sight of beings apparently human, and yet almost destitute of the ordinary marks of humanity. They were entirely naked. Each one was armed with a spear and tomahawk; some had battle-axes. They were fantastically tattooed on different parts of their bodies. Their hair, naturally coarse and black, like that of the Indians of America, was very long, and hung loosely over their shoulders, giving them a singular and frightful appearance. Their teeth were entirely black; rendered so, as we afterwards found, by chewing what they call "*abooak.*" The reader can judge of our feelings on finding ourselves in the hands of beings of this description. Our confidence in the honesty of our visitors did not improve on further acquaintance.

No sooner had they landed, than they commenced their depredations upon the few articles, which at that time constituted all our earthly riches. The nautical instruments, the musket, and a part of our clothing, they immediately appropriated to their own benefit. Fortunately a part of our clothing, the powder, and the cutlasses we had succeeded in concealing in a crevice of the rock. Taking with them their booty, they precipitately got into their canoe, and, beckoning to us, evidently with a view of inducing us to follow them, they steered directly for the wreck. Their first appearance, and this strong manifestation of their thievish disposition, so far from inclining us to cultivate their acquaintance any further, had given us an irresistible inclination to avoid them. Our minds were not long in coming to the conclusion, that an open sea, with Heaven to protect us, would be far preferable to a chance among beings like those. Accordingly, with the least possible delay, we launched our boat, and putting into it such things of value as we had saved, once more, surrounded by new difficulties and dangers, committed ourselves to the mercy of the waves.

The island before mentioned being now distinctly visible, we steered in a direction towards it; though we found it necessary to go a somewhat circuitous course, in order to avoid the reef. By the time we had succeeded in getting into deep water, the natives had been to the ship, and were returning with the five muskets which we had left on board. They soon passed us with great rapidity, and evidently with the intention of escaping with their booty unharmed. The cause of their precipitancy will soon be explained.

Just at this time there came in sight a number of canoes, perhaps thirty, filled with natives, who seemed no less intent upon plunder than those with whom we had already formed a disagreeable acquaintance.

Their language was to us entirely unintelligible, but we could gather from their somewhat significant gestures, that they most of all desired to possess themselves of fire-arms. They beckoned to us to go with them, and seemed quite anxious to avail themselves of our assistance; but we were not less so to escape; and with the hope of being able to do so, we continued to row towards the island. Some of them remained near us, while the rest made for the ship. At length, all, except those in one canoe, left us, and joined their companions.

These seemed particularly fond of our company, partly on account, as we afterwards learned, of their suspecting that we had something of value concealed about us, and partly for the purpose of making us their prisoners, and in that way gaining some advantage over the others. After a while they offered, with an appearance of friendship, to render us some assistance by towing our boat; and after some deliberation we concluded to throw them a line.

This greatly facilitated our progress, as their canoe, being made very light, skimmed over the water with incredible swiftness. No sooner was this arrangement completed than a chief, and one other of the natives, left their canoe and took their station with us; the chief with a somewhat offensive familiarity seating himself in the stern of the boat, near the captain. We were not long in doubt concerning the motive which had led them to this act of condescension.

Our bread was contained in a small chest, which had been placed in the bottom of the boat; this seemed to have excited their curiosity to the highest pitch, as they kept their eyes almost constantly upon it, and endeavored to persuade the captain to give them a chance to examine its contents. He declined gratifying them, thinking it better to keep their anxiety alive, rather than to expose to them the comparative worthlessness of the little that remained with us, of either the comforts or necessaries of life.

Probably owing to this show of resistance on our part, when we had approached to within five or six miles of the island, at a signal given by the chief, the sail of their canoe was suddenly dropped; and, seizing our powder canister, he jumped overboard and swam to the canoe. His companion, following the example of the thievish chief, seized a bundle of clothing and was making off with it; whereupon Mr. Nute, who had not yet become entirely reconciled to the fashion of going without clothes, like our new acquaintances, and conceiving that it might be well to insist upon having the rights of property respected, caught hold of the bundle and retained it.

Upon this they immediately hauled us alongside, and seized upon our oars; here again we had occasion to offer some resistance to their supposed right to plunder us, and we succeeded in keeping possession of these; the only remaining means of saving ourselves from premature death and a watery grave.

They had by this time become so exasperated, that we considered it altogether desirable to get ourselves out of the reach of their war clubs, spears, and battle-axes; and we took measures accordingly. We were still held fast to their canoe, and so completely within their reach that it required not a little courage to make any attempt to leave them; but Mr. Nute, whose resolution had been wrought up by the previous contest, took a knife and deliberately cut the line. Our intention was to throw ourselves astern, and then, by tacking directly about, and steering in the wind's eye, to escape from them, or at least to give them, for a time, some better employment than that of robbing their poor and suffering victims.

This we succeeded in accomplishing; not however without the expense of much toil, and some blows, which they dealt out at parting, with so much severity, that we shall not soon lose the recollection of their barbarous conduct towards us. Mr. Nute, by his intrepidity, seemed to have rendered himself an object of their particular dislike; they beat him unmercifully, for his resolution in retaining the bundle of clothes, and sundering the only cord that bound us to our tormentors.

Having but three oars, our progress was by no means as rapid as we could have desired; but perceiving that in going against the wind we had the advantage of our pursuers, and knowing that our only safety was in flight, we exerted our utmost strength, and soon had the satisfaction of leaving them at a safe distance from us. They seemed determined not to part with us, and continued to pursue us till about four o'clock, P. M.

It was with the greatest difficulty that we kept clear of them; at times it seemed impossible; and in this situation we could fully realize the force of the scriptural sentiment, "all that a man hath he will give for his life." Finding them too near us, and evidently intent upon taking vengeance for the crime we had committed in attempting to escape, though our wardrobe had been reduced to a few necessary articles of clothing, we resorted to the expedient of parting even with these, by casting one thing at a time upon the water, rightly judging that they might be detained in picking them up, and hoping by this management to keep our distance from them.

After they left us, we continued our course, which was directly into the open sea, until about sunset, when we discovered land ahead, apparently at the distance of forty miles. We continued to row on till about three o'clock in the morning, when we found that we were in shoal water, and near breakers. We contrived to throw the bight of a rope over a point of rock which was about eight feet under water, and we there remained until daylight. We then let go our hold, and pulled for land. At about four o'clock in the afternoon we succeeded in landing on a small island distant from the main land about half a mile, and drew our boat upon the beach. By this time our strength had become much exhausted, and we were suffering beyond description from the want of water.

Our first efforts were made to find some means for quenching our thirst; and, to our inexpressible joy, we soon found a spring, which, in that extremity of our sufferings, was of more value than a mine of gold. Poor Sedon was left lying in the boat in a state of complete prostration. We carried him some water, and he soon revived.

STRANDED

Having satisfied our most pressing wants, we next set ourselves at work to obtain food. We had with us a part of the bread brought from the wreck, and the preparation given us by the natives composed of the cocoa-nut pulverized and mixed with the sweet liquor extracted from the tree. Putting these together into a bucket-full of water, we made out the materials for a supper, which, though not of a kind to suit the delicate palate, was devoured with thankfulness and a good relish. Feeling refreshed and invigorated by our meal, we gathered ourselves into a group on the beach, and passed our moments of relaxation in conversing upon the melancholy vicissitudes through which we had passed, and the gloomy prospect which was at that unpromising moment spread out before us. Should we find it possible to procure the means of subsistence, it was thought best to remain where we were for a day or two, not knowing what reception we should meet with, were we to throw ourselves into the hands of the inhabitants of the main island, and feeling an unconquerable reluctance to come in contact with beings scarce less ferocious than beasts of prey. But fortune having commenced making us the sport of painful incidents, soon subjected us to another annoyance.

A canoe containing two living beings, in the form of men, in a state of nakedness, was seen, from where we sat, putting off from a point of land which projected into the sea a small distance below us. They had evidently discovered us, and were approaching the spot where we were, for the purpose of making themselves acquainted with us and our condition. When within hailing distance they stopped, and seemed afraid to come nearer. Thinking it best to be on friendly terms with them, we beckoned to have them approach. This seemed to please them; and, to manifest a friendly disposition, they held up a fish. To show them that we were inclined to reciprocate any acts of kindness, to the extent of our ability, we held up a crab which we had caught.

Upon this they immediately came near to where we stood. We presented to each one a jackknife, and indicated by signs, that they were at liberty to take anything we had. They appeared highly gratified, and their conduct was inoffensive. In a short time they returned to their canoe, and made signs to us to follow them; we thought best to do so, and accordingly soon placed our effects in the boat, and followed them towards a sort of harbor at no great distance. In consequence of the lightness of their canoe and their dexterity in managing it, they were soon ahead of us, and, turning round a point of land, they were speedily withdrawn from our view.

In a few minutes they returned, accompanied by a large number of canoes—the water seemed to be literally covered by this miniature fleet. The natives were all armed, much like those with whom we first became acquainted.

This instantaneous movement was occasioned, as we afterwards learned, by an alarm given by the two natives who had visited us on the small island. Intelligence of the fact, that a boat's crew of strange looking beings, as we doubtless appeared to them, had landed upon their territory, was given by sounding a shell. This aroused the multitude, and caused them to come out, to satisfy their curiosity, and assist in conducting us safely and speedily to a place of security. A large war canoe made directly towards us; and, on coming alongside, the head chief sprung into our boat, seized the captain by the shoulder, and struck him several times with a war-club; in the mean while giving him to understand, that it was his will and pleasure to have us row, with all convenient despatch, to the place whence they had issued.

He then commenced swinging his club over our heads with great apparent ferocity, for the purpose, as it seemed, of awing us into submission; occasionally striking some of our number. After pretty thoroughly convincing us that in this case our only course was submission, he began to strip us of our clothing. While this was going on, his associates in arms and mischief kept their canoe close alongside, and, standing up, held their spears in a position to enable them to pierce us through in an instant, if there had been any occasion for so doing.

We were soon in their miserable harbor; and, it being low water, we were compelled to leave our boat, and wade to the tableland through the mud. Our appearance, as the reader will naturally conclude, was not very creditable to the land which gave us birth; but since our destitute and miserable condition was not our choice, we could do no less than be thankful that it was no worse; and, making the best of it, we suffered ourselves to be ushered into the presence of the dignitaries of the island, in the way they thought most proper.

We were conducted to a platform, on a rise of land at a little distance from the harbor, on which were seated those who had power to dispose of us as they pleased. This platform was twelve or fifteen feet square, and was situated between two long buildings, called *"pyes."* These, as we afterwards learned, were used by the chiefs as places of carousal, and as a sort of harem for their women. They were constructed in a rude manner, of bamboo sticks, and covered with leaves.

They were sixty or seventy feet in length, and about twenty-four in width.

That something like a correct conception of this scene may be formed by the reader, it may be well to give, in this place, a brief account of the appearance, manners, and customs of the natives of this island. This was the island known to navigators as Baubelthouap, the largest of the group of the Pelew islands. It lies not far from the eighth degree of north latitude, is about one hundred and twenty miles in length, and contains probably not far from two thousand inhabitants.

The men were entirely naked. They always go armed, in the way before described, and carry with them a small basket, containing generally the whole amount of their movable property. The women wear no other clothing than a sort of apron (fastened to the waist by a curiously wrought girdle) extending nearly to the knees, and left open at the sides. The material of these garments (if such they can be called) is the bark of a tree called by them *"karamal."* This tree grows from thirty to forty feet high, and is two or three feet in circumference. The hair of both males and females is worn long; it is coarse and stiff, and of a color resembling that of the natives of North America. They make free use of the oil extracted from the cocoa-nut; with this they anoint their bodies, considering it the extreme of gentility to have the skin entirely saturated with it.

Their arms, and sometimes the lower parts of the body and legs, are ingeniously tattooed. Their complexion is a light copper. Their eyes have a very singular appearance, being of a reddish color. Their noses were somewhat flat, but not so flat as those of the Africans; nor are their lips so thick. They are excessively fond of trinkets. It would cause a fashionable lady of America to smile, to observe the pains taken by those simple daughters of nature to set off their persons. In their ears they wear a sort of ornament made of a peculiar kind of grass, which they work into a tassel; this is painted and richly perfumed. In their noses they wear a stem of the *kabooa* leaf, which answers the double purpose of an ornament and a smelling bottle; and their arms, in addition to being tattooed in the manner above mentioned, are adorned with a profusion of shells.

Our fair readers may judge how much we were amused, on finding that the copper-colored females of the island cut up our old shoes into substitutes for jewelry, and seemed highly delighted with wearing the shreds suspended from their ears.

Our further acquaintance with this extraordinary people confirmed us in the opinion, that the ceremony of marriage is unpractised and unknown among them. The chiefs appropriate to themselves as many females as they please, and in the selection they exercise this despotism over the affections without regard to any other laws than those of caprice. Reserving a more particular account of their manners, customs and mode of living for another place, I content myself with observing at this time, that the people of these islands, generally speaking, are in the rudest state imaginable. It is true that some sense of propriety, and some regard to the decencies of life, were observable; nor did they appear entirely destitute of those feelings which do honor to our nature, and which we should hardly expect to find in a people so rude and barbarous.

Such were the beings among whom Providence had cast our lot; and to think of remaining with them to the end of life, or for any great length of time, was like the contemplation of imprisonment for life in the gloomy cells of a dungeon.

From the rudely constructed wharf near the spot where we left our boat, we were conducted into the presence of a number of the chiefs, who were seated upon the platform above mentioned. The natives eagerly pressed forward to obtain a sight of us. That curiosity peculiar to the better portion of our race was, on this occasion, manifested by the females of the island. They clustered around us, and, placing their hands upon our flesh, seemed greatly to wonder that it should differ so much from their own. The fashion of wearing a skin so white as ours, seemed to them, no doubt, to be an offence against the taste and refinement of their portion of the world. To go at large without being tattooed, was to carry with us the palpable proofs of our vulgarity; and, to our sorrow, we were afterwards compelled to conform to the custom of the barbarians in this respect, and shall carry with us to the grave the marks of their well-meant, though cruel operation upon our bodies.

Judging from appearances, our case had become a concern of great importance. The chiefs seemed to have had under discussion the question, whether we were to be treated as enemies, and subjected to the process of beheading upon the block of the executioner, (which was there in readiness before our eyes) or regarded as friends, and welcomed to their rude hospitalities. Unable as we were to understand a word of their language, or to say anything by way of explanation or defence, the reader will conceive, better than we could describe, our painful situation. For a time we considered our case as hopeless. The women, who seemed to have taken an interest in our welfare, after observing, for a time, what was going on among the chiefs, began to utter their cries and lamentations, as if greatly distressed on our account.

Their grief had the appearance of being sincere; they wept, and in a variety of ways expressed emotions of deep and heart-felt solicitude. Whether this was their manner of interceding in our behalf, to avert some impending calamity, or was expressive of their regret on account of our doom having been already sealed, it was impossible for us to determine. Nor did we ever know the amount of our obligations to those female strangers for the interest taken in our welfare. A termination was put to our suspense, however, in the course of an hour.

At the close of the consultation, a large bowl was brought to us, filled with sweetened water, and richly ornamented with shells, so arranged as to form a sort of hieroglyphical characters. We drank of the contents of the bowl, in compliance with their request, from a richly wrought cup made of a cocoa-nut shell. This act of hospitality was regarded as a favorable indication of a friendly disposition on their part towards us; and our hopes were afterwards confirmed; for no sooner had we finished drinking, than the natives prepared to conduct us away. We afterwards learned, that a messenger had been despatched to a neighboring town, or settlement, to consult their prophetess in regard to the proper manner of disposing of us; and that she had directed them to send us to her. Of this important personage a more particular account will be given hereafter; suffice it, for the present, to say, that the respect paid to her by the natives of the island was of the most profound character, and her authority over them was almost unlimited.

We were conducted, through an inconsiderable place, to the town where the prophetess resided. In this place there were several dwelling-houses, scattered about without regard to order; and, besides the dwelling of the prophetess, two of their long buildings, or "pyes," gave it not a little importance in the estimation of these rude and uncultivated beings. We were halted in front of one of the "pyes," and directly opposite the house of the prophetess. Here, again, we were reminded of the fact, that we were in the presence of our superiors, as to power, by the platform on which were placed our judges, the chiefs, and the block standing near them, for the purpose of execution.

We were soon surrounded by a vast crowd of the natives, eager to see us, and to learn something of the nature of beings so different from themselves.

A short time after our arrival, a quantity of food was brought from the house of the prophetess, and placed in the centre of the platform. This consisted of a hog's head, boiled in sea-water, highly seasoned with cayenne and aromatic herbs, a plentiful supply of yams, and a large bowl of sweetened water. This meal was abundant and delicious; and we partook of it with an excellent relish.

THE ENGLISHMAN

An interesting incident now occurred. Just at the time when the servant of the prophetess brought out the materials for our repast, we observed, at a little distance, a singular looking being approaching us. His appearance was that of a man of sixty. His hair was long and gray, unlike that of the natives. His legs, arms, and breast were tattooed. His step was quick and firm; his motions indicating that he felt himself a person of not a little importance. His teeth were entirely gone, and his mouth was black with the use of "kabooa." Judge of our emotions on hearing this strange being address us in broken English! His first exclamation was—"My God, you are Englishmen!" He immediately said, "You are safe now;" but he gave us to understand, that it was next to a miracle that we had escaped being killed on the water.

This person was by birth an Englishman, and had been on the island about twenty-nine years. He told us that he had been a hatter by trade, and that his name was Charles Washington. He had been a private in the British naval service, on board the *Lion* man-of-war. Cruising in those seas, he had, while on duty, been guilty of some trifling offence; and, apprehending that he should be severely punished for it, had left the ship, and taken up his residence upon the island. He seemed to be contented with his situation, and had no desire to return to his native country. He had attained to great celebrity, and was the sixth chief among them. His authority seemed great, and he exercised it with exemplary discretion.

Observing the provisions before us, he told us that they were for our use, and desired us to partake of whatever we preferred. Seeing that we were likely to be somewhat annoyed by the crowd of young persons who had collected around us, he swung his battle-axe over their heads, and giving them to understand that we belonged to *him*, immediately caused them to disperse.

Arrangements were soon made for our accommodation. A part of one of the "pyes" was appropriated to our use, and we were furnished with mats, and other things for our comfort and convenience. Here we remained for about a month, and were regularly supplied by the natives with a sufficiency of provisions of various kinds, such as hogs, goats, fish, yams, cocoa-nuts, bread-fruit, preserved almonds, and occasionally with sweet potatoes.

A change seemed now to have come over us. We were, it is true, amongst a rude and barbarous people, cut off from all intercourse with the rest of the world, and deprived of many things which we had been accustomed to regard as essential to our happiness; but even then we found many reasons for being grateful to the Disposer of events. Our actual wants were supplied; and the natives soon evinced a disposition to consider us friends, and treat us as such. To the latest day of our lives we shall remember some of them with heartfelt respect and affection; and, most of all, regret our inability to requite them for the favors which they voluntarily bestowed upon us.

Especially should we rejoice to revisit that lonely spot of earth, and carry with us, to those children of nature, the means of civilization, and the blessings of Christian faith and Christian morality. And should the government of enlightened America ever see proper to extend to them some proof of its regard, it would afford us unspeakable pleasure to have it in our power to communicate to them the exalted principles, which might incline this highly favored nation to the performance of so noble a deed.

Finding it important to be able to converse with the natives, we improved every opportunity to become acquainted with their language. Having but little to occupy our attention, it was not long before we had acquired a tolerable knowledge of it; and we found our situation much more pleasant as we became familiar with it. Our great object was, as the reader will naturally suppose, to contrive some way of escape. Our only means of accomplishing this was by friendly and amicable negotiation, and to make them understand our wishes, and convince them that it would be for their interest to aid us in returning to our native land, were essential to our success.

We had not long been with them before we became acquainted with the fact, that upon the opposite end of the island there was another tribe, and that the two divisions of the inhabitants were not on the most friendly terms with each other. Intelligence had in some way been communicated to those who lived remote from the spot where fortune had thrown us, that we were desirous of leaving the island; and, probably with a view of gaining some advantage, they sent to us a message, informing us of their willingness to assist in constructing a boat sufficiently large to convey us across the water. The persons commissioned to make this proposal, and to persuade us to go to them, were two Englishmen, who, as we afterwards learned, had been on the island for several years, and were left there by English vessels. The particulars of their history we were unable to obtain.

An offer of that kind, coming as it did from their enemies, and being in itself calculated to offend the pride of those into whose hands we had fallen, greatly excited their feelings of animosity; and, in consequence of our having manifested some desire to satisfy our own minds on the subject, we were closely watched. On the whole, however, we had no reason to regret this state of things; for on finding that their neighbors were disposed to assist us, a spirit of emulation was aroused among them, and for a time we had some hopes that the excited energies of this tiny nation would lead to the performance of some exploit, which, in the end, might place at our disposal the means of deliverance.

Our maintenance had by this time become so great a tax upon their resources, that it was found expedient to cause some of our number to be removed to a settlement about a mile distant. Mr. Nute, Mr. Rollins, and myself were accordingly selected, and under a strong escort taken to the place. This did not please us, as we preferred remaining with our companions; but either expostulation or resistance would have involved us in worse difficulties, and we submitted. In our new situation we were well supplied with provisions, and kindly treated. We were allowed to visit our friends at the other town, and spent our time as agreeably as could be expected under the circumstances.

Previously to this, some steps had been taken towards constructing a sort of boat or vessel to convey us home. Finding the natives disposed to part with us, for a stipulated consideration, and to render us any assistance in their power, we left no means unemployed to induce them to exert themselves to the utmost; and, to their credit be it said, it was more owing to their inability than to their want of inclination that we were not entirely successful. An account of their proceedings cannot fail of being interesting.

After much deliberation, and many consultations upon the momentous subject, it was agreed to commence operations. Their prophetess had been duly consulted, and the assistance of their divinity had been implored with great formality. Before they ventured upon the undertaking, it was deemed advisable to hold a festival. An event of so much importance could not be suffered to transpire without being duly solemnized. Tradition furnished no account of anything equal to this attempt!

Accordingly large quantities of provisions were brought from various parts of the island, and an immense concourse of men, women, and children, attended the feast. On our part we had little confidence in the success of the plan; but, be that as it might, we were far from being displeased with their efforts to carry it into execution, and shared with them the festivities of the occasion, with not a little pleasure.

This part of the business having been duly attended to, the time had come for united and vigorous action; and accordingly the whole male population of that region repaired to the woods, to procure timber. In the meantime the females, animated by a spirit of emulation, betook themselves to the task of making mats, to serve as sails to our vessel, when it should be completed. In fine, the whole resources of the country, of every kind, were taxed to the last extremity, to accomplish the work.

Considering the means they had for carrying the plan into execution, it is surprising that they accomplished as much as they did. The best tools we had were a few old inch chisels, which served as substitutes for the broad-axe, in manufacturing trees into planks, and afterwards fitting them to their places. There were a few spikes on the island, but we had neither auger nor gimlet.

When news had been received that the timber was ready in the woods, orders were given to have it brought together. Seldom had we witnessed a more novel scene than that presented by the natives when they brought from the forests the rudely prepared materials for the boat. They were seen coming in from all quarters with loads of timber on their shoulders, of every size and shape that could be conceived of, and causing the hills and vales to resound with their shouts.

In due time the work of putting together the materials commenced. We succeeded in laying a sort of keel, and at length contrived to erect a kind of frame, which, though it might not be regarded as a first-rate specimen of naval architecture, nevertheless looked somewhat like the beginning of a water-craft. But when we came to the more difficult part of the business, that of putting on the planks, we found that not only our skill, but that of the whole nation, was completely baffled. We were compelled to abandon the undertaking; and despaired of ever being able to succeed in building anything of the kind.

During all this time the natives were sanguine in the belief that they should succeed, and repeatedly assured us that they could accomplish the work. Their sorrow and mortification, on being obliged to give it up, were great; for they seemed to realize, that now they must have fallen in our estimation, and thought that we should be anxious to avail ourselves of the assistance of their enemies, who, as they well knew, were extremely anxious to get us into their hands. The captain did not attempt to conceal his wish to go to the other part of the island. This greatly increased their dissatisfaction; and their murmurs became frequent and loud.

After considerable expostulation, they proposed to make a *canoe* sufficiently large to convey us away; and, having some confidence in the practicability of the plan, we consented to wait and assist them in their endeavors to supply us with this substitute for the more respectable craft we had contemplated building. After duly consulting the old prophetess, the principal chiefs were assembled, and having agreed to take for the purpose the largest bread-fruit tree on the island, the people were called upon to meet at the spot where it stood, and assist in cutting it down.

Matters of so great importance required deliberation in the operation of planning out the work,—but the accomplishment of an undertaking like that of felling so large a tree, with tools even less adapted to the business than the teeth of a beaver, was one that took several days. At length the herculean task was performed, and the tree fell! But judge of our feelings on finding that the trunk, which we had hoped to render so useful in conveying us to some place from which we could obtain a passage to our native land, had, in falling, become so split as to be good for nothing! It seemed to us that a cruel fate had ordained, that no labor of our hands should prosper. Another tree was selected, and with that we were more successful. We then commenced digging it out, and bringing it to a proper shape. The old chisels were now put in requisition; and, in twenty-eight days from the time we began, we had succeeded in bringing that part of our labor to a close. Of the other tree we made two wide planks, which we fastened to the upper edges of the canoe, thereby adding very considerably to its capacity. Two months more were consumed in fitting up our canoe with sails, and getting it ready for sea.

Having proceeded thus far, it was deemed proper by the natives to have another festival; and, as our labors, in this instance, had been attended with better success, extraordinary preparations were made for a feast that should do honor to the occasion. An immense quantity of fish had been obtained; the females brought large quantities of bread-fruit, cocoa-nuts, and yams; and the toil of months was forgotten in the universal joy which then prevailed.

THE DEPARTURE

By this time the natives had become nearly as anxious to part with us as we had ever been to leave them; and being mutually desirous to be rid of each other's company, we lost no time in preparing for our departure. Our object now was to get into the open sea, with the hope of falling in with some vessel on its passage to China or elsewhere, and thus be able, after a while, to find a conveyance to America. Provisions were furnished us by the natives; but we greatly needed a compass, and with much difficulty obtained one. Captain Wilson, who had been shipwrecked there many years before, left his compass with one of the chiefs, whom we finally succeeded in inducing to part with it. It had become much impaired by time and improper usage, but served as a tolerable guide.

It is proper here to state the particulars of our agreement with the natives of this island. They had, as before related, furnished us with the means of subsistence, and with comfortable lodgings; and, for the purpose of enabling us to return home, had been at great expense in fitting up a craft, such as they thought would answer to convey us wherever we pleased to go. According to their notions, we were persons of sufficient consequence in the estimation of our countrymen, to fulfil any engagement we might make with them, and to the extent to which, in our necessity, we were compelled to go, in order to obtain the object which we had in view, should the government consider itself bound; and it would be no less an act of justice than of humanity, to secure the friendship and confidence of these islanders; so that, should others unfortunately fall into their hands, their lives and property might be respected.

It is also important, that those who engage in commercial pursuits should have every protection extended to them. It would cost the government but a mere trifle to secure an amicable understanding with these islanders; and it is but reasonable to hope that no time will be lost in making the attempt.

Situated as we were, we did not feel ourselves at liberty to expostulate against the obvious unreasonableness of their demands. We were, in truth, indebted to them for our maintenance while among them, and for the assistance they rendered us in fitting up our craft; and, as a suitable requital for these favors, and to remunerate them for their hospitality, we solemnly assured them, that, should fortune so far prosper us, as to enable us once more to reach our native country, we would send to them two hundred muskets, ten casks of powder, with a corresponding quantity of balls and flints. Besides this, we gave them assurances of having several articles of ornament, such as beads, belts, combs, and trinkets of various kinds.

On the 27th of October, 1832, we set sail, having the boat in which we had escaped from the ship, and which we had repaired as well as we were able, and the canoe which had been constructed by the natives especially for our use. It was agreed, that three of our number, viz. Davis, Meder, and Alden, should remain on the island as hostages, and that three of the natives (two chiefs, and one of the common class) should accompany us, to see that the agreement made with them should be faithfully executed.

Fearing that the natives residing on the other part of the island might come upon us and prevent our going, we took our departure in the night.

We soon found that our boats leaked so badly that it would be next to madness to proceed, and we returned in the course of the night. Our unexpected return gave great offence; but we insisted that to go to sea in that condition would be certain destruction. They at length consented to assist in repairing the canoe and boat, and to suffer us to remain long enough to complete our arrangements more to our mind.

We were detained by these operations about a month, and then again took our leave of the spot where we had remained so long against our will; though we would not conceal the fact, that the rude kindness of the natives had so entirely overbalanced their faults, that, on parting with them, we experienced emotions of regret, and were quite overpowered with a sense of our obligations to them for the many favors which they had bestowed upon us. They had regarded and treated us as beings of a higher order than themselves; and our conduct had inspired them with a veneration and confidence almost unbounded. As a proof of this, three of their number were committed to our care, and were entirely willing to place themselves at our disposal.

Seven of our number now took the canoe, viz., Bouket, Sedon, Andrews, Hulet, and the three natives. Captain Barnard, Rollins, Nute, and myself preferred the ship's boat. We were accompanied on our passage the first day by a large number of the natives. At night, as we had then succeeded in getting beyond the reef, they left us, and we continued our course.

16

THE WRECK OF
THE *CITIZEN*

LEWIS HOLMES

*The dark, frigid and potentially lethal water was just the beginning
of the danger.*

On the 21st of September, we finished cutting in a whale, about
twelve o'clock, midnight, wind high from the north-east. The northern lights were uncommonly brilliant, which prognosticated a storm;
and the broken water and flying spray round the vessel seemed as if
composed of an infinite number of diamonds glistening in the rays of
the sun.

The season of the year had now arrived in which, in those high
latitudes, sudden changes and violent storms were expected. At three
o'clock on the morning of the 22d, the ship was put under short
sail; rough; unable to keep fires in the furnace; ship heading to the

south-east. We spoke with Captain Clough, who had just taken in a "raft" of blubber. We took a whale; and for a little time the wind moderated, which gave us hope that we should have favorable weather some time longer. Captain Clough left us that day, and turned his ship towards the straits, saying, "I am bound out of the ocean, and have enough." His ship was full; he had thirty-two hundred barrels of oil on board.

We concluded to remain on the ground a while longer, in lat. 68° N. The wind, which had in a measure subsided, now began to rise and increase, until it had reached a heavy gale. We saw in the distance several ships steering for the straits, and bound for the islands. On the 23d, it blew hard, and we were unable to boil.

We judged we were, at this time, about one hundred and fifty miles from land. The weather had been thick for several days past, and therefore we were unable to get an observation. We saw several ships lying to, and heading some one way and some another. The water, we perceived, was very much colored, which indicated that we were drifting towards the eastern shore of the Arctic. At twelve o'clock, wore ship, heading north-west by north. At the same hour that night, wore ship again, heading north-east.

We passed a ship, within the distance of half a mile, under bare poles, laboring very hard. On the 24th, four o'clock, wore ship north-north-west, wind blowing very heavily from the north-east. We saw great quantities of drift stuff, such as barrels, wood, &c., probably the deck load of some ship swept by the sea. At twelve o'clock, wore ship again; the wind appeared to lull somewhat, but the sea was very rugged; we judged we were about one hundred or one hundred and twenty miles distant from land; weather thick, with rain, sleet, and fog. About one o'clock, on the morning of the 25th, the wind increased, and swept over the ocean with the violence of a hurricane. The darkness of the night added to the tumultuous and mountainous waves that were running at that time; the surface of the ocean lashed into fury by the thickening storm, still gathering its strength; the noble ship now rising the crested billow, and then sinking into the watery valley beneath, and pressed down by the beating and overwhelming elements, made the scene one of indescribable grandeur and awfulness. With the return of morning light, an ugly sea struck the ship, and took her spars from the bow, and carried away one of the starboard boats.

The mate immediately reported to the captain, who was below at the time, that the ship was in shoal water. As soon as he reached the deck, he ordered to set the fore and mizzen topsails. About the same time, the fourth mate reported that there were rocks and breakers just before and under the bows of the ship. From the house, the captain saw projecting rocks through the opening waters, and land all around to the leeward, while the sea was breaking with tremendous violence between the ship and shore.

It now became a certainty, which no earthly power could change, that the ship must go ashore; and the only hope for any one on board was to avoid, if possible, the fatal reef, which appeared to extend out some distance from the land. To strike upon that reef was certain destruction; we saw no way of escape.

The man at the wheel was ordered to put the helm hard up, and at the same time command was given to the seamen to sheet home the fore topsail. The ship immediately paid off two or three points, when she was struck again by another sea that threw her round on the other tack.

The ship was now in the midst of the rollers, pitching and laboring dreadfully, while the sea was flying all over her deck, and the spray reaching nearly or quite to her fore and main yards. She was utterly unmanageable; and, at this instant, another sea boarded her, and took off three boats. The yards were ordered to be braced round as soon as possible; but, in the act of bracing them, a terrible blast of wind struck and carried away the fore and mizzen topsails, half-sheeted home. The foresail was now ordered to be set, the ship still pitching, tumbling, and rolling frightfully, and tossed about as a mere plaything at the mercy of winds and waves. In the act of setting the foresail, the weather clew was carried away, and with the next sea the ship struck aft very heavily, and knocked her rudder off, and sent the wheel up through the house. From five to eight minutes she struck forward with such stunning and overwhelming effect that the try-works started three or four feet from the deck, and opened a hole so large in her starboard bow that the largest casks came out.

About this time, the foremast was cut away, with the hope of temporarily relieving the foundering vessel. Shortly after this, the ship struck midships; and the dreadful crash which followed showed that her entire framework was shattered, while the standing masts bent to and fro like slender reeds when shaken by the wind. This was in effect the finishing blow; and what was to be done towards rescuing anything below deck must be done soon or never.

The captain, at this critical juncture, went into the cabin to secure what articles he could, such as clothes, nautical instruments, money, &c. While there, the stern burst in, and the water came in between the opening timbers in such torrents as to send him backward and headlong with the few articles he had hastily gathered, and scattered them in every direction. The floor of the cabin opened beneath his feet. There was no time for delay. His life was in imminent peril. He at once started for the deck, but was unable to reach it on account of the house having been thrown down upon the gangway, and the mizzen-mast having gone by the board, one part of which rested upon the rail. All access to the deck by the cabin doors was thus cut off.

Mr. Fisher became aware of the condition of the captain in the cabin, and called to him to come to the skylight; and as he jumped, he was caught by his arms, and drawn up by several who had come to his rescue. On reaching the deck, the captain saw at once the sad condition of his men. The sea was making a clear breach over the vessel, and they were huddled together round the forecastle and forward part of the ship, amazed, stupefied, cold, and shivering, and had apparently given themselves up to the fate which awaited them.

The fog having in a measure cleared away, the land was more plainly seen, and just at hand—not more than three hundred yards distant. The mainmast was still standing; and there was every indication that the entire top of the vessel, including the first and second decks, had become separated from her bottom, and was drifting in towards the shore. This proved to be the case. The standing mast was now inclining towards the shore, which seemed to present the only way to deliverance and life. The captain, therefore, encouraged his men to seize the first opportunity which should occur, and escape to land, and the sooner they did so the safer and better.

As the ship changed her position by the action of the waves, which swept over and around her with resistless fury, the end of the flying jib boom, at one time, was brought quite near the shore. The seamen were again urged to make an effort to save themselves. It was, indeed, a most desperate chance to venture an escape even from a present danger, with the liability of falling into another, unknown, and perhaps more to be dreaded. Though so near the solid land, towards which every eye looked and every heart panted, still the surging billows and receding undertow around the bow of the ship, were sufficient to appall the most courageous mind.

About this time, as near as can be recollected, the cooper and one of the boat steerers, having dropped themselves from the bow, reached land in safety. The captain, having observed that two had gained the shore, and knowing the utter impossibility of getting fire ashore if it was deferred until the breaking up of the ship, and without it all must unavoidably perish, even if they were saved from a watery grave, held up the lantern keg to attract their attention, and, making signs to them as far he was able for them to look after and save it, tossed the keg overboard. It was borne on the advancing and retreating waves back and forth for more than a quarter of a mile, before it was finally secured. In this keg, which was air-tight, there were candles, matches, tinder, and other combustible materials. It was indeed a most timely and fortunate rescue.

An effort was now made to get a line ashore. One of the crew fastened a line round his body, and attempted to reach the shore, the captain paying out the warp as was necessary. But in consequence of the great force of the current and undertow around the bow of the ship, the line swayed out so far that the man was compelled to let it go in order to save his life. It was with the greatest difficulty he reached the shore.

As the only and last resort which remained, offering reasonable prospect of deliverance, the mainmast was cut away. The ship was now lying nearly broadside to the shore, with her deck inboard, and so much heeled that it required the greatest attention to prevent one from falling off. The mast fell in the direction of the shore, and nearly reached land. The sea was still breaking with fearful power over the vessel, and its spray flying in dense masses over everything around us, and the din of the thundering billows, as they beat upon the wreck and upon the shore, drowned all human voices to silence.

Again the captain passed along to the forward part of the ship, and once more remonstrated, urged and entreated his men to exert themselves for their safety and lives, as they had now the same means of getting ashore that the officers had; and, furthermore, that in a short time the deck would go to pieces, and then there would be but little, if any hope of their being saved. He resolved he would not leave the wreck until he saw his men in a fair way of escape. Up to this time, no one, it is supposed, had been lost; several had reached land in safety, but those still on the wreck were exposed every moment to a watery grave.

At length, the steerage boy lowered himself down from the bow, and with manly efforts sought to gain the land. He was immediately swept away, and was never seen after. About this time, many began to crawl down on the mainmast, still lying in the direction of the shore. In working their way along on the mast, their progress was not only slow, but they were chilled, benumbed with cold, their clothes thoroughly wet to their backs, and the sea at the same time flying over them. It was with the greatest difficulty they could hold on. The sight was a most affecting one. It was a period of painful anxiety. How many of these seamen will be saved?—how many will be lost?

While attempting thus to escape upon the mast, the advancing or the returning waves would frequently wash numbers off, and then they would struggle with all their energies to regain the mast or the rigging; while those who were more fortunate, and had retained their hold, would aid them as far as possible in getting on to the mast again. It was a most trying and heart-rending scene.

The captain and Mr. Fisher were on the quarter deck, and observed a part of a boat hanging by the side of the ship; and they proposed to get into it, and, if possible, reach the land. Their purpose was to hold on to the boat, and thus be borne by the sea towards the shore. They did get into it; but whether it was carried towards the shore or not, or what became of the piece of the boat, they have no recollection. They were struck by a sea, and probably stunned. The first returning consciousness the captain had, he found himself floating alongside of the ship. He knew not what had become of Mr. Fisher until some time after. He regained a foothold on the quarter deck again, and seemed awakened more fully than ever to the conviction that he must do something, and that soon, in order to save his own life. He was chilled, benumbed, and exhausted; chances of escape appearing less and less probable, as a last resort, said Captain Norton, "I threw myself into the water, among casks, broken pieces of the wreck, and, besides, my own men floating all around me, that I might, if possible, gain the shore. I was probably insensible for some time. I knew nothing of what took place around me. When I came to myself, I found I was lying near the edge of the water, having been cast ashore by some friendly wave. I looked around, and the first man I saw was the fourth mate, floating about in the water a short distance from me. Mr. Fisher was washed ashore about the same time I was. We hastened to the fourth mate as soon as we were able; and one held on to the hand of the other, and hauled him ashore, supposing him to be dead. He, however, revived."

A heavy sea came along, and washed a number from the mast, and brought them ashore; but one man was carried off by the undertow outside the ship. The next sea brought him near to the shore again; and four of those on shore took hold of each other's hands, and ventured as far as safety would allow into the water, and succeeded in drawing him safe to land.

The condition of the carpenter was painful and distressing in the highest degree; yet no one could help him—no earthly power could afford him any assistance. He was plainly seen by those on shore. He was probably washed from the mast, with some others, and carried out to the deck again; and while there, he was doubtless caught in between the opening planks and timbers, and held fast by his legs; and it may be he was otherwise injured. He answered no signs made to him from the shore; he made no effort to free himself or to escape;

and, in his case, an escape was an impossibility. In that position, his head dropped upon his breast, and there he died. Soon after, another sea struck the deck, and broke it all to pieces. The largest part that could be seen was that from the bow to the fore chains.

Another painful occurrence was witnessed by those on the shore. A Portuguese sailor was discovered floating about among the broken pieces of the wreck, among casks, barrels, &c. His efforts for self-preservation were remarkable. His shipmates would most gladly have given him a helping hand, but it was impossible to do so. Every heart was moved with sympathy for him. As the towering wave would hurl towards him some piece of the wreck, or a cask or barrel, he was seen to dive, and thus avoid being crushed by it. This he did repeatedly, until, from exhaustion or injury, or both, he sunk to rise no more.

We had three dogs on board, but they were all either killed or drowned; and of three hogs, only one got ashore alive. Within two hours from the time the ship first struck, the wreck was piled up on shore, opposite to where the disaster occurred, to the height of ten feet or more. Spars, timbers, planks, casks both whole and broken, shooks, &c., were thrown together in frightful confusion; and in this promiscuous mass we saw what was once our home and hope on the deep. Here we saw before our eyes a striking illustration of the feebleness of man's frail bark, and with what ease it is torn to pieces, and scattered far and wide, by the resistless power of the elements.

All who were living of our number had reached the shore. Those that were saved had become greatly chilled, and some were nearly perishing. Notwithstanding it was storming at the time, one of the first efforts of a part of our men was to make a fire over a cliff some little distance from the shore, affording a partial protection from the wind and rain.

In searching for articles as they came ashore, we discovered a small keg of spirits, which, in our condition of cold and destitution, was somewhat reviving to all our minds. Five casks of bread, also, were cast upon the beach; but neither beef nor pork was found. The latter probably sunk where the ship left her bottom.

The whole company was soon gathered round the fire, in order to dry our clothes, and, if possible, to obtain some additional warmth. All, however, of our former number were not there; it was a solemn gathering, and the appearance of all of us indicated that we had a narrow escape. Alas! some of our comrades and fellow-seamen were left behind in the surges of the deep, or mingled with the floating wreck, or cast with it upon the shore. The roll was called by the captain, and thirty-three answered to their names; five were numbered with the dead.

The few hours of the past had been full of painful and distressing interest. The majority of our number had been mercifully rescued; but we were cast shelterless, with a small supply of provisions, with no clothing, only what was upon our backs, upon the most barren and desolate region of the earth.

What were our present prospects? They were dark and ominous indeed. A new voyage, in effect, was just opening before us, with diminished numbers, of the progress and termination of which we could not even entertain a reasonable conjecture; yet one thing was certain—its commencement was inauspicious. And, though hope might measurably sustain our minds, still the prospective view before this company of castaway seamen—the rigors of the arctic winter before us, wholly unprepared with clothing to withstand the merciless and long-continued cold of the north, uncertain whether there would be any deliverance for us by any friendly sail, or what would be our reception among the natives,—indeed, the prospect before us was anything but cheering and encouraging.

But here we were, in the providence of God, vessel and boats gone, at an unknown distance from civilized life and from the settlements of the natives; this was our present lot. Self-preservation, therefore, prompted us to make immediate efforts, in anticipation of what we might need in the future. A common misfortune united all our interests and exertions.

The captain ordered that everything of value to them in their present circumstances found among the wreck—such as provisions, casks of sails, pieces of canvas, ropes, broken spars, tools, whale gearing, &c.—should be selected, and brought out of the reach of the surf and the accumulation of ice upon the shore. More than a thousand barrels of oil had drifted ashore, and could have been saved had some vessel arrived about that time. A temporary tent was erected as soon as possible, in which various articles could be stored, as well as afford some protection to us from the inclemency of the weather.

There were two circumstances exceedingly favorable in our disaster. It might have been much worse, and no one might have lived to relate the sad event. We realized, upon the review, that this would have been our certain fate, had the ship gone ashore in the night time. It was, however, daylight, and thus we had a clear view of our condition, danger, and prospects. Had it been otherwise, and the same general features of the wreck been transferred to the darkness of night, we do not believe that one soul of us would have been saved.

The other favorable circumstance was, we were not cast upon a rocky part of the coast, or against some high and precipitous cliffs, which lift their bold and defiant fronts against the surges of the ocean far into deep water; to strike against such as we saw, would, at the first concussion, have been the last of the ship and of all on board.

In the good providence of God, however, we drifted upon a part of the coast which presented, for half of a mile or more, quite a plain, sandy beach. We were, therefore, wrecked in the most fortunate spot. On both sides of us, to the west and south-east, cliffs began to rise, and broken and abrupt ledges extended some distance into the sea. Though five of our number found a watery grave, yet the fact that so many of us reached the shore was a matter of profound gratitude to that God who controls the elements, and before whom the sparrow does not fall to the ground without his notice.

The first night we spent on shore was a very stormy one. There were rain, sleet, and high winds above and around us; below us, on the ground, ice, snow, and water in abundance. Our tent, which was a hasty and temporary construction, afforded us, after all, but little permanent shelter. The water came through and under it in every direction. Here we found an additional exposure, and the prospect of increased suffering both from the cold and wet. Had it not been for our oil, we could never have kindled a fire at first, nor continued it afterwards.

But necessity gives origin to many inventions and improvements. It suggests new plans, and urges to more favorable shifts and expedients. If, therefore, our arrangements for the first night's lodging on land should seem somewhat novel, or even unheard of before, let it be remembered that sad necessity drove us to this device.

If our frail tent with a few yards of torn sails stretched over us cannot shield us from the drenching rain, something else can. Most of us, on that sad and sorrowful night, got into empty casks; some were oil, others water or bread casks; it mattered not what, if we could only be protected from the violence of the storm, or rest in some place, instead of making the icy earth our bed.

With one head of the cask knocked out, and resting upon its bilge, one or two would get into each cask, and find within it quite a dry retreat. At the same time, a fire was kept burning not far from the open heads of the several casks, placed in a circle around the fire, and thus we were made as comfortable, perhaps, as our circumstances would permit. This was our first night's experience on land.

The next day, arrangements were made to form parties of exploration. We knew not where we were. Of this, however, we were quite certain—that we were north of the straits; but upon what part of the arctic coast we were cast away, we could not tell.

Therefore, our first object was, if possible, to ascertain our true position. The thick, foggy, and stormy weather which had prevailed for many days before the wreck, contributed greatly to mislead us. Neither sun, moon, nor stars had appeared for some time, by which we might have been guided in our course through the trackless deep. All above us had been shrouded with dense clouds, while strong and variable winds, approaching to the severity of tornadoes, and even hurricanes, had carried our ship far out and beyond her true course.

The last, and not the least perhaps, of the causes which resulted in our wreck, was the current, which appeared to change its course during the storm, as it not unfrequently does. At this time, it set from the eastern to the western shore of the Arctic. Under the combined influence of the current coming from the north and east, and a severe gale of wind, accompanied with hail, rain, and fog, our ship was constantly pressed upon the western shore, until she struck and went to pieces.

Two companies were now formed, one to take an easterly course, and the other a westerly one. Those who were left behind were to be employed in making sacks out of canvas, for the purpose of carrying bread and other provisions in our anticipated travels. This expedition was intended only as an introductory one to our final removal from the place, when we should ascertain more particularly where we were.

It was the opinion of some that we were cast away upon an island; and in so far as we could judge at this time, this opinion was rather confirmed.

The captain with his party took their departure towards the east, and Mr. Fisher and his party went towards the west.

Each man was armed with whatever defensive and offensive weapon he could well carry along with him. These weapons were neither guns nor swords, but a few knives, a hatchet, a broken whale lance, and a spade. We knew not with what we should meet, whether savage beasts, or more savage men.

The parties, as they traveled in opposite directions, soon found they were not upon an island, as they at first imagined, but merely upon an extended projection, as it appeared to be, from the main land.

The captain's party, after having traveled in an easterly direction about ten miles, discovered tracks of dog teams, and the footmarks of those who accompanied them. These facts assured the explorers that human habitations of some sort were not probably far distant. They therefore returned immediately to the tent to inform their companions, and to make particular arrangements for more extended researches. The western party also returned to the tent soon after the other, having made no very definite discoveries.

We became satisfied at this time, from the direction of the coast, and the general aspect of the country, that we were north of East Cape; but how far distant from it, we had no means of determining. It was likewise a matter of equal uncertainty whether we were east or west of East River. If we were west of this river, the prospect of our liberation the coming winter, or of meeting with any friendly sail, was extremely small. If, however, we were east of the river, we had strong hopes of deliverance before the winter should fairly set in, and that we should be able to reach East Cape in season to intercept some ship bound out of the ocean.

Thus we reasoned upon and discussed those matters which pertained to our speedy deliverance, or our bondage for months to come in the dreadful and merciless winter of the polar region; or it may be that no one of our number would escape to tell the wreck of the ship, and the catastrophe which would befall his fellow-companions.

Besides, considerations were urgent and pressing why we should make all possible haste, either to find some suitable habitation for the winter, or, perchance, fall in with some friendly vessel. With the advance of the season, we were assured that traveling would become more and more difficult, and that Borean storms would soon burst upon us with resistless fury. And hence, to remain where we were first cast upon the shore, without persevering efforts to save our lives, would be the height of presumption. With nothing more to protect us than the frail tent which we had erected, thinly clad, and all we had on our backs, a limited supply of provisions from the wreck, if we should remain at our first landing place until deliverance should come to us, then, indeed, before the opening of another spring, all of us would have fallen victims to inexorable death.

At this distance from the place where the scene of our sufferings commenced, how little can our readers appreciate what were then our condition, wants, and prospects! Indeed, ice and snow already began to largely increase, though we were in the region of eternal frosts, where they never wholly disappear. Both upon the shore, and as far as the eye could reach in an inland direction, the ice and snow were perennial occupants of the country. Neither the rains of spring nor the suns of summer are able to melt away and dissolve the deep foundations of a polar winter.

The surface of the country was much broken and uneven, and especially in the interior, alternating in valleys, deep gorges, precipitous cliffs, rugged and rocky eminences, one elevation rising above another, until the remote horizon exhibited lofty mountain ranges. The entire panoramic view presented an aspect at once sublime and frightful to behold.

It should be remembered that, amid our hopes and fears, we stood at this time on the borders of human habitations; and beyond this locality, as we afterwards ascertained, especially on this coast, there was but one known settlement of the natives to the north of us.

The dead hog that drifted ashore was skinned and roasted for supper on the second night after the wreck, and for breakfast next morning. Utensils for cooking were very scarce; only a few small articles had come ashore. The hog was suspended over the fire, and turned over and around when necessary, until it was baked suitable for eating.

Preparations were made on the coming day for another traveling-exploring expedition, in which all were to be included as one company. The grand purpose we now had in view was to find a passage to East Cape, or to fall in with the huts or settlements of the natives.

Before leaving, however, a grave question arose as to what should be done with the live hog, which had thus far shared with us in our deliverance from the wreck, and from his general deportment seemed to realize his forlorn condition.

This was a "pet hog" among the seamen; he knew his name, and appeared to have more than ordinary intelligence; at least, this was his reputation on board of the ship. His weight was not far from twelve score. He was washed from the deck at the time it was broken up by the sea, and discovered, by Mr. Fisher, floating about in the surf, and supposed to be dead. He went to him, and struck a smart blow upon his back, and said to him, "Jack, what are you doing here?" He immediately gave a grunt or two, started upon his feet, and struggled for the shore. He went with us to the tent, and made that his home. He would frequently wander forth some distance from the tent, apparently ruminating upon the sad state of things; and after a while he would return and take up his position at the entrance of the tent. In the estimation of the crew, he was indeed one of the "*learned* hogs."

When the question came up, what should be done with "Jack," many at once resolved they would never eat him, because he knew so much; and being so strongly attached to him, he really seemed like one of our number: "Old Jacky must not be eaten."

A different counsel finally prevailed. If we should leave him behind, he would soon be destroyed by wild beasts, and especially bears, that swarm the region; or he would perish with hunger. In view of these considerations, it was decided to kill the favorite hog, more from necessity than choice. He was accordingly killed and roasted, and a division made of him, each man taking his proportionate share. A cheese was also divided into as many parts as there were men, and distributed to each. Each man carried a sack containing thirty biscuits, in addition to other articles of provision just mentioned.

We were particular also before leaving, though it was quite uncertain whether we should ever see the spot again, to save from the wreck and stow away in the tent whatever we thought might be necessary for future use. This was a judicious precaution. As a last resort, if all other sources of deliverance should fail us, neither finding the settlements of the natives, or being received by them, nor seeing any ship to take us off, then we must return to the wreck, and make the best of what we had, and live as long as we could.

We furthermore agreed to travel seven days from the wreck, and if we found no help or deliverance from any quarter, then we would return, which would require seven days more—about as long as we supposed our provisions would last us.

The direction we took was towards the east and south, along shore, which was less difficult to travel than farther back in the country; besides, there were less snow and ice on the seaboard at that time.

We had traveled, as was supposed, about fifteen miles, when we saw two natives, some little distance before us, in an inland direction.

At first they were unwilling to stop, probably aware from our appearance that we were foreigners. While we all kept together the natives continued on their way.

Captain Norton and two of his officers separated themselves from the rest of the company, making signs, thus indicating peaceable intentions, and advanced towards them. The natives then stopped. The captain and those with him approached them and shook hands with them. The natives appeared to understand the signals and signs, and at once desired that all the company that was behind some distance would come forward to them. This they did.

The natives pointed in the direction of their settlement, and furthermore desired all the company to follow them. We followed them until we came in sight of their huts. Here the whole company was requested to stop, with the exception of the captain and two of his officers. We went with the natives into the settlement, and were immediately conducted into the presence of a very old woman, who marked one side of our faces with two lines, and our hands in the same manner, with a burnt stick. After this singular manœuvre was over, she made signs to the captain to call all his men, and they also were marked upon their faces and hands.

It is altogether probable that the marking of our faces and hands by this old woman with a burnt stick was some sacred rite, and that she might have been a sort of priestess or prophetess among the natives, and that the ceremony was a mark of her approval, or that she secured the protection of some divinity in our behalf.

It was ascertained afterwards, that this old woman was held in very high repute among the natives, and that she was supposed to be a personification of a certain deity which inhabited some remote mountain in the interior of the country.

We also learned that the purpose she had in view in marking our faces and hands, was, that we might not *poison* those with whom we should eat, or contaminate anything we should take hold of with our hands.

We were distributed among the several huts, and remained there that night. The natives set before us something to eat in the form of whale and walrus blubber, and deer meat. This "bill of fare" had not the recommendation of being cooked, but in its original state, with no other condiment than what age imparted to it. But whether the whole company found their appetites or necessities such as to pass immediately into this new regimen, was quite, if not altogether, improbable.

This settlement appeared to be of a temporary character; the natives with their families having come from another region or section of the country for the purpose of trading and hunting. There were but five huts in all. Our company, therefore, of thirty-three persons, occupied all the room they had to spare. It was close stowage but far better for us than to be exposed and unprotected during a long and chilly night.

After our arrival at this settlement, and sometime during the night, word was sent by the natives, as we afterwards learned, to another and larger settlement, to inform the natives there that a company of ship-wrecked mariners (*raumkidlins*) had come, and wanted shelter.

Accordingly next morning, ten or fifteen dog teams, with their drivers, made their appearance, having come from a settlement east of us for the purpose of transporting us, with our effects, to new and larger quarters. We arrived at this latter place about four o'clock in the afternoon, distance about twenty miles.

The captain, with two others, went directly to the head man of the settlement, whose name was *Taunty*, and made him understand, by signs and gestures, that they wished him to take care of the whole company.

He readily assented to our request. He manifested a most kind and obliging disposition. He showed a degree of sympathy for us in our destitute and dependent condition wholly unlooked for, and altogether unexpected. Such accommodations as he and his people had were promptly offered to us.

In this instance of cordial reception by the natives, the hand of a good and merciful Providence can be easily discovered. What if, at this time of our need, the natives had thrust us away from their dwellings, and refused us shelter for the night, or a protection from the storm? or if they had exhibited towards us the spirit of hostility and war? Augmented sufferings would have been added to our otherwise unhappy lot. There would have been no escape for us from the arctic region. But we found friends when we most needed them.

We were distributed among the natives in the following manner: four men and one officer were to constitute a company; and in this proportion we occupied our respective huts, lived with the families, and shared in their accommodations.

Compared with the first settlement, where we stopped for the first night in our travel, this one was quite respectable, numbering twenty or more huts.

We had no intention of making this settlement a permanent resting place for the winter, if by any means we could find a more southern locality. We cherished strong hope of being able to reach East Cape, and thus being taken off by some ship passing through the straits, before the approach of winter. Nor was there any time to be lost towards completing such an arrangement as this.

One of the first things which we did, was to make known our wants to the head man of the settlement. So far as we were able, we conversed with him by signs, and thus endeavored to explain to him what we wished to do. He gave us to understand that it was impossible for us to travel down to East Cape this season of the year, and that the distance to the cape was very great, and it was therefore impossible to get there.

Not knowing our precise locality upon the coast, we could not tell whether the cape was three or five hundred miles from us. We concluded it would be safer to remain where we were than to venture upon such an uncertainty. It was afterwards ascertained that we were distant from East Cape about two hundred and fifty miles.

The head man gave us to understand, in his way, that there was a very great river to cross before we could get to East Cape, and that it could not be crossed now; and still further, if we should perish on the way, great ships (*laloutoutlines*) would come, kill him, and destroy all their huts.

On the whole, we judged that it was the desire of the head man that we should remain with him and his people, and live among them for the present; and nothing occurred in all our subsequent acquaintance with the natives in this settlement to remove this impression from our minds. It may be, however, that they anticipated some remuneration for their attention to us, which, by the way, they had a right to expect. This was not unlikely a motive which induced them to desire that we might live with them.

We sincerely hope the time may speedily come, when they shall be amply recompensed by our government for their kindness towards *thirty-three American seamen*, whom they protected, clothed, and fed, during three quarters of a year.

The prospect of reaching East Cape for the present was at length abandoned. A conclusion was arrived at, from the necessity of our condition, which was full of disappointed hope, and which required an unusual degree of patient courage to sustain our minds under the painful conviction that we must, after all, spend the next three quarters of a year, if we should live, in the northern regions. How the mind of man becomes shaped and adjusted to meet certain conditions of his being! If viewed in the light of unavoidable necessity, we see the force and independence of mind grappling with adverse circumstances, thus proving its original superiority over all outward disadvantages. It is, however, the province of *Christian* faith in the providences of an all-wise God, which secures to the mind true reconciliation, imparts hope in adversity, and awakens unearthly joy in seasons of sorrow and disappointment.

The next day after our arrival at our new habitations, the whole company rested, and got somewhat recruited as to our bodies, and, not the least in our circumstances of anticipated captivity for months, our minds became partially settled that we must make the best of a common disaster and a common destiny.

The day following, preparations were made by ourselves, in connection with the natives and their dog teams, to visit the wreck. One of the first questions asked, and the principal one in which the natives were more interested than in any other, was, whether there was any rum at the wreck. A keg of spirits had been washed ashore, as before stated, and a part of it had been used, and the remainder was in the keg in the tent, stowed away with other articles from the wreck.

A difficulty was now apprehended. If the natives should find the keg of rum, and become intoxicated, as they probably would, serious and perhaps fatal consequences might take place. To avoid any fears of this sort, and remove all grounds of contention, the captain sent two of his men ahead, with orders to knock in the head of the rum keg. It was done as commanded; no further difficulty, therefore, could arise from this source.

Self-preservation prompted to this; but in a multitude of instances no less striking, where property, reputation, and even life itself are concerned, a like decision, to knock in the head of the rum keg, or break jugs and bottles, and pour the source of evil upon the ground, would be highly commendable, and fraught with the most happy results.

In due time we reached the wreck, and, as was expected, the natives began to search for spirits; but for their advantage, as well as ours, they found none. They sought everywhere for it, ransacked every nook and corner, hauled over wreck stuff, looked into barrels, knocked to pieces oil casks, &c., to find it, but all in vain.

It appeared, furthermore, as if the natives supposed they had a *right* to whatever they could lay their hands upon, and what they found among the wreck, or on shore, was a lawful prize. Several pieces of white and blue cotton cloth had washed ashore since the wreck was last visited; these the natives appropriated to their own use. A slate was found, and upon it we wrote the name of the ship, her captain, and where the crew could be found, and placed it in a prominent position near the wreck, hoping that it might possibly meet the eye of some deliverer, though an event so much desired could now hardly be expected.

The company remained in the vicinity of the wreck until towards night, and then each man took with him a bag of bread, and, with the natives and their dog teams, we left for the settlement, which was about fifteen miles distant.

It was exceedingly hard to visit the scene of our recent disaster, and behold the desolation and end of the noble ship that had withstood so many storms and weathered so many gales, but now a promiscuous mass of broken timbers, planks, and spars; besides, her cargo thrown upon the beach. If possible, it was even harder to leave what remained of her behind, and to carry away a small quantity of provisions to eke out an existence which, under the most favorable circumstances, among the natives, must be most trying and painful. And then, again, all the provisions we expected to obtain from the wreck could last us but a few months, at the longest. If our lives, therefore, should be prolonged, we saw before us the only alternative of living as the natives did, being constant spectators of their extreme filthiness in person and habits, and sharing with them in the peculiarly offensive and disgusting character and preparation of their food.

The next day, the company remained in the settlement, wearied with the labor of the preceding day, and, the greatest calamity of all, oppressed in our minds, as we contemplated the future; and as we began to realize more and more what would probably be our destination for many long months to come.

"Hope deferred maketh the heart sick;" but hope revived—when well nigh abandoned and ready to expire, like the last flickerings of the lamp—hope revived imparts new life, and sends a thrill of joy through languishing minds. Thus the weak become strong, and the disheartened are animated and encouraged to put forth more earnest efforts. Hope revived under the circumstances in which these shipwrecked mariners were placed was like the introduction of light, comfort, and home into their wintry habitations. What intelligence more to be desired and sincerely asked for than the announcement of a sail in sight?

Think of them, as brooding over their anticipated doom; settling it, or having settled it in their minds, that their abode was doubtless fixed for the present; thoughts of home now and then rushing into their minds with overwhelming force, or, it may be, with the only exception of their sleeping moments, never out of their minds; indeed, their very dreams shaded, colored, and made treacherously illusive with joyous meetings of companions, parents, relatives, and friends! Think of them at such a time as this, when the hope of deliverance had taken its lowest dip, like the wintry sun of the Arctic passing below the horizon, its light and comfort quite departing; so hope in the minds of this company of wrecked mariners had fallen beyond any reasonable expectation of deliverance.

Severe and terrific storms of wind, rain, hail, and snow had swept over the northern ocean, and ere this it was supposed that every ship had sought a more southern and genial clime.

What, then, was our unexpected and glad surprise, on the following day, when, amid the tumult and confusion, as well as the excitement of the natives, both in and around the huts, it was announced that a *sail* was in sight!

With all possible speed we hastened to a high cliff bordering the sea shore, and there we saw, indeed, what our eyes delighted to behold, and our bosoms swelled with grateful emotions to contemplate—a ship under sail, some ten or twelve miles distant, and standing in directly for the shore. As we looked, never before with more exhilarated spirits and reviving hope, on, on the vessel came, approaching nearer and nearer, until her davits were plainly seen, and men walking to and fro on deck. The ship now was not more than two miles distant. She came to, main yard hauled back, and lay in that position a quarter of an hour or more.

With these indications, all doubt had nearly or quite left our minds that the intentions of those on board were to take us off. Still, no boat was lowered, nor was there any answering signal. This surely was mysterious, and betokened fear. And yet could it be that within so short a distance no deliverance would be extended? It was contrary to reason to believe so; the thought must not be cherished a single moment. We should soon tread a friendly deck, and share again a sailor's home on the deep. Thus whispered hope, suddenly revived in all our hearts.

But in order to make the case doubly sure, and remove all suspicion in the minds of those on board that those on shore were not all natives, two colors, one white and the other blue, were raised upon poles to the height of full thirty feet. It was plainly seen by those on board, as subsequent testimony from the officers abundantly proved. Besides, these were signals of civilization, of common brotherhood, of pressing emergency, and strongly excited hope. But, alas! they met with no response from that vessel's deck.

Lest there should be a lurking distrust in the minds of the captain and officers of the ship that these signals were a mere trickery or device of the natives to get on board of the ship, or for the ship to send a boat ashore, the company on shore separated themselves from the natives, so that with the aid of a glass, or even with the naked eye, a distinction in manner, movement, and dress could be easily seen by those on shipboard. This expedient also failed.

As another resort to attract attention, a fire was kindled; and yet the rising and curling smoke met with no cordial response, no friendly salutation; no boat came to our rescue. Shortly after, the ship filled away, passed down the coast, and was seen no more.

We felt, what no language can adequately express, that this was an instance of cold, deliberate, and even infamous neglect. Could it be they were ignorant of the ordinary laws of humanity, and wilfully misconstrued the most obvious signs of needy and suffering seamen? Instances have, indeed, occurred, in which vessels at sea have been known to pass near shipwrecked mariners, and yet they were not discovered. They were upon a low raft, perhaps, or had no means of raising a signal, and were therefore passed. The imploring cries and stretched-out hands of the sufferers were alike unheeded; not from any intentional neglect, by any means, but simply because they were not seen from the vessel's deck.

It is sad to contemplate an oversight even like this, in which the hopes and lives of a number of unfortunate seamen were suspended upon the bare possibility of being recognized by the passing ship.

How many, many have doubtless perished in mid ocean, whose eyes beheld again and again the approaching and departing sail, whose hearts alternately rose in hope and sunk in despondency, and yet at last died without the precious boon of deliverance!

Other instances have, however, occurred, of a far different character. Suffering, exhausted, and dying mariners, either upon wrecks or rafts, have been left uncared for and abandoned by the passing ship.

If the records of the past did not furnish conclusive evidence of the truth of the foregoing statement, it would seem that the bare announcement of the fact would be sufficient not only to appall the hardest heart, and cover with deep and lasting shame the perpetrators of such a deed, but to place it in the frightful category of those events absolutely beyond both human experience and credulity.

Revelation informs us that "the sea shall give up its dead;" so will there be a resurrection both of the good and bad in human conduct. A virtuous and benevolent act performed upon the ocean will never be concealed. The winds, as they sweep over its surface, will declare it. And so, on the other hand, an act of inhumanity, capriciousness, cruelty, or turning a deaf ear to the expostulations and entreaties of the dependent and suffering, will never slumber. The mighty waves, as they traverse the great deep, will speak in thunder tones that the deed lives.

The hopes of *thirty-three* persons in the cold and dreary region of the north, in the province of perpetual ice and snow, were suddenly and unexpectedly revived by the near approach of a ship within trumpet hail; signals of wrecked mariners on shore, the ship remaining more than fifteen minutes with her yards back, and those on board beholding the demonstrations of intense anxiety of those on shore that deliverance might be sent to them, and yet not one motion made for our rescue! The ship is soon on her way, and out of sight. If hope was ever suddenly and unexpectedly revived, it was then; if hope was ever suddenly cast down to its lowest depths, it was then.

Nor could our eyes hardly believe what we were beholding. Was it all illusion, dream, or magic? No; it was a reality. We had been tantalized. The cup of the greatest earthly blessing had been held to our lips, and yet we were not allowed to drink of it, but it was dashed to the earth in our very presence. The departure of that ship was the departure of mercies to us, to procure which we would have been willing to make the greatest earthly sacrifice.

What a day of joy and sorrow was that to us! How many hitherto downcast countenances were lighted up! What words of good cheer passed from one to another! How many hearts bounded with thankfulness and gratitude at the thought of so speedy a deliverance!

Our families and friends at home were thus far ignorant of the distressing scenes through which we had passed, and also of our present condition; but ere long, as we believed, on our arrival at the islands, we should communicate to them the wreck of our ship, the loss of the voyage, and the fortunate rescue of so many of our number from a watery grave.

We felt that we had much for which to be thankful to God, and that soon we should be able to send to anxious ones at home the happy intelligence that we were among the saved.

Such is hope when strongly excited. It ennobles and invigorates the human soul; it adorns the horizon with the gorgeous drapery of morning clouds; it paints the evening with the glories of departing day; it forgets the past; it is the elixir of life itself; without it man lives only in the present, and anticipates no future good.

But that was a day of sorrow too! It seemed as if we should sink into the very earth, and that we were unable to stand, with such a load and pressure upon our spirits. We were crushed both in body and mind. Contending emotions of indignation, abandoned hope, unmitigated grief, and poignant sorrow, swayed and strongly agitated every bosom. The whole company wept like children.

It may be asked, "Why did not the officers and crew avail themselves of the canoes of the natives, and go off to the ship?" It is true there were several canoes near the shore, but the natives were unwilling they should be touched; from what cause we could not understand. Our acquaintance with them, and theirs with us, had thus far been very slight; and it may be they had serious suspicions in their minds that we designed some evil towards them. They were doubtless governed by some notions, in refusing us the aid of their canoes, in keeping with their half-civilized or barbarous natures.

The captain and others offered to hire the canoes, at the same time presenting to them some little articles they had with them, as a pocket or jack knife, but all to no purpose. They resisted every proposition.

The officers and some of the crew were so anxious to get to the ship that they proposed twice to the captain to take forcible possession of the canoes, and follow the ship; and they would have done it, and risked all the consequences, had the captain approved of it. He, however, opposed this plan, on the ground that though a few might succeed in reaching the ship, yet those who were left behind, being entirely unarmed, would probably be instantly killed, and, therefore, it was bad policy to expose the lives of a majority of the company for the safety of only a few. Or, it may be, in their first efforts to seize the canoes, and before they could even get them into the water, the natives would fall upon us, and massacre the whole company on the spot. And still farther, we were wholly in their power, both for the present and for months to come, and without their kindness and good will we had no sort of chance for life; therefore the least misunderstanding or violent collision between the parties might lay the foundation for causes which would result, if not now, yet in some future time, in the destruction of the whole company. These considerations, suggested by the captain, dissuaded his men from attempting a forcible seizure of the canoes of the natives; and, therefore, for the good of the whole, that means whereby a few possibly might have reached the ship, was given up.

We leave this painful reminiscence of the past by copying from *The Polynesian*, published at Honolulu, November 19, 1853, the following card.

"The undersigned, late master of the whale ship *Citizen*, of New Bedford, feels it a duty he owes alike to the living and the dead to make known the following circumstances.

"On the 25th of September, 1852, in the Arctic Ocean, in lat. 68° 10' N., the ship *Citizen* was wrecked, and five men were lost; himself and the balance of the crew reached the shore, without any thing but the clothes they stood in. It was very cold, and they kept alive by burning casks of oil that had floated ashore from the wreck that they lived near the wreck until October 3, when the whale ship *Citizen*, of Nantucket, Captain Bailey, hove in sight; they immediately hoisted a flag upon a pole thirty feet high, and made every signal they could of distress; that the ship at first stood in as though she saw them, then hauled up and shivered in the wind, and afterwards filled away and left them. She was so close at one time that those on shore could see her davits. The feelings with which they saw the vessel leave them are indescribable, as no hope was left them but to endure the rigors of a winter's residence in that cold, bleak, and desolate region, if they should escape the tomahawk of the savage. That their signals were seen by Captain Bailey there can be no doubt, as Captain B. reported seeing his signals last fall. The mate of Captain Bailey's vessel reported to Captain B. that he could see sailors on shore, and requested a boat to go to their relief, which Captain B. refused.

"Through the inhumanity of Captain Bailey, we were compelled to remain *nine months* in that barren region, destitute of clothing and food, other than the natives could supply us from their scanty stores of blubber and furs. During this time, two of the crew perished from cold, and left their bones to bleach among the snows of the north, as a monument of 'man's inhumanity to man.'

"The natives were humane, kind, and hospitable to us, though wretchedly poor.

THOMAS H. NORTON."

SOURCES

"The Wreck of the *Equator*" from *Old Times on the Upper Mississippi*. George Byron Merrick. Cleveland, OH: The Arthur H. Clark Company, 1909.

"The *Essex* and the Whale" from *Narrative of the Most Extraordinary and Distressing Shipwreck of the Whale-Ship* Essex. Owen Chase. New York: W. B. Gilley. 1821.

"Mainers Marooned and Murdered" from *Narrative of the Shipwreck of the Brig* Betsey. Daniel Collins. Wiscasset, ME: John Dorr. 1825.

"Death on the Columbia Bar" from *Narrative of a Voyage to the Northwest Coast of America*. Gabriel Franchère. New York: Redfield. 1820.

"The Burning of the *Morro Castle*" from *Men, Wind, and Sea*. Riley Brown. New York: Carlyle House. 1938.

"On the Rocks in Alaska, Twice" from *A Voyage Round the World from 1806 to 1812*. Archibald Campbell. Charleston, SC: Duke & Browne. 1822.

"The Last of the *Monitor*" from *The* Monitor *and The* Merrimac. J. L. Worden, Lt. S. D. Greene, and H. Ashton Ramsay. New York: Harper and Brothers Publishers. 1912.

"The Wreck of a Slave Ship" from *Thrilling Narratives of Mutiny, Murder, and Piracy*. New York: Hurst & Company.

"The *General Slocum* in the Gates of Hell" from *The History of the* General Slocum *Disaster*. J. S. Ogilvie. New York: J. S. Ogilvie Publishing Co. 1904.

"The Loss of the *Bonhomme Richard*" from *John Paul Jones*. Hutchins Hapgood. Boston and New York: Houghton, Mifflin and Company. 1901.

"The Burning of the *Philadelphia*" from *Hero Tales from American History*. Henry Cabot Lodge and Theodore Roosevelt. 1896.

"The Loss of the Brig *Tyrell*" from *Thrilling Narratives of Mutiny, Murder, and Piracy*. New York: Hurst & Company.

"The Last Cruise of the *Saginaw*" from *The Last Cruise of the* Saginaw. George H. Read. Boston and New York: Houghton Mifflin Company.

"Bark *Kathleen* Sunk by a Whale" from *Bark* Kathleen *Sunk by a Whale*. Thomas H. Jenkins. New Bedford, MA: H. S. Hutchinson & Co. 1902.

"Wrecked, Stranded, and Captured" from *A Narrative of the Shipwreck, Captivity, and Sufferings of Horace Holden and Benjamin Nute*. Horace Holden. Boston: Russell, Shattuck, and Co. 1836.

"The Wreck of the *Citizen*" from *The Arctic Whaleman*. Lewis Holmes. Boston: Wentworth and Company. 1857.